DICTIONARY

OF

ECONOMIC TERMS

DICTIONARY
OF
ECONOMIC TERMS

By

ALAN GILPIN

B.Sc. (Econ.), M.Inst.F., M.I.P.H.E.
of the Queensland Public Service, Australia.
Formerly of the Development Policy Branch, Planning
Department, Central Electricity Generating Board;
Visiting Lecturer in Applied Business Economics,
Borough Polytechnic, London.

SECOND EDITION

LONDON
BUTTERWORTHS
1970

ENGLAND: BUTTERWORTH & CO. (PUBLISHERS) LTD.
                 LONDON: 88 KINGSWAY, W.C.2

AUSTRALIA: BUTTERWORTH & CO. (AUSTRALIA) LTD.
                 SYDNEY: 20 LOFTUS STREET
                 MELBOURNE: 343 LITTLE COLLINS STREET
                 BRISBANE: 240 QUEEN STREET

CANADA: BUTTERWORTH & CO. (CANADA) LTD.
                 TORONTO: 14 CURITY AVENUE, 374

NEW ZEALAND: BUTTERWORTH & CO. (NEW ZEALAND) LTD.
                 WELLINGTON: 49/51 BALLANCE STREET
                 AUCKLAND: 35 HIGH STREET

SOUTH AFRICA: BUTTERWORTH & CO. (SOUTH AFRICA) LTD.
                 DURBAN: 33/35 BEACH GROVE

First published   *April,* 1966
Reprinted with corrections   *September,* 1967
Second edition   *February,* 1970

Standard Book Number: 406 73001 6

Printed in Great Britain by R. J. Acford Ltd., Chichester, Sussex

PREFACE TO THE SECOND EDITION

While the fundamental truths of economics are valid for all time, the details of their manifestations are constantly changing. In consequence an extensive revision of this dictionary has been necessary while the opportunity has been taken to incorporate terms relating to new developments, particularly in the field of public policy.

I am grateful to those members of staff of the Universities of Cambridge, Bristol, Kent, Lancaster, Birmingham, Nottingham and Dublin, and of the West London College and the Derby and District College of Technology, and to other readers, who have written either to myself or the publishers with helpful suggestions and comments. Comment in relation to the Second Edition will be welcomed and appreciated also.

A.G.

November, 1969.

PREFACE TO THE FIRST EDITION

This book has been inspired by my professional acquaintance with applied economics in a major industry and my experience as a lecturer in economics and allied subjects over many years.

It is intended primarily for economists and students of economics, but it is hoped that it will prove of value and interest also to planners and engineers in industry who, faced with the growing impact of positive national economic planning, are having to give more constructive thought to the long-term development of their own industries and the implications of such development for the economy as a whole.

I would like to thank my wife for scrutinising and typing the manuscript and the many organisations who have assisted by supplying information on their activities. In particular, I should like to thank the Board of Trade, the Commercial Banks, the Monopolies Commission, the National Economic Development Council, the Stock Exchange and the United Nations Organisation.

The terms in this dictionary are those used largely in the United Kingdom, but a number in use in the United States of America and other countries have also been included.

A.G.

December, 1965.

TO MY MOTHER

A

A Priori An expression commonly used in economics, it relates to speculation or reasoning which is prior to actual experience. As reasoning it proceeds deductively from cause to effect; such speculation or reasoning stands in contrast to an appeal to evidence.

"A" Shares *See* STOCKS AND SHARES PREFIXED OR AFFIXED "A", "B", ETC.

A1 at Lloyd's First class in Lloyd's Register of Shipping (q.v.); the first in a series describing the condition of a vessel, the letter referring to the state of the hull and the figure to the condition of the stores and equipment. A first class guarantee to Lloyd's (q.v.) for marine insurance purposes.

"Above-the-Line" Payments and Receipts Payments and receipts contained in that part of the Government's Budget dealing with expenditure to be met out of revenue raised mainly from taxation. The payments cannot be made by borrowing from some other source. Payments and receipts of this kind are:

    Payments (a) Consolidated Fund Services (e.g. debt service, Civil List, Judges' salaries); and,

            (b) Supply services, defence and civil expenditure.

    Receipts (a) Produce of taxation; and,

           (b) Miscellaneous revenue receipts.

Since 1947 it has been customary for the British Budget to contain a full statement of the estimated expenditure and revenue for the following year, some items being shown as "above-the-line", as above, and others as "below-the-line" (q.v.). Most current items appear above-the-line and most capital items below. The out-turn of the Budget for 1964–65 was an above-the-line surplus of £420 m. and a below-the-line deficit of £848 m., resulting in a borrowing requirement of £428 m. Since 1965 the terms "above-the-line" and "below-the-line" have not appeared in the financial statement (q.v.).

Abrasion Loss of weight in coins caused by wear and tear.

Absentee Landowner who resides away from his estate, drawing rents from tenants and managing his affairs through an agent.

Absenteeism Absence from work which may be involuntary due to sickness or other causes, or voluntary.

Absolute Monopoly The control of the entire output of a commodity or service, for which there is no substitute, by a single producer or supplier. This kind of situation rarely occurs in real life. *See* MONOPOLY.

Abstinence In an economic sense, the sacrifice of current consumption to enable resources to be directed to the production of capital goods. As this means that in the long run the flow of consumer goods will be increased, abstinence may be regarded as the sacrifice of some current consumption in favour of greater future consumption.

Abstinence or Agio Theory of Interest A theory that interest (q.v.) is a payment for abstaining from current consumption. This is but a partial explanation as there are other reasons for saving. *See* LIQUIDITY-PREFERENCE; PROPENSITIES TO CONSUME AND SAVE.

Accelerated Depreciation The depreciation (q.v.) of new plant or machinery over a shorter period than normal. Firms in development areas (q.v.) have been authorised to do this. *See* FREE DEPRECIATION.

Accelerator, The The process by which changes in the demand for consumer goods bring about even larger variations in the demand for the capital equipment used to make them. The accelerator is a factor which tends to accentuate booms or slumps in the economy. The demand for capital equipment is the aggregate of two distinct demands, (a) the demand arising from the need to replace worn-out or obsolete capital equipment, and (b) the demand for the provision of additional productive capacity if there is a growing demand for goods. As an example of the effect of the accelerator, envisage a plant manufacturing 1 million units of a commodity per year. Assume that 10 per cent of the productive capacity requires replacement each year. Now if the market demand for the commodity increases from 1 million units to 1.1 million units, the productive capacity will have to be increased by 10 per cent to meet the additional demand. Thus the effect of a 10 per cent increase in consumer demand is an increase of 100 per cent in the demand for capital equipment. Conversely, if demand for the commodity fell by 10 per cent, then the producer need not carry out his normal replacement of plant at all, and the effect of this relatively small fall in demand for the commodity is to reduce the demand for capital equipment to zero. In practice, the effect may not be as sharp as this. An increase in demand, if temporary, may be met by running down stocks; there may be reserve productive capacity which can be brought into use; existing plant may be used more intensively; and the cost of durable equipment may not be great in relation to materials and labour, reducing the importance in the economy of large variations in the demand for equipment.

Acceptance The agreement of the drawee of a bill of exchange (q.v.) signified by his signing the bill, to carry out the order of the drawer. An acceptance may be general (i.e. without qualification), or qualified (i.e. conditional or partial). After acceptance the drawee is known as the acceptor.

Acceptance Credit A method of payment used in international trade. If the credit of a foreign import merchant is considered satisfactory an Accepting

2

House (q.v.) may open an acceptance credit for him in London. A purchase from a British exporter may then be financed by means of a bill of exchange (q.v.) drawn on the Accepting House. The exporter can then obtain his money quickly as the bill can be easily discounted in the London discount market.

Accepting House A financial institution which "accepts" bills of exchange; with such backing the bills command a higher price. Most accepting houses were originally merchant houses engaged in trade before specialising in financial operations. In addition to accepting bills, accepting houses engage in ordinary banking business and function as investment advisers and issuing houses. See ACCEPTANCE; ACCEPTANCE CREDIT; ISSUING HOUSE.

Accepting Houses Committee A committee representing seventeen accepting houses conducting business in Britain. The principal qualifications for membership are: (a) a substantial part of the business of an applicant must consist of accepting bills of exchange to finance the trade of others; and (b) the applicant's acceptances must command the finest rates in the market and be eligible for rediscounting at the Bank of England (q.v.). See ACCEPTANCE; ACCEPTING HOUSE; MERCHANT BANKS.

Accommodating Movements Transfers of gold and convertible currency abroad to meet deficits in the total balance of payments (q.v.) of a country.

Accommodation Bill A bill drawn, accepted or endorsed for the sole purpose of discounting it, no goods being given or received for it, thus providing short-term cash accommodation.

Account Day The day on which all bargains (q.v.) done on the Stock Exchange (q.v.) must be settled, being usually seven days after the close of dealings at the end of the previous account period (q.v.). Also known as settlement day, and occasionally as pay day.

Account Period A period during which transactions take place on the Stock Exchange (q.v.). The year is divided into twenty-four account periods; these are normally fortnightly periods, but there are four three-week periods in each year to cover Christmas and other holidays. See ACCOUNT DAY.

Accounting The recording of the transactions of a business to reveal the financial position of the business, permit the computation of tax liabilities, and provide management with information essential to the efficient control of the business. See MANAGEMENT ACCOUNTING; SOCIAL ACCOUNTING.

Accounting, Management See MANAGEMENT ACCOUNTING.

Active Balance A favourable balance of payments (q.v.) when receipts from the export of goods and services exceed expenditure on the import of goods and services.

Active Circulation That part of the note issue of the Bank of England (q.v.) in circulation at any given time.

3

Active Market A market for a particular class of stock or shares in which there are frequent and regular dealings.

Activity Rate The proportion of civilian employees (employed plus registered unemployed) in a given population age group. Low activity rates may be regarded, to some extent, as an indication of "concealed" unemployment. *See* UNEMPLOYMENT.

Actuary A member of the insurance profession, specially skilled in the application of mathematical and statistical techniques to the problems of insurance of all types.

Ad Valorem "According to value".

Ad Valorem Tax A duty imposed on commodities in proportion to their value, i.e. a duty expressed as a percentage and not a flat amount. It is commonly used in respect of import tariffs. In Britain values are assessed on the c.i.f. (q.v.) values, plus landing charges, or alternatively on the market value when landed. In Canada the value used is that which is considered to be the fair market value on such or like goods sold for home consumption. When a fair market value cannot be ascertained, production cost plus a reasonable mark-up is accepted.

Advance Factories Factories constructed in advance of requirements by Industrial Estates Corporations (q.v.) in development areas (q.v.) in order to attract industry. The construction of these factories is authorised under the Local Employment Acts 1960 to 1966 (q.v.).

Advance Refunding (U.S.) A technique of the U.S. Treasury to hold traditional bondholders; the Treasury offers holders of expiring bonds especially attractive terms to buy its new bond issues. In this way it does not compete with private borrowers for the inflow of new savings.

Advances *See* BANK LOAN; BANK OVERDRAFT; PERSONAL LOANS FROM BANKS; TERM LOANS.

Advertising The publicising of a good or service to create, maintain or enlarge the effective demand (q.v.) for it, presenting the qualities of the good or service in an attractive manner coupled with an invitation to buy; the form of presentation may often be skilful, appealing and informative, tending frequently to exploit weaknesses in the psychology of mankind. Advertising is usually the principal selling cost (q.v.). It has been estimated that the cost of advertising in Britain is a little over 2 per cent of the national income (q.v.) with proportions varying considerably according to the commodity and type of market. For example, advertising accounts for 45 per cent of the price of patent medicines, 35 per cent of patent foods and toilet requisites, 10 per cent of food and household goods, but is negligible in respect of fuel and light. There is much to be said for and against advertising. In its favour it may be argued that advertising disseminates useful information about what

4

is available and that it stimulates the total demand for goods. Again advertising helps create a continuous demand for an article which assists in lowering its costs of production and its price. Advertising also helps in guaranteeing goods of standard and uniform quality. Against this it may be argued that many advertisements do not even pretend to give any details of the composition and quality of the goods concerned; the appeal is to the emotions rather than to good sense. Advertising may go even further in attempting to endow a product with a virtue that it does not possess; and it may be a product which on health grounds people should consume less of, not more. If a product establishes itself in the public mind through advertising, in preference to similar but less well known makes, it may be sold at a monopoly price.

Advice   A note sent by one merchant to another advising him of the despatch of goods ordered.

Aggregate Demand   The total effective demand or expenditure of all purchasers of capital and consumer goods within a given market.

Aggregate Supply   The total physical volume of goods and services currently coming on to a given market.

Aggregated Rebates   *See* DEFERRED REBATES.

Aggregation   The bringing together or summing of primary data. For example, the national income is an aggregate, in contrast with the income of an individual.   *See* AGGREGATE DEMAND; AGGREGATE SUPPLY.

Aggregative Index   An index number which is constructed by aggregating a number of items, e.g. Laspeyres' Index (q.v.) and Paasche's Index (q.v.). *See* INDEX NUMBERS.

Aggregative Model   An econometric model in which the variables are themselves constructed from groups of individual variables, as when a price index number is substituted for a set of prices.   *See* ECONOMETRIC MODELS; INDEX NUMBERS.

Agistment   The feeding and taking care of cattle for reward.

Agreement, Information   *See* INFORMATION AGREEMENT

Agricultural Marketing Act 1931   An Act authorising the setting up of a Marketing Board in respect of any agricultural commodity where the producers of a large proportion of the total output of the commodity are in favour of such a scheme.   *See* MARKETING BOARD.

Agricultural Mortgage Corporation   A finance corporation set up under the Agricultural Credits Acts of 1928 and 1932 to provide long-term finance for the agricultural industry in England and Wales. Its equity shareholders are the Bank of England and nine joint-stock banks. Loans are advanced for periods of from twenty to sixty years for the purpose of purchasing farms or for use as general working capital. In addition to the capital provided by the equity shareholders, additional funds for lending have been obtained by the public issue of debenture stock. A similar service has been provided in Scotland by the Scottish Agricultural Securities Corporation. *See* FINANCE CORPORATIONS.

Agricultural Subsidies Payments to the farmers by the Government for the purpose of encouraging home production of foodstuffs while maintaining reasonable retail prices to consumers. About two-thirds of United Kingdom farm subsidies are known as "deficiency payments" and are paid in respect of produce sold on the home market at prices less than the guaranteed prices negotiated annually between the farmers and the Government. These guaranteed prices are fixed at an Annual Review. The farmer sells his produce to private buyers on the home market at prices competitive with imported supplies. The Agricultural Acts of 1947 and 1957 laid down that the object of Government intervention was to ensure the production of as much as it was desirable to produce in the national interest with "proper remuneration" for farmers and farm workers and an adequate return on the land and capital employed. The United Kingdom level of agricultural production is very much higher than before the Second World War and self-sufficiency has been achieved, or nearly so, in liquid milk, pork, poultry, eggs, barley, potatoes and hops. About 70 per cent of the total supply of beef and veal is home-fed.

Agricultural Wages Board A statutory body responsible for negotiating the wages of agricultural workers. *See* MINIMUM WAGE LEGISLATION.

Aid-Tying An obligation which may be imposed by a donor government upon a recipient to use aid funds for purchasing goods and services in the contributing country.

Air Consignment Note Where goods are transported by air an air consignment note replaces a bill of lading (q.v.). This is not a document of title to the goods, but merely a copy of the consignment contract.

Algol Abbreviation for "algorithmic oriented language"; an international computer programming language for science and mathematics. *See* COBOL; COMPUTER; HARDWARE AND SOFTWARE.

Allonge Slip of paper attached to a bill of exchange (q.v.) to provide additional space for endorsements, should this be required.

Allotment Act of allotting newly issued debentures, or shares between applicants who have responded to an offer for subscription.

Allotment Letter Letter advising an applicant how much stock or how many shares he has been allotted and specifying the amounts due and dates of payment in respect of them.

Allowed—Or Standard—Times Prescribed times for the completion of a task, based on time-study data.

Alternative-Cost *See* OPPORTUNITY-COST.

Amalgamation The merging or combining of two or more firms.

"American Economic Review" The quarterly journal of the American Economic Association.

American Federation of Labour and Congress of Industrial Organisations (A.F.L.-C.I.O.) An amalgamation, achieved in 1955, of two American rival federations of trade unions. The combined federation comprises over one hundred national unions and over five hundred local unions, with a total membership of over fourteen million trade unionists.

American Loan *See* WASHINGTON AGREEMENT.

Amortization (a) The gradual repayment of a debt by means of a sinking fund (q.v.); (b) The annual writing down of the value of an asset by depreciation.

Anglo-American Council on Productivity An organisation set up shortly after the Second World War to study the experience of the United States in raising productivity, and to consider which of the methods adopted there could be applied or adopted to the needs of British industry. Some sixty-six teams, representing management, technicians and operatives, drawn either from specific industries or from experts in certain techniques of service to industry generally, went to the United States for this purpose. All these teams prepared comprehensive reports and recommendations. *See* BRITISH PRODUCTIVITY COUNCIL; PRODUCTIVITY.

Anglo-Irish Free Trade Agreement 1965 An Agreement, operating from 1st July, 1966, under which the United Kingdom ceased to charge protective duties on goods originating in the Irish Republic.

"Annual Abstract of Statistics" A publication of the Central Statistical Office covering the main features of the British economy.

Anthropology, Economic *See* ECONOMIC ANTHROPOLOGY.

Anti-Trust Laws (U.S.) A series of Acts introduced by the United States Federal Government to check and control the formation of trusts (q.v.). The first was the Sherman Anti-Trust Act of 1890. The Clayton Act 1914 sought to check the development of monopolies by prohibiting the amalgamation of firms producing a large proportion of the total output of a commodity.

Application Money The amount of money which must accompany an application for a new issue of stocks or shares.

Applied Economics Branch of economic science devoted to the study of practical problems, utilising the principles and tools of economic analysis provided by theoretical economics (q.v.).

7

Appreciation An increase in the value of an asset. For example, an increase in (a) the value of property in relation to other assets during a period of growing demand; (b) the value of stocks held by merchants and manufacturers during a period of rising prices; (c) the value of a currency when its value increases in relation to the values of other currencies; or (d) the value of stocks and shares in general, or particular categories, on the stock exchange.

Apprenticeship The system under which young persons training in a particular occupation have to "serve their time", usually for five years, before being recognised as skilled.

Appropriation Account A business account showing how the net profit has been apportioned between dividends, reserves, profit-sharing scheme, pension fund, and so on.

Appropriation-in-Aid An item in the estimates of a Government Department which records any revenue received from the sale of goods and services to the public; the effect of such an item is to reduce the amount of money required from the Exchequer (q.v.) during the coming financial year.

Arbitrage Dealing in commodities, currencies or securities between two or more markets to take profitable advantage of any differences in the prices quoted for such commodities, currencies or securities.

Arbitration A method of settling industrial disputes. Both sides to a dispute agree to refer the matter to an impartial person or body for adjudication, there being a formal or informal agreement to accept the decision or recommendation.

Arithmetic Mean Figure computed by aggregating a series of figures and dividing by the number of items included in the series.

Arithmetic Progression A series of quantities taken in order which increase or decrease by a constant amount known as the "common difference", e.g. 1, 3, 5, 7, 9, ... in which the common difference is 2. The nth term $= a + (n-1)d$, where a is the first term and d the common difference. The sum of the terms, $S = n/2\ [2a + (n-1)d]$ where n is the number of terms being considered. Both the first term and the common difference may be positive or negative.

Articles of Association A document which must be submitted to the Registrar of Companies when seeking registration of a company. The articles determine the internal constitution of the company, either accepting the standard articles suggested in the Companies Act or setting out special terms of their own. Articles cover such important matters as:
   (a) issue and transfer of shares,
   (b) alteration of capital,
   (c) borrowing powers,
   (d) shareholders' meetings and voting rights,

(e) appointment and powers of directors,
(f) presentation and auditing of accounts.

See COMPANIES ACTS 1948 AND 1967; COMPANY, LEGAL FORMATION OF; MEMORANDUM OF ASSOCIATION.

Asset Backing The net assets of a company divided by the number of issued shares. For example, if the ABC Co. Ltd. has £100,000 net assets and 10,000 shares issued, the asset backing is £10 per share.

Assets The property of a business; they may be classified as :
   (a) Current Assets, consisting of cash, stock and book debts;
   (b) Fixed Assets, consisting of buildings, plant and machinery;
   (c) Intangible Assets, being the value of goodwill or patents.

At Discretion A term qualifying an instruction given by a client to his stockbroker (q.v.) to buy or sell stocks or shares, it gives the broker discretion as to price.

At Limit A term qualifying an instruction given by a client to his stockbroker (q.v.) to buy or sell stocks or shares, it places a specified limit on either the highest price that may be paid, or the lowest price at which a sale may be made.

At Par Stocks and shares the market price of which is the same as the nominal or face value. If new stock is issued at par, then £100 of such stock can be bought for £100.

"At the Back Door" Description of assistance to the money market by the Bank of England (q.v.), which injects cash into the market by the purchase of bills through the special buyer (q.v.), when it wishes to provide the market's requirements of cash without exerting pressure upwards or downwards on the rates of interest in the market. If the Bank does not wish to provide cash in this manner, and the discount houses can obtain the cash they require in no other way, then the discount houses may borrow direct from the Discount Office of the Bank of England. This is known as assistance to the market "at the front door". *See* LENDER OF LAST RESORT; MONEY MARKET; PENAL TERMS.

"At the Front Door" *See* "AT THE BACK DOOR".

At the Market A term qualifying an instruction given by a client to his stockbroker (q.v.) to buy or sell stocks or shares, it indicates that the broker may buy or sell at about the market price prevailing at the time the instruction is given.

Auction A method of determining prices employed in the sale of objects which cannot be standardised, e.g. horses, fish, cattle, vegetables, etc. Specified quantities or "lots" are open to public bids, buyers competing to complete a purchase. The general system is for the price to start low and for bidding to raise it, although there may be a reserve price below which the seller reserves the right to withdraw the goods from sale. In a Dutch auction, however, the bids come down from a high price instead of rising from a low price. This method is used extensively in Holland for the sale of agricultural commodities.

Auctioneer An agent employed by a seller to sell his goods at an auction (q.v.).

Audit The examination of the account books of an organisation, by an accountant or other competent person, to ascertain their correctness.

Audit Office The office of the department of the Comptroller and Auditor-General. The department is responsible for the annual audit of the accounts of the Government departments.

Australian Banking System The Australian banking system consists of a central government bank (The Reserve Bank of Australia), the Commonwealth Banking Corporation, private trading banks (all joint stock companies) and various other commercial and savings banks.

The Reserve Bank is responsible for the issue of notes, regulation of bank lending and of bank interest rates, the movement of foreign currency and the operation of Government Securities.

There is a system of statutory deposits through which the Reserve Bank regulates the liquidity of the Trading Banks and hence their capacity to make advances. The Trading Banks have also agreed to maintain a minimum level of liquidity in their own hands.

Australia has adopted the English system of branch banking.

Austrian School of Economists Name given to a group of 19th Century economists at the University of Vienna, among whom were Carl Menger (1840–1921), Friedrich von Wieser (1851–1926) and Eugen von Böhm-Bawerk (1851–1914). Their contribution rested largely in the development of the utility theory of value, refuting the cost of production theory of value of the older Classical School of Economists. *See* VALUE, THEORIES OF.

Autarky An ideal of self-sufficiency, a country attempting to be as independent as possible of imports from other countries. A costly policy for those who try it and an unrealistic one for most.

Authorised Clerk Stockbroker's clerk allowed to deal on the floor of the Stock Exchange (q.v.).

Automation A system of automatic machine control extending over an entire series of manufacturing operations or other productive activities; an advanced form of mechanisation achieving various levels of sophistication. The general effect is to reduce manpower requirements. In the motor industry, automation has been described as the "automatic handling of parts between progressive production processes". It has permitted the extension of mechanisation into areas which previously had defined such changes, e.g. banking and insurance.

Autoregression A series of observations in which the value of each observation is partly dependent upon the values of those observations immediately preceding it. Each observation stands in a regression relationship with one or more of the immediately preceding observations.

Average Cost The average cost of producing each unit of output, i.e.

$$\frac{\text{cost of producing (n) units}}{\text{(n)}}$$

The greater the proportion that fixed costs (q.v.) bear to variable costs (q.v.) the more rapid the decline in average costs as the total output is increased. In economics, costs include "normal profit" (q.v.), this being a necessary payment in respect of the special type of labour called "enterprise".

Averaging The practice of buying more of a security when its price has fallen in order to lower the average cost of a holding.

B

Back-Door Operations *See* "AT THE BACK DOOR".

Backwardation (a) A payment made by a bear (q.v.) to a bull (q.v.) for refraining from demanding delivery of shares sold by the former to the latter. Opposite to contango (q.v.).

(b) In the commodity markets, the amount by which the spot price of a commodity (plus the costs of carrying the commodity over time) exceeds the forward price. *See* SPOT PRICE; FUTURES MARKET.

Balance of Payments The relation between the payments of all kinds made from one country to the rest of the world and its receipts from all other countries. For the world as a whole, imports must equal exports. For Britain, while the value of visible imports normally exceeds that of visible exports, the addition of invisible earnings (q.v.) usually results in a current account (q.v.) surplus. As a consequence of the War, British overseas earnings declined considerably (mainly due to the sale of overseas assets to finance the war) and this loss of earnings had to be matched by an increase in exports. Inflationary trends and high consumer demand at home have encouraged imports of raw materials and finished goods, while the same inflationary pressure in raising the prices of British exports has tended to weaken the competitive position of British goods in the export markets.

British exports and earnings comprise two elements, the "visible" and the "invisible". Visible exports are by far the most important element, consisting of tangible goods such as plant and machinery, consumer goods, aircraft and coal, etc. Invisible earnings are receipts for services rendered. For example, British shipping earns large sums for carrying goods for other countries; banks, insurance companies, civil airlines, etc. perform useful services for foreign firms and nationals; the investment of capital overseas earns interest and dividends; tourists from abroad also add to earnings. At the same time debts are incurred by Britain not only in respect of imported goods, but in respect of interest and profits earned by foreign firms and governments. In addition, British tourists spend money abroad, and payments have to be made to foreign countries for the maintenance of the British Forces overseas.

The "current account" is that part of the balance of payments account which shows all payments made or received in respect of goods and services, including payments of interest on past lendings or borrowings. The "capital account" is that part of the balance of payments account showing all payments made or received by way of settling old debts or creating new debts. *See* BALANCING ITEM; CAPITAL ACCOUNT; MONETARY MOVEMENTS; UNREQUITED EXPORTS.

Balance of Revenue Term used by the Electricity Council (q.v.) for the financial surplus or profit of the electricity supply industry. It is additional revenue deliberately secured as a contribution to capital development, i.e. for investment in plant and other assets. The word "surplus" in the industry's earlier accounts had caused unnecessary confusion since it implies quite incorrectly a sum of money over and above that required.

Balance of Trade The relationship between the values of a country's imports and its exports, i.e. the "visible" balance. These items form only part of the balance of payments (q.v.) which is also influenced by (a) "invisible" items and (b) movements of capital.

Balance Sheet An ordered statement of:
    (a) the economic resources or assets of a company or other business organisation, each item having a value set upon it;
    (b) the financial claims of persons or organisations upon the value of these assets.
All assets are, by definition, owned by someone; consequently, the total claims equal the value of the assets.

Balancing Item An item entered in the balance of payments (q.v.) accounts to make the account balance; it is the net total of the errors and omissions in other items.

Baltic Mercantile and Shipping Exchange A London market devoted to shipping services and cargoes; it is international in scope and the largest market of its kind in the world. As a commodity exchange it specialises in the grain trade, with a well-established "futures" market. In respect of shipping almost any business connected with ships and cargoes is transacted. It is also concerned with the arranging of air freight. The Exchange has over 2,000 members.

Bank Bill A bill of exchange (q.v.) carrying the names of two accepting houses (one a member of the Accepting Houses Committee) eligible for discount at the Bank of England (q.v.). *See* ACCEPTING HOUSE.

Bank Charter Act 1844 Following a series of banking crises during the period 1825–1837, an Act introduced to control the issue of bank-notes.
    The chief provisions of the Act were:
    (a) the work of the Bank of England (q.v.) was to be divided into two departments (i) Issue Department, and (ii) Banking Department;
    (b) there was to be a small fiduciary issue (q.v.) of about £14 millions; all notes above this amount were to be backed by gold;
    (c) no new bank was to be allowed to issue notes and existing issues were not to be increased; note-issuing powers were withdrawn from any business as soon as the number of partners exceeded six, and from

any issuing bank becoming bankrupt, ceasing to carry on the business of banking, or otherwise discontinuing note issue;

(d) the Bank of England (q.v.) was to be allowed to increase its fiduciary issue by two-thirds of the lapsed issue of any other bank; and

(e) the Bank of England had to publish a weekly return for both its issue and banking departments.

In 1844 there were 72 banks of issue in England, but by 1914 the number had been reduced to 13. By 1921 the Bank of England had become sole bank of issue in England; eight Scottish Banks continued to issue notes. *See* CURRENCY AND BANK NOTES ACTS 1928–1954.

Bank Deposit A liability of a bank to a customer; a sum of money credited to a customer who may demand payment at any time. The money may have been deposited by the customer, or have been credited to the customer by way of an overdraft or loan or by way of payments from other sources. A current account (q.v.) or a demand deposit (q.v.) forms part of the money supply (q.v.) of a country together with coins and notes. *See* CHECKING DEPOSIT; CHEQUE.

Bank for International Settlements (B.I.S.) Established at Basle in 1930, as a result of a recommendation of the Young Committee, the B.I.S. undertook initially certain functions of collecting and disbursing Reparations and Allied War Debt payments; the intention was that the Bank would develop into a clearing house for central banks and eventually into a "central bank for central banks". These earlier hopes were not realised and since the Second World War the International Monetary Fund (q.v.) has been performing many functions which might have been performed through the B.I.S.

The B.I.S. remains in existence, and since the Second World War has been largely concerned with short-term operations between European central banks, taking short-term deposits of gold or currencies and giving short-term credits. In addition, the B.I.S. was appointed Agent for the Organisation for European Economic Co-operation (q.v.) for the operation of the European Payments Union (q.v.) (and, subsequently, the European Monetary Agreement) and carries out certain operational functions for other international institutions, including the International Monetary Fund (q.v.) and the European Coal and Steel Community (q.v.). The Bank of England, as central bank of the United Kingdom, is a member of the B.I.S. *See* BASLE AGREEMENT.

Bank Giro A scheme for the improvement of money transfer services offered by the British clearing banks; the improved services include direct debiting arrangements, a particularly useful service for large organisations receiving frequent payments from the holders of bank accounts. *See* GIRO.

Bank Interest Interest paid and charged by the commercial banks for money deposited with or borrowed from them. Deposit accounts usually earn a rate of interest some 2 per cent less than Bank Rate (q.v.); bank overdrafts carry a rate of interest of 1 per cent above Bank Rate. *See* BANK LOAN; BANK OVERDRAFT; DEPOSIT ACCOUNT.

14

Bank Loan A loan of a fixed amount for a specific purpose, carrying a definite date for repayment. Such a loan is usually made on approved security, the interest charge tending to be lower for larger concerns. *See* BANK OVERDRAFT.

Bank Note Paper currency issued by the Bank of England, or other bank of issue, carrying the promise of the bank "to pay the bearer on demand" a stated sum of money. Note issue in Britain is regulated by the Currency and Bank Notes Act of 1954.

Bank of England The British central bank. Its functions and duties are as follows:
   (a) It carries out the monetary policy (q.v.) of the Government, and keeps the country's gold reserves;
   (b) It is responsible for the issue of bank-notes in England;
   (c) It is the bankers' bank. The commercial banks (q.v.) keep about 50 per cent of their reserves with the Bank of England;
   (d) It is the Government's bank. It receives the proceeds of taxation and makes payments on behalf of the Government. It manages the National Debt (q.v.) and floats new loans for the Government. By "ways and means advances" (q.v.) it lends money direct to the Government;
   (e) It influences the money market (q.v.) by changes in the Bank Rate (q.v.) and by "open market operations" (q.v.);
   (f) It is the "lender of last resort" (q.v.);
   (g) It carries on a little ordinary banking business;
   (h) It manages the Exchange Equalisation Account (q.v.), foreign exchange control, and conducts transactions between Britain and the rest of the world.

The Bank of England was established as a joint-stock company in 1694. The Bank Charter Act of 1844 (q.v.) gave the Bank a virtual monopoly of note issues. In 1946, the Bank was nationalised, the capital being acquired by the state. The Bank is managed by a Governor, Deputy-Governor and sixteen directors (four of these are full-time). The Bank publishes a weekly statement of account known as the Bank Return.

Bank of Issue A bank, authorised by statute to issue bank notes. *See* BANK CHARTER ACT 1844; CURRENCY AND BANK NOTES ACTS 1928–1954.

Bank Overdraft A loan from a bank made on current account (q.v.). Often a means of financing trading requirements on a short-term basis, an overdraft is of no definite duration and is repayable on demand. The interest charged on a bank overdraft is usually 1 per cent above Bank Rate (q.v.); it is levied on a day-to-day basis, i.e. on the actual amount borrowed and not on the agreed maximum. *See* BANK LOAN.

Bank Rate The minimum rate at which the Bank of England (q.v.), acting as "lender of last resort" (q.v.) will discount first-class bills or make advances

15

MINIMUM LENDING
RATE (OCT 1972)

to a discount house against "eligible paper" (q.v.). Bank rate governs the movement of market rates of discount, although these remain somewhat below bank rate. By custom, bank rate also governs the movement of many administered interest rates, e.g. the rates on commercial bank deposits and advances, and the rates of lending by the Exchequer to local authorities and nationalised industries. The Bank Rate is announced every Thursday morning by the Court of Directors of the Bank of England.

The effect of raising the bank rate is to check or reduce bank advances; lowering the bank rate means that borrowing is cheaper and an expansion of credit is encouraged. It is thus a monetary instrument for influencing the activity of the economy; its effectiveness is often assisted by " open market operations" (q.v.).

At one time bank rate fluctuated frequently, but between 1932 and 1951, save for a short period in 1939, it remained steady at 2 per cent. This was the era of "cheap money". In 1951 the bank rate was raised to $2\frac{1}{2}$ per cent, and in March 1952 to 4 per cent. Since then it has risen to higher levels, varying between 5 and 8 per cent.

Bank Return A weekly statement of accounts by the Bank of England (q.v.).

Bankers' Deposits The portion (about half) of the cash reserves of the commercial banks deposited with the Bank of England (q.v.).

Banker's Draft A cheque drawn by a banker at the request of his customer. It differs from an ordinary cheque, however, in being regarded as cash and cannot be returned unpaid; a banker's draft is payment.

Bankers' Industrial Development Company An agency set up by the Bank of England (q.v.) and the commercial banks (q.v.) during the Great Depression, 1929-35 (q.v.). for the purpose of assisting industry. It played an important part in the financial reconstruction of the cotton, shipbuilding and steel industries. It was placed in voluntary liquidation in August, 1945. *See* FINANCE CORPORATIONS.

Banking The business of holding deposits and lending money. The British Banking System comprises the Bank of England (q.v.); the Commercial Banks (q.v.); and the savings banks and other banking institutions.

Banking and Currency Schools Following a series of banking crises during the period 1825-1837, two schools of thought which developed on the best form of parliamentary intervention to control the issue of bank notes. The Currency School believed that strict measures were needed to restrict the note issues of the banks and that the entire note issue should be fully backed by gold. If a fiduciary issue (q.v.) was permitted, then it should be kept very small. The Banking School believed that the note issue should be flexible and made to suit the needs of business at any time. The Bank Charter Act of 1844 (q.v.) was a victory for the Currency School. Neither group at that time could foresee the future development of the cheque (q.v.) as a money medium much more flexible than bank notes.

Banking Legislation Legislation affecting the British banking system. It includes the Bank Charter Act 1844 (q.v.); Bills of Exchange Act 1882; Stamp Act 1891; Bank of England Act 1946; Currency and Bank Notes Acts 1928 to 1954 (q.v.); Companies Acts 1948 and 1967 (q.v.); Cheques Act 1957; Trustee Savings Banks Acts 1954 to 1968; Decimal Currency Act 1967.

Bankruptcy The inability to meet the demands of creditors. Bankruptcy may be followed by adjudication in which a bankrupt's property is divided among his creditors. *See* LIQUIDATION.

Banks A general term for certain financial institutions. It includes:
  (1) Joint Stock Banks: ordinary banks which accept deposits and usually have a large number of branches, i.e. the "Big Four" (q.v.) and the smaller joint stock banks, the Scottish banks, a few once private banks now controlled by joint stock banks, and one surviving private partnership, Hoare & Company.
  (2) "Merchant Banks", also called "Accepting Houses" or "Issuing Houses" which are concerned chiefly with the financing of international trade and with the issuing and servicing of home and overseas loans.
  (3) Overseas banks, i.e. the London offices of banks operating in foreign countries or the Commonwealth.
  (4) Savings banks, such as the Post Office and Trustee Savings Banks which accept deposits from the general public but do not grant the same cheque-drawing and other facilities that ordinary banks provide.

Bargains Deals done on the Stock Exchange. Every day, *The Times* and other newspapers print a list of "bargains marked". The term bargain does not imply "cut-price".

Barlow Report The Report of the Royal Commission on the Geographical Distribution of the Industrial Population, published in 1940. The Report urged the importance of preventing further industrial congestion in Greater London, and the need for encouraging a greater diversity of occupation in areas which had become too dependent on specialised industries.

Barratry Any wilful act of wrongdoing by the master or mariners against their ship and its cargo.

Barter The exchange of goods for goods, without the use of money (q.v.). The method is cumbersome as every transaction requires a "double coincidence of wants" (q.v.), and the sub-division of goods may be difficult or impossible so that "change" cannot be given.

Barter Terms of Trade *See* TERMS OF TRADE.

Basle Agreement An Agreement announced on 9th September, 1968, whereby Britain can draw United States dollars and other foreign currencies from the Bank for International Settlements (q.v.) should the sterling balances of the

17

overseas sterling area fall below an agreed starting level. The facility, totalling $2,000 million, will be administered by the Bank for International Settlements (q.v.); it will be available for ten years and the net amount ultimately drawn under it will have to be repaid between the 6th and 10th years. The purpose of the facility is to ensure that U.K. reserves will not be run down as a result of large-scale movements out of sterling by countries which hold some of their reserves in sterling. An earlier arrangement of June, 1966, will terminate in 1971.

Batch Production The production of articles in batches; to be distinguished from job production (q.v.) and mass production (q.v.).

Bear A person who, believing prices are about to fall, sells shares in the hope of buying them back again at a lower price thus making a profit. If the bear does not possess the securities he sells he is said to have "sold short"; to complete his manoeuvre he must purchase them again within the same account period. If a bear does possess the securities he sells, he is known as a "protected" or "covered" bear. *See* BACKWARDATION; BULL; CONTANGO.

Bear Market A market in which prices are falling.

Bearer Stocks or Bonds Securities (q.v.) the ownership of which can pass from one person to another without formal deed of transfer (q.v.) or re-registration of ownership by the company concerned.

Belgium-Luxembourg Economic Union (B.L.E.U.) An economic union formed between Belgium and Luxembourg on 25th July, 1921. Following the creation of Benelux (q.v.) this economic union continued to exist independently.

"Below-the-Line" Payments and Receipts Payments and receipts contained in that part of the Government's Budget dealing with capital items.
  They are payments in respect of which Parliament has given the Treasury (q.v.) specific power to borrow, and receipts which Parliament has given the Treasury specific power to use for the service of debt. Payments and receipts of this kind are:
  Payments (a) Payments of a capital nature (mainly loans, e.g. loans to the nationalised industries and the Public Works Loan Board) which Parliament has specifically authorised to be paid from the Exchequer and which do not have to be voted annually; and,
  (b) That part of interest payable on the Government's own debt which is met from interest received on loans made by the Government.
  Receipts (a) Repayments on loans and advances made by the Government; and,
  (b) Interest on loans made by the Government.
  Since 1947 it has been customary for the British Budget to contain a full statement of the estimated expenditure and revenue of the Government for

the ensuing year, some items being shown as "above-the-line" (q.v.) and others as "below-the-line". Most current items appear above the line and most capital items below. Since 1965, the terms "above-the-line" and "below-the-line" have not appeared in the financial statement (q.v.).

Benefits, Social *See* SOCIAL BENEFITS.

Benelux A customs union established between Belgium, Luxembourg and the Netherlands in successive stages between 1944 and 1948. The purpose of the union was to abolish tariff duties within the union and to apply a common tariff to imports from other countries. A final treaty of economic union was ratified in 1960. Belgium, Luxembourg and the Netherlands are members of the European Economic Community (q.v.). *See* BELGIUM-LUXEM-BOURG ECONOMIC UNION (B.L.E.U.).

Best Profit Equilibrium The point at which the marginal costs of a firm's production and its marginal revenues from sales balance. In mass production markets, small outputs may involve costs which exceed total revenue. As output increases, marginal and average costs per unit of output fall (due to increasing returns to scale) and the point of maximum profitability is also approached. At very large outputs, average and marginal costs per unit of production may tend to rise (due to decreasing returns) while selling price continues to fall.

In general, the optimum or most efficient firm tends to survive and prosper best.

Betterment An increase in the value of land and buildings arising from the action of other developers, or from restrictions imposed on the use of land elsewhere by the public authorities.

Betterment Levy *See* LAND COMMISSION.

Beveridge Plan A plan presented by Sir William Beveridge in 1942 for the revision and improvement of the British social insurance system. The plan provided for eight primary causes of need: (a) unemployment; (b) disability; (c) loss of means of support when not regularly employed; (d) retirement; (e) marriage; (f) expenses of childhood; (g) funeral expenses; (h) sickness or incapacity. *See* SOCIAL INSURANCE.

Bid The price a person is willing to pay. On the stock exchange (q.v.), the lower of the two prices quoted by a stockjobber. *See* OFFER.

Bid-Filing After a contract has been allotted, an arrangement whereby firms who competed for the contract notify a central agency of the prices submitted on tender. These prices are subsequently circulated to all members of the agency.

"Big Four", The Barclays, (including Martins), Lloyds, Midland, and The National Westminster (including The District) Banks.

Bilateral Monopoly A sole purchaser buying from a sole seller in any given market.

Bilateral Trade Trade between two countries; strictly interpreted the value of the goods and services exported by country A to country B must be exactly matched by the value of the exports from country B to country A. The development of bilateral, as distinct from multilateral, trade dates largely from the Great Depression (1929–35) (q.v.). In the post-war years it has tended to recede with increasing efforts to remove barriers to international trade by commercial treaties such as the General Agreement on Tariffs and Trade (q.v.).

Bill of Exchange An order for the making of payment, mainly used in international trade. It is addressed by the drawer to a second party, the drawee, as an instruction to pay a third party, the payee, a certain named sum of money at a certain date. To be valid, a bill of exchange needs to be "accepted" by the drawee; this is done by the drawee signing his name across the face of the bill.

Bills of exchange are of two types, "term" or "usance", and "sight". A term bill may not be payable until, say, ninety days after acceptance; a sight bill is payable upon acceptance.

An accepted bill is negotiable, i.e. can be sold at a discount. Indeed, a bill may change ownership several times. The use of inland bills of exchange has declined in importance during the 20th century. *See* ACCEPTANCE; ACCEPTING HOUSE.

Bill of Lading A document of title to goods received for shipment. It usually gives a brief description of the goods which have been received for shipment and states the terms on which they are to be carried; it is signed by the shipowner or his agent, and normally bears the name of the consignee. Usually two or three copies of a bill of lading are signed and the exporter or his agent sends these, together with other necessary documents, to the consignee. In addition unsigned, or non-negotiable copies, are supplied to the master of the ship and to those who handle the goods prior to shipment. Signed copies give the right to collect the goods at their destination.

Bimetallism A monetary system in which the units of currency are expressed in terms of two metals, usually gold and silver. The metals exchange in a specific ratio and are accepted in unlimited quantities for coinage. *See* MONOMETALLISM.

Binary Code A method of expressing numerical values by a numbering system based on two instead of ten as in the normal decimal system; thus as one moves to the left, the numbers ascend in powers of two instead of powers of ten. For example:

$$000\ 011 \text{ means } 2+1 = 3$$
$$000\ 101 \text{ means } 4+0+1 = 5$$
$$001\ 110 \text{ means } 8+4+2+0 = 14$$
$$111\ 111 \text{ means } 32+16+8+4+2+1 = 63$$

Letters and mathematical signs may be symbolised by allocating a number in binary code to each; a system used in computers. *See* COMPUTER.

Black Market The buying or selling of goods at prices above prices fixed by a Government during emergency conditions, e.g. war-time or famine.

Block Grant A non-specific contribution to local authority services by the central government, each local authority determining its distribution between services.

Block Tariff A method of charging for gas or electricity in which the price per therm or unit is highest for a specified initial number, or block, of therms or units consumed within a prescribed period, and lower for additional quantities of therms or units consumed within the same period.

Blocked Account Bank deposits, payments from which are restricted to certain legally defined purposes. This device was used to prevent the export of sterling by countries that supplied Britain with goods and services during the Second World War. When hostilities ceased Britain's creditors held blocked sterling accounts to the value of £3,500 millions. Subsequently, Britain made agreements for the gradual release of some of these blocked sterling accounts.

"Blue Button" An Unauthorised Clerk on the floor of the London Stock Exchange. *See* AUTHORISED CLERK.

Blue Chip High class industrial share.

Blue Sky Laws A popular description for laws enacted in various States of the United States of America intended to protect the public against security frauds. The term is thought to have originated when a judge ruled that a particular stock had about the same value as "a patch of blue sky".

Board of Trade A British government department which, under the President of the Board of Trade, has a general responsibility in respect of the United Kingdom's commerce, particularly overseas trade, including commercial relations with other countries; import and export trade; protective tariffs; consumer protection; the shipping and shipbuilding industries; aviation; distribution and retail trades; insurance; tourism; and the administration of certain regulatory legislation.

Board of Trade Journal Weekly publication which gives authoritative information about export opportunities; tariffs, customs and imports regulations of overseas countries; international trade exhibitions and fairs; U.K. production, etc. Reports from H.M. Government's commercial representatives throughout the world are published to assist industrialists to increase their trade. Also contains statistical articles dealing with many important aspects of the national economy. It contains a monthly index of wholesale prices.

Boiler Room (U.S.) A room lined with desks or cubicles, each with a telephone, salesmen engaging in high-pressure peddling over the telephone of company stocks and shares of dubious value.

Bond A security issued by a Government, public body, corporation or company carrying a fixed rate of interest. The terms of repayment are usually printed upon the bond. A bond may be secured or unsecured and the date of maturity varies considerably. Some bonds are undated and irredeemable. *See* SECURITIES.

Bonded Warehouse Warehouse in which dutiable articles may be stored without previously paying duty. Thus, if the goods are re-exported, the duty need not be paid at all. On the other hand, if goods are removed to be consumed in the country, i.e. taken out of bond, duties are then payable.

Bonus Issue *See* SCRIP OR BONUS ISSUE.

Bonus-Penalty Contract A type of contract under which the contractor is guaranteed a bonus, usually a fixed sum of money, for each day the project he has undertaken to construct is completed ahead of a specified date, while he agrees to pay a penalty for each day of delay in completing the works after the specified date.

Boom A period of expansion of business activity. Opposite of slump or recession. A boom reaches a peak when the economy is working at full capacity.

"Borrowing Short to Lend Long" Incurring short-term liabilities to purchase long-term assets.

Bottomry The pledge of a ship and its cargo to secure a loan to enable the ship to continue its voyage. Respondentia is the pledge of the cargo only. Bottomry is named after the bottom or keel of a ship.

Bounty A payment (i.e. a subsidy) given by the state to merchants or manufacturers to encourage particular branches of business activity, e.g. the building of ships, or the export trades.

Bourse The equivalent of the English Stock Exchange, and is a term applied not only to the Paris Exchange but also to the Exchanges of such places as Zurich, Milan, Frankfurt and Amsterdam.

Boycott An economic sanction which may be used for political or economic ends. It takes the form of one party refusing to supply goods or service to, or to purchase goods and services from, another party.

Bradburys Treasury notes of the period 1914–19, signed by John Bradbury, Secretary for the Treasury (q.v.).

Branch Banking A feature of the British and Australian banking systems in that relatively few large banks maintain a large number of branch banks throughout the country. In Britain there are over 14,000 branches. Branch banking has shown considerable development in the United States of America in recent years, but the basic pattern is one of a very large number of banks each possessing only a very small number of branches. *See* COMMERCIAL BANKS.

Branding   An attempt to create or enhance differences between similar products, or between groups of products, by the use of a distinctive name or symbol. *See* ADVERTISING; PRODUCT DIFFERENTIATION.

Brassage   A charge once made by the Mint (q.v.) to cover the expense of converting bullion into coin. Abolished in 1666.

"Break-Even" Chart   A chart which shows the profitability or otherwise of an undertaking at various levels of activity, indicating a point at which neither profit or loss is made, i.e. the "break-even" point. *See* Figure 1.

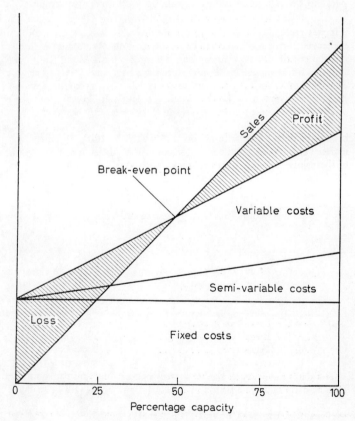

FIGURE 1.   BREAK-EVEN CHART

23

Breaking Bulk   The function of a wholesaler (q.v.) in dividing up a commodity into quantities or sizes to meet the particular requirements of individual retailers.

Break-up Value   Net worth of a company: the value of physical assets less current liabilities and prior charge capital (q.v.).
If the break-up value greatly exceeds market valuation of company's equity, there is scope for a take-over bid (q.v.).

Bretton Woods Agreement   An international monetary and financial conference held at Bretton Woods, New Hampshire, U.S.A., in July, 1944, which resulted in an agreed statement of aims for post-war monetary policy. These aims were:

    (a) to make all currencies freely convertible and thereby encourage multi-lateral trade (q.v.);
    (b) to keep exchange rates stable; and,
    (c) to provide some means of assisting a country with temporary difficulties with its balance of payments (q.v.).

It was recognised that during the immediate post-war years a degree of exchange control would have to be accepted. A direct result of the Agreement was the creation of two institutions, the International Monetary Fund (q.v.) and the International Bank for Reconstruction and Development (q.v.). The Bretton Woods Agreement was essentially a compromise between two plans, one advanced by Lord Keynes of the British Treasury and the other by Mr. White of the American Treasury.

British Employers' Confederation   Established in 1919, a confederation of national employers' organisations which dealt with labour questions in most of the principal industries, other than the nationalised industries. In August, 1965, its functions were taken over by the new Confederation of British Industry (q.v.).

British Funds   Issues of British Government stock. They include the following:

Exchequer $6\frac{3}{4}\%$	1971
British Electric 3%	1968–73
Savings Bonds 3%	1965–75
British Electric $3\frac{1}{2}\%$	1976–79
British Transport 3% ..	1978–88
Funding 4%	1960–90
Treasury $6\frac{3}{4}\%$	1995–98
Funding 6%	1993
British Gas 3%	1990–95
Treasury $5\frac{1}{2}\%$	2008–12
Consols $2\frac{1}{2}\%$	undated

The dates show when the stock will mature and the loan be redeemed. Double dates indicate a period in which the repayment will be made.

British National Export Council   A national co-operative body set up in 1964 to keep the overall national export effort under constant review and to guide and inspire the best results in all actual and potential markets. The Council aims to provide finance and common services towards this end. The membership of the Council comprises representatives from Government departments particularly concerned and from national organisations.

British Productivity Council Successor to the Anglo-American Council on Productivity (q.v.) which conducted many studies on both sides of the Atlantic during the years immediately following the Second World War into the factors governing productivity. *See* PRODUCTIVITY.

British Savings Bond Introduced in 1969, a savings bond which carries a rate of interest of 7 per cent per annum with a 2 per cent tax-free bonus if held for five years.

British Steel Corporation A public corporation formed on 27th April, 1967, to implement the Iron and Steel Act 1967, and assume ownership and control of fourteen major British steel companies and their subsidiaries. The aims of the corporation are: (a) to strengthen the marketing and technological position of the nationalised steel industry as a whole; (b) to provide British industry with products that are competitive in price, quality and service; and (c) to ensure the efficient and socially responsible use of human resources. The corporation intends to retain substantial planning and policy-making authority at the centre, while allowing the four groups into which the industry is divided the greatest degree of operating autonomy. A common system of pricing is maintained throughout the nationalised steel industry, although the groups compete with each other on costs, service, quality and productivity. *See* IRON AND STEEL CORPORATION OF GREAT BRITAIN.

British Transport Commission A body set up in 1947 to take over and control the railways, docks and inland waterways, road transport, London transport, and hotels owned and operated by the railways. The Transport Act, 1962, replaced the Commission by four Boards—the British Railways Board, the London Transport Board, the British Waterways Board and the British Transport Docks Board.

Broker An intermediary between two or more persons engaged in a business transaction. Brokers include import brokers, issue brokers, insurance brokers and stockbrokers. *See* STOCKBROKER.

Brokerage Commission charged by a broker for selling or buying shares, commodities or insurance on behalf of a client.

Brookings Institution An institution for research and graduate training in economics and government established in Washington, D.C., in 1928 upon the merging of three research organisations. The Institution is named after Robert S. Brookings (1850-1932), businessman and philanthropist, who played a prominent part in its establishment.

Bucket Shop A slang term denoting a firm dealing in stocks and shares, not a member of the Stock Exchange, whose business is highly speculative and disreputable; much of this type of business was eliminated upon the passing of the Prevention of Fraud (Investment) Act 1939.

Budget, British An estimate of national revenue and expenditure for the ensuing fiscal year, announced by the Chancellor of the Exchequer in the April of each year. In times of economic crisis, it is sometimes necessary to introduce an "interim Budget" before the end of the fiscal year. The Budget has become a major instrument of social and economic policy. The Chancellor presents a review of fiscal policy against a background of general economic policy; he reviews the Government's income and expenditure for the past year, and presents a forecast of income and expenditure for the coming year. He then announces changes in taxation, if any, necessary to achieve the Government's policies. It is no longer the Government's aim to simply balance its revenue and expenditure; Budget surpluses, or deficits, may be created to influence the economy as a whole, e.g. by "siphoning off" excessive purchasing power in an attempt to combat inflation, or to inject additional purchasing power into the economy to stimulate demand and trade. The full details of each Budget are contained in a Financial Statement (q.v.), commonly known as the Budget White Paper.

Budget, Business A financial and quantitative statement, prepared in advance, of the policy to be pursued during a defined period of time to serve specified objectives. The budget plays a leading part in the cycle of events in managing a business; it is in fact an evaluation of the intentions of management. The final budget, or master budget, adopted by a company for the ensuing period is the result of integrating budgets prepared for each of the main sections of the business. *See* BUDGET, CAPITAL; BUDGET, MANUFACTURING; BUDGET, MASTER; BUDGET, OFFICE AND ADMINISTRATION; BUDGET, RESEARCH; BUDGET, SALES AND MARKETING.

Budget, Capital A business budget covering: (a) development expenditure, such as the purchase of new plant and buildings, sales promotion and advertising schemes; (b) provision for the depreciation of fixed assets; and (c) finance. *See* BUDGET, BUSINESS; FINANCE.

Budget, Manufacturing A business budget covering: (a) the anticipated output in quantity and value of the company's products; (b) the purchases of raw materials; (c) stocks of raw materials, work in progress and sundry stores; (d) factory labour costs; and (e) the factory overhead expenses. *See* BUDGET, BUSINESS.

Budget, Master A business budget integrating several separate budgets, such as the capital budget, sales and marketing budget, manufacturing budget, research budget, and office and administration budget. *See* BUDGET, BUSINESS.

Budget, Office and Administration A business budget covering: (a) the salaries and expenses of office management and staff; and (b) other expenses such as legal expenses, audit fees, etc. *See* BUDGET, BUSINESS.

Budget, Research A business budget covering: (a) the salaries and expenses of research staff directly employed by the company, and (b) contributions to research conducted by outside agencies (if any) for the company. *See* BUDGET, BUSINESS.

Budget, Sales and Marketing A business budget covering: (a) anticipated sales in quantity; (b) anticipated realisable prices of sales; (c) expected turnover, being the product of (a) and (b); (d) selling and distribution expenses; (e) expenditure on publicity; and (f) the quantity and value of the stocks of finished products. *See* BUDGET, BUSINESS.

Budget Surplus An excess of Government income over Government expenditure. This may be achieved deliberately in order to drain off purchasing power for consumer goods and reduce inflationary pressure. The surplus may be retained by the Government or invested in productive activities.

Budgetary Control An important aspect of management accountancy which consists of the comparison of achieved trading results with the results assumed in the budget in order to ascertain or ensure that the objects of the plan are being achieved, or to provide a starting point for the investigation of discrepancies which could lead to revisions of the budget. *See* BUDGET, BUSINESS.

Buffer Stocks Stocks of raw materials and commodities held for the purpose of reducing fluctuations in the prices of primary products. Buffer stocks may be used to match the supplies coming on to a market with the current demand in order to narrow the movement of prices. Usually a "ceiling" and a "floor" price is fixed for a commodity; when the ceiling price is reached stocks are released on to the market and, conversely, when the floor price is reached stocks are increased. Such schemes, which are generally international in scope, are only suitable for commodities which can be stored cheaply and with little risk of deterioration. Schemes in the past have been run solely for the benefit of producers, but the larger schemes now provide for consumer representation.

Building Society A society which is a source for the provision of long-term loans on the security of houses and land, and a channel for the investment of small personal savings; the building society in Britain enables large numbers of people to buy their own houses. Building Societies are regulated by the Building Societies Act 1962; over three hundred societies are members of the Building Societies Association. The investment facilities offered to the public take the form of "shares" and "deposits". The shares are not dealt in on the stock exchange (q.v.) and carry a rate of interest which may be varied from time to time. Deposits carry a rate of interest usually $\frac{1}{4}$ per cent less than that paid on shares; deposits may be withdrawn at shorter notice than shares. Advances are made on the security of freehold or leasehold property, the society retaining a legal interest in the property until the loan is repaid. The advances are usually repayable by fixed monthly or quarterly instalments, which include both capital and interest.

Bulk Supply Tariff A preferential tariff for the purchase of supplies of a commodity or service in bulk. The Central Electricity Generating Board (q.v.) sells electricity in bulk to the Area Electricity Boards who then re-sell it to the consumer. The tariff is based upon the aggregate costs of generation incurred by the Generating Board, and its share of the balance of revenue (q.v.) to be earned. It is a two-part tariff with a kilowatt demand charge and a running charge per kilowatt-hour.

Bull A person, who, believing prices will rise, buys shares with a view to selling them at a higher price. A "tired" or "stale bull" is a person who has made a purchase but has found no early opportunity to sell at a profit. *See* CONTANGO, CARRY OVER, CONTINUATION.

Bull Market A market in which prices are rising.

Bullion Name given to gold and silver in bulk, whether in the form of bars or lumps of refined metal, or coins, medals or dust.
In Great Britain, until 1925, anyone taking gold bullion to the Royal Mint had the right to have it made into coins free of charge.
This right was abolished, but even up to 1931 anyone could still sell gold to the Bank of England (q.v.) at fixed prices.

Bullion Market A market in which gold bullion is bought and sold. The London bullion market comprises five firms of bullion brokers who meet daily to fix an official price; dealings are also carried on between banks and authorised dealers.

Business Economics The study of the ways in which commodities are produced and distributed.

Business Saving Saving out of profits, or "ploughing back" (q.v.), and provision for depreciation (q.v.).

Business Statistics Office (B.S.O.) A British Government organisation whose main task is to introduce and maintain a co-ordinated and comprehensive system of industrial statistics which will meet the needs both of the Government and industry. The B.S.O. came into operation on 1st January, 1969. *See* CENTRAL REGISTER OF BUSINESSES.

Buyers' Market A market in which producers, suppliers and dealers experience difficulty in selling the goods which are available.

Buying-In A procedure adopted by the Stock Exchange to assist a seller who is unable at the due date to deliver shares sold, by buying an equivalent amount of stock in the market, charging the cost and extra expenses to the seller.

By-Product A useful product which results from the production of some other commodity but is not the main purpose of the activity.

C

Call Options *See* SHARE OPTIONS.

Callable Preferred Stock (U.S.) Preferred stock (q.v.) which can be called in for payment at a stated price.

Calls Instalment payments on new shares. A company does not necessarily require immediately the full amount on the shares it has issued, and may instead call-up the additional capital as it requires it.

Cambridge School Appellation for a school of economists consisting of Alfred Marshall (1842–1924) and his followers. Marshall was Professor of Political Economy at Cambridge between 1885 and 1908. As a result of his efforts a separate School and Tripos in Economics and associated branches of Political Science was established at Cambridge in 1903. Marshall's famous work *Principles of Economics* (1890) and other works placed him in line with the Classical School (q.v.), particularly Adam Smith and John Stuart Mill. The more striking contributions to economic science made in his *Principles of Economics* were:

(a) the clarification of the respective roles played by demand and by costs of production in the determination of value;

(b) the general theory of economic equilibrium in which all the elements of the economic world are kept in their places by mutual counterpoise and interaction, a theory strengthened by two subsidiary concepts— the "margin" and "substitution" (q.v.);

(c) the explicit introduction of the element of time as a factor in economic analysis, with the concepts of the "short" and "long" period;

(d) the distinction between "external" and "internal" economies;

(e) the doctrine of "normal profit" (q.v.) assisted by the concepts of "quasi-rent" (q.v.) and the "representative firm" (q.v.);

(f) the concept of consumer's surplus (q.v.);

(g) the introduction of the idea of "elasticity";

(h) proof that laissez-faire (q.v.), regarded as a principle of maximum social advantage, breaks down in certain conditions, theoretically and not merely practically; and

(i) an examination of the effects of monopoly.

Marshall's successor was A. C. Pigou. *See* CLASSICAL SCHOOL; KEYNESIAN REVOLUTION.

Cambridge Theory of Money A "cash balance" form of the quantity theory of money (q.v.), developed by the Cambridge school of economists and contained in the equation:

$$M = kPT$$

where M = the amount of money (bank notes, etc. plus bank deposits); k = the reciprocal of the velocity of circulation; P = the general price level; and T = the total number of trade transactions. If the velocity of circulation of money is four times in a given period, then k is one-quarter of expenditure; k is the proportion of the community's expenditure on goods and services which on average is held as cash during the period. There are no fundamental differences between Fisher's quantity theory of money and the Cambridge theory of money, but the "cash balance" approach emphasises that changes in the demand for money (k) may be as important as the quantity of money (M) in determining the general price level (P). The influences determining the general level of prices are more complex than both forms of the quantity theory envisaged. *See* LIQUIDITY PREFERENCE.

Canons of Taxation *See* TAXATION, ADAM SMITH'S CANONS OF.

Capacity The estimated maximum level of production from a plant on a sustained basis, allowing for all necessary shut-downs, holidays, etc.

Cape Scrip Union of South Africa shares.

Capital One of the factors of production (q.v.) and may be defined as "wealth used for the production of further wealth". Capital is described as "real" when it consists of machines, factories, railways, stocks of raw materials, etc. Real capital may be sub-divided into:

(a) *Fixed Capital*—factories, warehouses, offices, shops, and other buildings used in industry and trade; plant and machinery and equipment; means of transport and communication;

(b) *Floating or Circulating Capital*—raw materials, fuel, goods in process of manufacture, stocks held by producers or traders. Alfred Marshall described circulating capital as "fulfilling the whole of its office in the production in which it is engaged by a single use";

(c) *Specific Capital*—equipment which cannot normally be used for any other purpose than that for which it was originally designed and constructed;

(d) *Non-specific Capital*—equipment which can be used in a variety of processes.

The term "capital" is commonly used for the money subscribed by shareholders or stockholders, or lent by banks, for use in a business. This is more correctly described as business finance, although Adam Smith argued that "a person's capital is that part of his stock from which he expects to derive an income".

Capital Account An element in the balance of payments (q.v.) account which deals with financial transactions, the buying and selling of securities, investment abroad and non-residents' investment in the U.K.

Capital Accumulation An increase in man-made equipment such as machinery, tools, buildings and other structures, and stocks of goods, used for or capable of being used for the production of goods and services.

Capital Allowances Deductions from gross business profits for the purpose of covering the depreciation of assets permitted by the tax authorities when calculating taxable income.

Capital—Authorised, Nominal or Registered Synonymous terms for capital fixed by the Memorandum of Association (q.v.) of a company.

Capital Charges Charges which include interest on the amount of capital employed, and provision for depreciation or repayment of principal.

Capital Consumption *See* CAPITAL FORMATION AND DEPRECIATION; DEPRECIATION.

Capital Cost Component In relation to the total production cost of each unit of output, the capital cost component is given by:

$$\frac{\text{Capital Charges}}{\text{Units of Output}}$$

where the capital charges are the sum of the annual interest charges on capital employed (q.v.) and the annual depreciation charges, and the units of output relate to the year under consideration.

Capital, Cost of The cost of obtaining the total capital employed (q.v.) by a business, expressed as a rate of interest.

Capital, Deepening *See* INVESTMENT, DEEPENING.

Capital Employed The capital in use in a business; it consists of the total assets *minus* the current liabilities. Current liabilities are those liabilities providing resources for less than a year; their exclusion helps avoid fluctuations in total assets which might otherwise impair comparisons based on several years' trading. *See* CAPITAL EMPLOYED, RETURN ON.

Capital Employed, Return On The relating of profit to the estimate of average capital employed (q.v.) to give a ratio, commonly called the primary ratio, as follows:

$$\frac{\text{Profit}}{\text{Capital}}$$

It is essential that the long-run return on capital employed in a business should be sufficient to ensure a fair return to shareholders, provide for the normal expansion of the business, attract new capital when required and retain the confidence of creditors and employees.

Capital Expenditure Expenditure of a non-recurrent nature resulting in the acquisition of assets. *See* CURRENT EXPENDITURE.

31

Capital Formation and Depreciation Capital formation in a given time period is the expenditure on fixed capital assets (buildings, plant and machinery, vehicles, etc.) either for replacing or adding to the stock of fixed assets. Expenditure on repairs and maintenance is excluded. During a year fixed capital resources are also used up, or "consumed", due to wear and tear, obsolescence, etc. Thus from the value of gross capital formation, there must be deducted the value of capital consumption or depreciation, thus leaving a value for net capital formation. *See* DEPRECIATION.

Capital Gains Profits made from the sale of investments or property, due allowance being made for any decline in the value of money during the period which elapsed between buying and selling.

Capital Gains Tax A tax imposed by the Government on capital gains (q.v.). Previously untaxed in Britain, the Finance Act of 1962 introduced a short-term capital gains tax on the purchase and sale of property (including shares) excluding personal belongings and owner-occupied houses, if the sale took place less than six months after the purchase (three years in the case of land and buildings). In 1965, the law was extended to cover capital gains realised over any period of time, but with similar exceptions from the tax.

Capital Gearing The ratio of fixed interest capital including prior charges (q.v.) to ordinary share capital. If a company's capital contains a large proportion of fixed interest stocks, the company is described as "highly-geared". In these circumstances a small change in profits can make a large difference to the amount available for distribution to ordinary shareholders; yields may be well above or well below the average yield on the whole capital involved. *See* LEVERAGE (U.S.).

Capital Goods Goods made for the purpose of producing consumer goods (q.v.), and other capital goods, e.g. machinery of all kinds. Synonymous with "producer goods".

Capital-Intensive Description of forms of production in which there is a considerable use of capital equipment per person employed. In a capital-intensive industry, capital charges may account for 50 per cent or more of production costs, excluding the value of raw materials or fuel. In chemical processes, the value of capital equipment per worker is very high. In the British coal-mining industry, which is comparatively highly-mechanised, wages still account for over half the costs of production. *See* LABOUR-INTENSIVE; RESEARCH-INTENSIVE.

Capital Issues Committee A non-statutory body created to advise the Treasury (q.v.) as to whether consent should be given to individual applications for permission to borrow on the capital market (q.v.). Introduced in 1939 as a war measure, the control of investment was given an extended life by the Investment (Control and Guarantees) Act 1946. The aim was to enable the Government to plan both public and private investment. No firm was permitted to issue new shares, above a specified total value, without the sanction of the Treasury acting on the advice of the Capital Issues Committee. Before recommending a licence, the Committee would consider whether the proposed project would further the Government's investment programmes, whether it would assist the expansion of exports or whether it would assist the policy of diversification of industry in one or other of the Development Areas (q.v.). The regulatory functions of the Committee were brought to an end in February 1959, save that overseas borrowers must still apply for consent for issues over £50,000 in any twelve months.

Capital Levies Once-for-all capital taxes. Death duties (q.v.) are a form of capital levy.

Capital, Marginal Efficiency of See MARGINAL EFFICIENCY OF CAPITAL.

Capital Market A market comprising institutions which deal in the purchase and sale of securities, e.g. the new issue market and the stock exchange (q.v.). See FINANCE.

Capital Movement The movement of money capital from one country to another. See HOT MONEY.

Capital-Output Ratio, Incremental For a given industrial technique, the ratio of the capital cost of the technique to the value added by the additional output. If the ratio is 3:1 then a £300 addition to capital equipment will yield a £100 increase in output per annum. Thus, if an economy invests 12 per cent of its income, and has a capital-output ratio of 3:1, it can expect a 4 per cent increase in output per annum.

Capital Recovery The process by which the original investment in a physical asset is recovered over its economic life (q.v.). In the absence of inflation (q.v.), capital recovery is achieved through depreciation allowances.

Capital Reserves See RESERVES.

Capital, Risk See RISK CAPITAL.

Capital, Security See SECURITY CAPITAL.

Capital, Social See SOCIAL CAPITAL.

Capital Stock (U.S.) Shares in the proprietary interest in a corporation (q.v.).

Capital Structure The types and numbers of stocks and shares which are to be issued, or have been issued, by a company.

Capital Surplus (U.S.) The amount paid by stockholders in excess of the par value of each share.

Capital Transactions The lending or borrowing of sums of money, or the transfer of assets accumulated in the past.

Capital, Venture *See* RISK CAPITAL.

Capital, Widening *See* INVESTMENT, WIDENING.

Capitalisation The amount and nature of the capital of a company.

Capitalisation Issue *See* SCRIP OR BONUS ISSUE.

Capitalisation Ratios The proportions of each kind of security issued by a company. *See* CAPITAL STRUCTURE.

Capitalised Value The capital equivalent of an annual payment. Capital values are determined by the rate of interest and the rent produced. Thus, if the prevailing rate of interest for investments is 5 per cent and a parcel of land has a rental of £50, the capitalised value will be £1,000. If the rate of interest falls, then the capital value increases, the rent still being regarded as corresponding to the current rate of interest. At 2½ per cent the land mentioned would have a capital value of £2,000. If the site has prospects of development, however, the market value may greatly exceed the capitalised rental value.

Capitalism A social system in which the means of production, distribution and exchange are wholly or substantially owned by private persons. *See* INDIVIDUALISM; SOCIALISM.

Capitation Tax Also known as a poll tax, a tax levied on each member of the community equally irrespective of wealth or income.

Captive Market A market in which the supplier of a good or service is in a monopolistic position, the consumer being unable to obtain suitable substitutes or to do without. Until a few years ago, the gas industry, using no other raw material save coal, was a captive market for the National Coal Board (q.v.).

Carry-Over *See* CONTANGO, CARRY-OVER, CONTINUATION.

Cartel A central selling organisation which assigns to each of its members a specific share in the total output of a commodity. Members are bound by a code of rules; if the specified output is exceeded a fine is inflicted.

Cash Money (q.v.) in the form of coin and bank-notes.

Cash Flow The passage of money into and out of a business enterprise. The term is used by American and Canadian companies to describe net earnings, plus depreciation and other allowances, expressed as an amount per share.

Cash Generation The net cash flow (q.v.) arising from an investment by a business enterprise, assuming this to be positive.

Cash Ratio (a) The ratio of 8 per cent which British banks conventionally maintain between their liquid assets either in till money (notes or coin) or on account at the Bank of England (q.v.), and their total deposits. Prior to

1946 this ratio was maintained at 10 per cent. As a bank must always be able to pay cash on demand the maintenance of a satisfactory cash ratio and a satisfactory liquidity ratio (q.v.) have proved essential to sustain public confidence in a bank's ability to do this.

(b) A measure of the ability of a firm to meet its obligations in the short-term, being expressed in the form:

$$\frac{\text{Cash in hand plus payments due from customers}}{\text{Current liabilities}}$$

Census of Distribution and Other Services A census conducted for the first time in 1950 of wholesale and retail distribution and a limited number of service trades in Britain. It did not cover hotels, entertainments and business services. All the businesses covered by the Census were required to supply details of sales, purchases, stocks, employment, wages and salaries, and certain additional information appropriate to the type of business. The results of the Census were published in 1953 in the main Report (Vols. I, II and III) and a short Report. In addition, a special Report entitled "Britain's Shops" was published in 1952. The Census was repeated in 1957, 1961 and 1966.

Census of Population An enumeration of inhabitants. A census of the population of the United Kingdom has been taken every tenth year since 1801, with the exception of 1941. From 1966 a census will be taken every five years. Estimates of population for the intervening years are made by the Registrar-General. The modern census is a means of obtaining a great deal of information about people, their occupations and their social conditions.

Census of Production A census of the output and related affairs of the manufacturing industries, mines and quarries, building trades and productive services carried on by public utility undertakings. Until 1968 a full census was not taken every year, but in those years when a full census was not taken a sample census was relied on. The census provides information useful in estimating consumers' expenditure, fixed capital formation, stocks and work in progress and national income (q.v.) statistics. The census also provides a basis for the calculation of the monthly index of industrial production and the indices of wholesale prices (q.v.). Since 1968 the business statistics office (q.v.) has collected quarterly or, in some cases, monthly, production figures, supplemented by annual inquiries into such matters as total sales and purchases, fixed investment and changes in stocks and work in progress. *See* INDEX NUMBERS OF INDUSTRIAL PRODUCTION.

Central Bank A bank which in any country is (a) banker to the Government, (b) banker to the commercial banks and (c) implements the currency and credit policy of the country.

Central Electricity Generating Board (C.E.G.B.) Established under the Electricity Act of 1957, which reorganised the electricity supply industry, the Board's statutory responsibilities are " to develop and maintain an efficient, co-ordinated and economical system of supply of electricity in bulk for all parts of England and Wales." The Board own and operate some 230/240 power stations (both conventional and nuclear), and the main transmission lines for the bulk supply of electricity to the twelve Area Electricity Boards. The Board undertakes the planning and construction of new generating and transmission capacity. By 1970 the C.E.G.B. had eight completed nuclear power stations in operation. The Nationalisation Act of 1947 did not embrace private generation by industrial establishments, but these account for no more than one-ninth of the total national output of electricity.

Central Register of Businesses A register, prepared by the Business Statistics Office (q.v.), of the names and addresses of all business establishments in Britain and other "units" which make statistical returns; each entry is coded to indicate its location, industrial classification and size. The Register is a "data bank" for all the principal Government inquiries, and a basis for sample surveys.

Certificate of Incorporation A certificate issued to companies who have complied with all the statutory requirements for registration. *See* COMPANY, LEGAL FORMATION OF.

Certificate of Inspection A certificate, which may be required under the terms of a contract or the laws of an importing country, stating that goods shipped are in sound condition. This applies particularly to perishable goods.

Certificate of Origin A declaration by an exporter or by a Chamber of Commerce stating the country of origin of goods shipped. Such a declaration is often necessary in order to obtain preferential tariff rates, e.g. Imperial Preference in British Commonwealth countries.

"Charging What the Traffic Will Bear" A system of charging based upon the upper limit of what any particular traffic can afford to pay, subject to the lower limit of what a transport system can afford to carry it for. In practice, this means that some rates are so low as to barely cover running expenses, while other rates are sufficiently high, not only to cover running costs but also to leave a surplus available as a contribution towards the unapportioned expenses of the low class traffic. This principle also forms the basis of the system of taxation which aims, not at equality of payment by each taxpayer, but rather equality of burden or sacrifices.

Charter Party A contract to convey goods by sea to a special place for a stated sum.

Cheap Money A description applied to money when the Bank Rate (q.v.) is low. Between 1932 and 1951, save for a short period in 1939, the Bank Rate was kept down to 2 per cent in order to stimulate borrowing. The use of the Bank Rate as a flexible instrument of monetary policy was restored in 1951. *See* MONETARY POLICY, OBJECTIVES OF.

Checking Deposits (U.S.) Demand deposits held by commercial banks; the largest element in the supply of money. The system of demand deposits enables payments to be made by cheque (q.v.). *See* DEMAND DEPOSIT; TIME DEPOSIT.

Cheque A bill of exchange (q.v.) drawn on a banker and payable on demand; an instruction to a banker to pay without delay a stated sum of money to the person to whom the cheque is payable. If payable to the "bearer" a cheque is a negotiable instrument (q.v.); but it is not negotiable if it is endorsed "not negotiable". If a cheque is "crossed", having two lines drawn parallel across its face, the amount will be paid only into the payee's account. If "open" or uncrossed, a banker will pay cash to the person presenting the cheque. A cheque is not legal tender (q.v.). Banks honour cheques by reducing the deposit of the person writing the cheque and increasing the deposit of, or paying cash to, the person in whose favour the cheque is written.

Choice A fundamental principle underlying all economic activity. The private individual must decide on the distribution of his income between expenditure and saving, and on the distribution of his expenditure between different goods and services; the businessman must decide on what he intends to produce and the methods of production to be adopted, as well as the location of the production facilities; the State must decide how the resources of the nation are to be best deployed. All these decisions involve often difficult choices between alternatives.

C.I.F. Cost, insurance and freight. Term used of goods shipped where the price includes shipping and insurance charges. A C.I.F. quotation means that the seller must ship the goods, meeting all charges up to "on board" and paying freight, insurance, etc. He must supply the buyer with all the documents required to enable the goods to be imported. The buyer must pay all expenses, customs duties, etc. on arrival of the goods at the port of destination. *See* F.O.B.

Circuit Velocity *See* VELOCITY OF CIRCULATION.

"City, The" The City of London, commonly known as the "Square Mile". Hobson has defined the four fundamental functions which the City performs:

(a) The City provides a mechanism by which payment of any sum of money, large or small, may be made with safety and dispatch, without the use of actual notes or coins;

(b) The City provides the money which enables foodstuffs and raw materials to be produced, to be transported about the world, and to undergo processes of manufacture until they are finally sold as finished, consumable articles;

(c) The City collects the country's savings and provides for their investment;

(d) The City provides a mechanism, consisting of the Foreign Exchange market (q.v.), assisted by the Gold Bullion Market by which the money of one country can be exchanged into the money of another.

Civil List Money voted annually by Parliament for the Sovereign and for the expenses of the Royal household.

37

Civil Partnership Partnerships formed in the Province of Quebec, generally by firms of lawyers, chartered accountants or other professional men. They differ from general and limited partnerships in that members are jointly liable, but not jointly and severally liable for the debts of the partnership. If a civil partner makes a contract in the name of the partnership without authority expressed or implied by his co-partners, he binds only himself and not the other partners, unless it can be shown that the partnership as a whole has benefited from the act.

Classical School Appellation for a group of writers on economics during the second half of the 18th century and the first half of the 19th century. They were the first to formulate a systematic body of economic principles, seeking to explain uniformities in economic activity which are not the result of deliberate design by a central planning body, but the product of the interplay of separate decisions by individuals and groups. In general they supported the philosophy of laissez-faire (q.v.) in opposition to mercantilism (q.v.) prevalent in the early part of the period. Their doctrines became the philosophical basis of the Manchester School (q.v.) which was ardent in support of free trade between nations. The principal members of the group included:

ADAM SMITH (1723–90). Professor of logic and moral philosophy at Glasgow University. In 1759 he published his *Theory of the Moral Sentiments*. This was followed in 1776 by his great work *An Inquiry into the Nature and Causes of the Wealth of Nations*. This was the first comprehensive treatment of the subject, examining the forces through which the market process directed the distribution of resources between different industries and the manner in which competition produced a kind of order based on specialisation and division of labour. He explained the value of commodities in terms of the quantity of labour employed in their production and examined the three elements which entered into price—wages, profit and rent. Smith's philosophy was individualistic, seeing self-interest as a proper criterion of economic action. Thus, the pursuit of self-interest would contribute to the public interest. Nevertheless, he introduced some important exceptions to the doctrine of laissez-faire (q.v.), for example, state administration of the post office and compulsory elementary education. He strongly advocated freedom of trade and sharply criticised the restriction of competition whether by government regulation or by combination of producers.

THOMAS ROBERT MALTHUS (1766–1834) In the year 1798 Malthus became curate of Albury in Surrey. In the same year appeared his *Essay on the Principle of Population* in which he argued that population tended to increase beyond the means of subsistence and that checks on this increase were necessary. The *Essay* re-appeared as a second edition in 1803 embodying somewhat less dismal conclusions. The work caused a storm of controversy. *See* MALTHUSIAN THEORY OF POPULATION.

DAVID RICARDO (1772–1823) After making a fortune on the London Stock Exchange, Ricardo devoted himself to a study of economics. With James Mill (1773–1836) he founded modern economic theory, although his work was somewhat impaired by building on Smith's theory of value. In 1817 he published his main work, *Principles of Political Economy and Taxation*, a work largely concerned with the causes determining the distribution of

38

wealth. In it he developed his famous theory of rent. *See* RENT, RICARDO'S THEORY OF.

NASSAU WILLIAM SENIOR (1790–1864) Professor of political economy at Oxford University, 1825–30 and 1847–52. In addition to important political articles, he published *An Outline of the Science of Political Economy* in 1836. Senior stands somewhat outside the orthodox classical tradition.

JAMES MILL (1773–1836) Although educated for the ministry, Mill became a journalist. In 1818 he published his *History of British India,* and, subsequently, obtained a high post with the East India Company. He was closely associated with Jeremy Bentham and David Ricardo, helping to found modern economic theory. In 1821 his *Elements of Political Economy* appeared. This was followed by his *Analysis of the Human Mind* in 1829. Mill was the father of John Stuart Mill.

JOHN STUART MILL (1806–1873) Son of James Mill. He formed the Utilitarian Society and in 1825 edited Jeremy Bentham's *Treatise upon Evidence.* In 1843 he published his *System of Logic;* and in 1848 his *Principles of Political Economy,* which became the most influential book on the subject during the second half of the 19th century. Subsequently, in 1859, appeared his essay *On Liberty* and in 1873 his autobiography.

JEREMY BENTHAM (1748–1832) A lawyer by training, but a reformer and philosopher by inclination. In 1776 he published his *Fragment on Government* embodying a theory of government. In 1789 appeared his *Introduction to the Principles of Morals and Legislation.* In addition he produced a number of works on ethics, jurisprudence, logic and political economy. He developed the philosophical theory that all human action, especially action by the government, should aim at the greatest happiness of the greatest number of people. Bentham's "Utilitarianism" led him to regard a great deal of state intervention at that time as mischievous, buttressing all manner of privileges. He supported the economists' view that all regulation should be swept away which impeded the free course of industry and commerce.

Clayton Act *See* ANTI-TRUST LAWS (U.S.).

Clearing Banks, London Five banks who are members of the London Bankers' Clearing House, an institution which originated in the late 18th century for clearing or settling inter-bank transactions. Inter-bank payments are limited to net deficits arising from each day's business. Nearly all the domestic banking business of England and Wales is in the hands of these five banks, which are Barclay, (including Martins), Lloyds, Midland, the National Westminster (including the District), and the National and Commercial Bank. *See* "BIG FOUR", THE.

Clearing Dollars Units of account which may be used by two countries who have set targets for the quantity of goods they will buy from each other; each side is credited for its sales in clearing dollars which are earmarked for purchases from the other party. Bilateral trade agreements may stipulate a maximum "swing" in the payments balance, setting a limit to surpluses and deficits. Clearing dollars are not United States dollars, being units of account only. *See* BILATERAL TRADE.

Clearing House A banking institution where interbank debts are cancelled out.

Closed Shop   A condition imposed by trade unions or employers that all employees of a firm shall be members of the appropriate trade unions.

Some local authorities have made it a condition of employment that men shall be members of the trade union concerned.

Those in favour of the "closed shop" argue that those who are not members of the union should not enjoy the benefits obtained by the union for its members.

Non-unionists (and many unionists) assert that insistence on the closed shop is an infringement of the liberty of the individual.

Closing Prices   Prices of securities at the close of a day's business on the floor of the Stock Exchange (q.v.)

Coal Equivalent   The heat content of any quantity of a fuel, other than coal, expressed in terms of a quantity of coal of the same heat content. For example, it is often assumed that a heavy residual fuel oil may be converted to coal equivalent at 1.7 tons of coal per ton of oil.

Cobol   Abbreviation for "common business oriented language"; an international computer programming language for accountancy and business purposes. *See* ALGOL; COMPUTER; HARDWARE AND SOFTWARE.

C.O.D.   Cash on delivery.

Cohen Report   The *Report on Company Law Amendment*, 1945. *See* COMPANIES ACTS 1948 AND 1967.

Coincidents   *See* ECONOMIC INDICATORS.

Collateral Security   Security for an advance or loan, collateral usually consists of Stock Exchange securities, but advances may also be made against life insurance policies, commodities or property.

Collective Bargaining   Negotiations between employees and employers, conducted through representatives, on the terms and conditions of employment.

Collusive Tendering   A restrictive practice (q.v.) in which firms tendering for a particular job agree to submit a common price, or to allow one of their number to submit a lower tender, thus allocating orders between themselves.

Colombo Plan   A plan devised at a conference of Commonwealth Foreign Ministers held at Colombo, Ceylon, in January, 1950, for the industrial and general economic development of the countries of south and south-east Asia. The plan came into operation on 30th June, 1951. Membership of the organisation was originally limited to Britain, Canada, Australia, New Zealand, India, Pakistan and Ceylon. Later the United States of America and Japan joined the organisation, together with several south-east Asia countries. A Council for Technical Co-operation, with headquarters in Colombo, offers assistance in planning public administration, health services, scientific research, agricultural and industrial activities, and the training and equipment of personnel. Funds come from the assisted areas, Commonwealth countries, the United States and the International Bank for Reconstruction and Development (q.v.).

Combination, Horizontal and Vertical *See* HORIZONTAL INTEGRATION; VERTICAL INTEGRATION.

Comecon *See* COUNCIL FOR MUTUAL ECONOMIC ASSISTANCE.

Coming Out Price The price at which new shares are issued.

Commercial Banks Joint-stock banks whose principal function is to receive deposits and make loans. These loans are usually of a short-term nature and are mainly required as working capital (q.v.) in businesses. In addition to ordinary banking business, the commercial banks offer many ancillary services, e.g. executor and trustee services, foreign currency transactions, bill discounting, investment management services, personal loans, credit cards, and custody of valuables. The joint-stock banks are limited liability companies subject to the Companies Acts; the privilege of limited liability was extended to banking concerns in 1862. Today, six banks account for over 80 per cent of the banking business in the United Kingdom. While the number of banks is small, they maintain over 14,000 branch banks in Britain. *See* "BIG FOUR", THE; CLEARING BANKS, LONDON; SCOTTISH BANKS.

Commercial Bill *See* BILL OF EXCHANGE.

Commission A broker's charge on the shares which he sells and buys for his clients; the amount of commission is established by a fixed scale. *See* STOCKBROKER.

Commission Broker (U.S.) A partner of a member firm of a U.S. Stock Exchange, e.g. the New York Stock Exchange. A broker executes orders for his customers, and for his services charges a commission. The equivalent of an English stockbroker (q.v.).

Commission on Industrial Relations A Commission set up under the Industrial Relations Act 1968 to stimulate the reform of collective bargaining (q.v.), and in particular to work towards the improvement and extension of satisfactory arrangements for handling and resolving industrial disputes. *See* DONOVAN REPORT.

Committee on Public Accounts A Select Committee of the House of Commons which receives and considers the annual reports of the Comptroller and Auditor-General. *See* AUDIT OFFICE.

Commodity A good or service which satisfies a particular, distinct want felt by consumers.

Commodity-Currency The adoption of a commodity as a currency, e.g. tobacco, furs, cereals, sugar, rum, cotton, etc.

Commodity Restriction Scheme Schemes, common during the period 1922–1935, to restrict world output of such important commodities as rubber, tin, sugar, coffee and cotton.

Commodity Terms of Trade *See* TERMS OF TRADE.

Common Carrier A person who is prepared to carry goods for anybody. He has certain statutory rights and obligations.

Common Pricing The fixing of identical prices for goods by agreement between otherwise competing firms selling through wholesale or retail channels of distribution.

Common Stock (U.S. and Can.) Shares representing ownership of a business, with the common stockholders sharing all distributed earnings after the prior claims of the bondholders and preferred stockholders, if any, have been met; the equivalent of British ordinary shares. *See* ORDINARY SHARES.

Common Stock Ratio (U.S.) The ratio of common stocks to the total of all bonds and stocks issued by a corporation.

Commonwealth Development Corporation (C.D.C.) Formerly known as the Colonial Development Corporation, an organisation established by Act of Parliament in 1948 to assist the economic development of dependent territories of the Commonwealth. The Commonwealth Development Act of 1963 gave the corporation full powers of operation in all those Commonwealth countries which had achieved independence since 1948, and changed the name to Commonwealth Development Corporation. The Corporation is empowered to undertake, either alone or in association with others, projects for the promotion or expansion of a wide range of economic enterprises; it is organised to operate commercially and has a statutory obligation to pay its way taking one year with another. C.D.C. has powers to borrow up to £150 m. on a long- or medium-term basis and £10 m. on short-term; loans up to £130 m. may be outstanding at any one time from the United Kingdom Exchequer.

Commonwealth Development Finance Company Ltd. (C.D.F.C.) A private enterprise institution, established in 1953 to assist in the financing on a commercial basis of sound productive developments in Commonwealth countries, including dependent territories. The company's shares are held by a number of industrial, shipping, mining and banking companies, the Bank of England (q.v.) and certain Commonwealth and other central banks The company's participation in projects consists largely of debenture stocks and loans and some equity investment; its portfolio covers a wide variety of manufacturing and other productive activities. *See* FINANCE CORPORATIONS.

Companies Acts 1948 and 1967 The Companies Act 1948 revised and consolidated company law in Britain, giving legal force to most of the recommendations of the 1945 Report of the Cohen Committee on Company Law Amendment (Cmnd. 6659). The Act introduced " consolidated accounts" which lump together all subsidiary companies with the parent company. It created the " exempt private company " which was exempt under certain conditions from filing accounts annually with the Board of Trade (q.v.). Over 70 per cent of registered companies were in this category. In 1962 the Jenkins Committee reported, its findings leading to further amendments of company law embodied in the Companies Act 1967. This Act abolished the exempt private companies and has compelled companies to reveal much more information than hitherto. The additional disclosures which must now be made include: (a) the naming of each subsidiary company and its country of incorporation (if other than Britain); (b) trade investments, if more than 10 per cent of the capital of a company; (c) the naming by subsidiaries of the country of ultimate holding company; (d) the Chairman's pay, the Directors' pay in income "bands" and shareholdings, and the pay of highly-paid employees; (e) turnover, profits and allocation between different activities; (f) charitable and political payments; (g) number of people employed and average pay; (h) exports. In addition, the Act requires that new insurance companies will need to seek Board of Trade permission to start business, and any permission granted may be subject to conditions.

Company, Legal Formation of a A legal process requiring the completion of two documents, the Memorandum of Association (q.v.) and the Articles of Association (q.v.), followed by registration of the Company. An application for registration should be addressed to the Companies' Registration Office of the Board of Trade in respect of a business to be registered in Great Britain, or to the Ministry of Commerce in respect of a business to be registered in Northern Ireland. The Memorandum of Association and the Articles of Association should accompany the application, together with certain statutory declarations and certificates. Upon issue by the Registrar of a Certificate of Incorporation (q.v.) the company becomes a legal entity. On the issue of this Certificate a private company can start business at once; a public company requires an additional document known as a "Trading Certificate". The Registrar may refuse to register a company if its objects are illegal, or the proposed name is that of some other Company or is otherwise undesirable or misleading.

Company Limited by Guarantee Company in which liability is determined by the amount which each member guarantees to provide in the event of the liquidation of the company.

This type of company is rare, since the company limited by shares is regarded as more suitable for normal business purposes.

Company Promoter A specialist in the launching of new businesses.

Company Reserves Profit set aside for "ploughing back" into a business.

Company Taxation In Britain, taxes charged on the trading profits of a company, whether distributed as dividends or retained as reserves. Formerly, companies paid two taxes on their profits:

(a) Profits tax at 15 per cent; and
(b) Income tax at the current standard rate.

Thus company taxation absorbed about half of a company's taxable profits. Beginning in the tax year 1966/67, profits tax and income tax were replaced by a "corporation tax". This tax falls on the whole of the taxable profits of a company whether distributed as dividends or not. In addition, dividends are also subject to normal rates of income tax, which is deducted by the company. The general effect of the corporation tax is to differentiate between distributed and non-distributed profits, taxing the former much more heavily than the latter and thus encouraging the retention of profits in a business. The purpose is to stimulate new capital investment.

Comparative Cost Method A method of comparing the profitability of alternative projects. The method takes account of the initial cost of alternative projects only; it is possible to use this method only where the output and life of each competing scheme is the same.

Comparative Costs, Principle of A principle which is the basis of all international trade. Thus, countries tend to specialise in the production of those goods in which they have the greatest advantage over other countries, to the mutual advantage of all countries. Through the medium of free trade the world may hope to derive the maximum advantage from the operation of this principle.

Competition *See* IMPERFECT COMPETITION; PERFECT COMPETITION; PHANTOM COMPETITION.

Complementary Goods Goods which are necessarily used in conjunction with each other, e.g. pens and ink, knives and forks, petrol and motor-cars.

Components Manufactured goods which are incorporated into a final product without further processing.

Composite Demand The total demand for a product which arises when it is required for a number of different purposes, e.g. steel is demanded by the engineering, construction and ship-building industries.

Composite Supply The total supply of a number of products which satisfy a particular demand, e.g. tea, coffee, lemonade and beer, provide a composite supply of beverages.

Computer A fast automatic calculator. A computer has five main functions: (a) acceptance of information; (b) storage of information; (c) mathematical operations; (d) output of information in the form required; (e) control of its own operation. Computers are grouped into two main types; (a) analogue and (b) digital. Computers are an aid to raising productivity and may be justified where calculations are highly repetitive or the calculations are too complex and/or would take too long to do by hand.

Computers are designed by manufacturers for commercial data processing and scientific data processing. Commercial data processing is characterised by large volumes of input/output data and small amounts of calculation, whereas scientific data processing is characterised by long and complex calculations and relatively modest quantities of input/output. *See* BINARY CODE; HARDWARE AND SOFTWARE; PROGRAM; PROGRAMMER.

Concentration A situation in which the control of economic activity within a market (q.v.), whether on the supply or demand side, has moved into the hands of one company or a small number of companies.

Concentration Ratio A measure of the concentration (q.v.) of an industry, e.g. the extent to which the largest sellers control the bulk of the sales of the industry. Concentration ratios may be expressed as the percentage of value of sales accounted for by the largest firms in the industry, e.g. the largest 4, largest 8, largest 20 firms, The concentration ratio of an absolute monopoly (q.v.) is 100 per cent. The concentration ratios for different industries assist in assessing their positions in the spectrum ranging from pure competition to pure or absolute monopoly.

Confederation of British Industry (C.B.I.) Founded in August, 1965, the representative organisation of British Industry. The Confederation combines the roles previously played by the British Employers' Confederation (q.v.), the Federation of British Industries (q.v.) and the National Association of British Manufacturers (q.v.). The Confederation seeks to express the views of industry as a whole and to offer advice to the Government on all aspects of Government policy which affects the interests of industry. Membership of the C.B.I. consists of some 14,000 companies and 300 trade associations and employers' federations. In addition to these full members the nationalised industries and commercial undertakings are able to apply for associate membership. The governing body of the C.B.I. is the Council which is assisted by some 30 expert standing committees. There is also a Regional Council for each industrial development region in the United Kingdom. The C.B.I. provides its members with a wide range of services and practical advice. Member companies pay subscriptions, the amount varying with the numbers employed.

Confirming Houses Agencies in Britain through which overseas buyers may import goods. A confirming house will usually pay a producer for his goods and then attend to the necessary documentation and shipment. A confirming house in Britain normally acts solely in the interests and under the instructions of principals overseas.

Conscious Parallelism Firms co-ordinating sales and output policies one with another without formal understanding or agreement.

Consolidated Fund Standing Services An item in the British Budget consisting of expenditures which have been authorised by specific legislation and which do not have to be voted annually by Parliament but which are otherwise similar to Supply Services (q.v.). By far the greater part of this item consists of interest payable on the National Debt. *See* BUDGET, BRITISH.

Consolidated Loan Funds An item in the British Budget covering expenditures which do not have to be voted annually by Parliament, although the total sums that can be advanced to particular categories of borrowers are usually limited by statute. These loans are distinguishable from Consolidated Fund Standing Services (q.v.) by the fact that statutes authorising the loans also empower the Treasury (q.v.) to borrow for the purpose. *See* BUDGET, BRITISH.

Consols Funded Government securities or stock which the Government need not repay until it wishes. The term is an abbreviation for "consolidated annuities". The purchase of £100 nominal of 2½ per cent Consols brings a perpetual annuity of £2.50, subject to the Government's right to redeem it at its discretion. An investor in Consols can however sell them at prices reflecting the yield on securities of comparable security.

Constant Returns, Law of A statement that when all the productive services are increased in a given proportion, the amount of product is increased in the same proportion. *See* VARIABLE PROPORTIONS, LAW OF.

Consular Invoice An invoice certified by the consul of an overseas country relating to goods shipped to that country. In many parts of the world, customs authorities require consular invoices for every shipment; they permit certification of values so that correct ad valorem (q.v.) import duties may be levied.

Consumer Behaviour, Principles Governing The generalisations made in economic analysis relating to the behaviour of a consumer in distributing his limited income amongst an infinite variety of goods and services available to him. It is assumed that (a) he will so arrange his expenditure that the relative marginal utility of all the goods he consumes will be in the same proportion to their relative prices; (b) a fall in the price of a good or service, other things being equal, will increase his consumption of it, while a rise in its price will have the opposite effect; and (c) a rise in his real income will normally result in an increased consumption of goods and services, a fall in real income having the opposite effect. While exceptions to these generalisations do occur, and people vary enormously in the efficiency with which they spend their incomes, they are of sufficient validity to be regarded as reasonable assumptions in analysis.

Consumer Council A Council established by the Government in March 1963, following the Report of the Molony Committee on Consumer Protection which called for a Consumer Council to act as a forceful and independent authority on behalf of consumers. A grant-aided but otherwise independent body, it consists of 12 members drawn from various walks of life and different areas of the country, who serve in their individual capacities and not as representatives of particular interests. The Council is served by a full-time secretariat.

The Council's duties include informing itself about the problems of the consumer and matters affecting his interest; to consider action to further or safeguard the consumer's interest and to promote that action, and to provide advice and guidance for the consumer. It is specifically excluded from handling individual complaints, from doing comparative testing of goods and from entering into legal actions on behalf of consumers. *See* CONSUMERS' COUNCILS.

Consumer Credit Loans to members of the general public to finance the purchase of goods. These loans take the form of credit from suppliers, hire-purchase and personal loans from banks (q.v.).

Consumer Durable A good (q.v.) of reasonably long life, such as a refrigerator or piece of furniture; as distinct from, say, foodstuffs.

Consumer Goods Products in the actual form in which they will reach domestic consumers.

Consumer Preference, Theory of Used in modern economics, a theory of consumer preference in which the consumer is asked if he "prefers" one set of goods to another, or is "indifferent" between them. The theory is not concerned with by *how much* the consumer prefers one set of goods to another. *See* UTILITY.

Consumers' Councils Councils set up under the Nationalisation Acts, e.g. coal, gas and electricity, to provide a defence for consumers against statutory monopolies. The Coal Nationalisation Act provided for two Consumers' Councils, an industrial and a domestic consumers' council. Under the Electricity Act and the Gas Act these Councils were known as Consultative Councils. The Councils are not allowed to spend any money and their usefulness has been limited. *See* CONSUMER COUNCIL.

Consumers' Sovereignty The influence of consumers exercising freedom of choice in a free market over the activities of producers of goods and services. To succeed in business, producers must direct their activities to meeting precise consumer requirements; the consumer passes judgment by buying or not buying, and in varying the amounts bought. In times of national emergency, such as the Second World War, the consumer loses his sovereignty and must buy just what is available. *See* PRICE MECHANISM.

Consumer's Surplus A consumer's surplus is the excess of the price which a person would be willing to pay rather than go without an article, over that which he actually does pay; it may be called Consumer's Rent.

Consumption The use of goods and services for the satisfaction of wants (q.v.). Consumption was described by Keynes as "the sole end and object of all economic activity".

Consumption Goods, Collective Goods and services provided collectively by the community and paid for out of taxes, e.g. national defence, police protection, public health measures and other public works, etc.

Contango, Carry-Over, Continuation Synonymous terms for a charge levied on a "bull" (q.v.) for deferring payment for stocks and shares bought from one settlement day (q.v.) to the next. *See* BACKWARDATION.

Contango Broker Broker (q.v.) who lends to other brokers who need money for settlement of accounts. A loan is not advanced, however, in the ordinary way; for a consideration the shares in question are "carried over" until the next settlement day.

Contango or Making-up Day The first day of the three day settlement period for Stock Exchange transactions. On this day arrangements can be made to postpone payment until the next settlement period. Contango is the charge made for postponing payment.

Contract An agreement, either oral or in writing, whereby one party undertakes to do something for the other party to the contract.

Contract Note A legal document relating to the sale or purchase of shares. It contains full details of the transaction.

Contract of Employment Act 1963 An Act which entitles British workers to a statutory minimum period of notice and a written statement of the main terms of their employment. The Act applies to nearly all employees who normally work for their employers for 21 hours a week or more, but some employers in certain occupations are not covered, e.g. those employing registered dock workers, merchant seamen and fishermen. The Act lays down that every worker who has been with his employer for 26 weeks or more will have a right to at least one week's notice; if he has been with his employer continuously for two years or more he will have a right to at least two weeks' notice; and for those who have been in continuous employment for five years or more the period of notice will be at least four weeks. In return, the worker is required to give his employer at least one week's notice if he has been working for him for 26 weeks or more. The Act came into operation on the 6th July, 1964.

Contra-Cyclical Movements Generally increases in public investment to counter a downward swing in economic activity.

Contribution The difference between sales value and the marginal cost of sales. A term particularly associated with the marginal costing (q.v.) technique.

Control of Office and Industrial Development Act 1965 An Act to assist in the relief of congestion in the London Metropolitan Region and any other designated area by imposing restrictions on the development of offices. The Act gives the Board of Trade (q.v.) power to control office development by means of granting or refusing office development permits required for planning permission of office development of over 3,000 sq. ft. gross in any area to which the control applies. Control has been extended to the West Midlands conurbation.

Conversion Issue Issue of new stock by Government or other borrower, offered to holders in exchange for an existing stock which is, or will shortly become, due for repayment. *See* ADVANCE REFUNDING (U.S.)

Convertibility The freedom to exchange any currency for another currency at the ruling rate of exchange.

Convertibility of Sterling In relation to sterling, convertibility means that sterling received in any part of the world for goods sold to the Sterling Area (q.v.) could itself be used as a medium of payment in transactions with any part of the world. One of the conditions of the Washington Loan Agreement 1945 (q.v.), was that sterling should be made freely convertible by not later than July, 1947. The way was prepared for the convertibility of sterling in 1947 by a series of separate agreements with other countries, providing for the transferability of the sterling accruing to them from current transactions. The sterling balances accumulated during the Second World War were to remain blocked. In consequence of the introduction of convertibility every country which received pounds sterling in the course of current business

48

could gain access to American supplies by turning pounds into dollars. However, there was such a rush to make the conversion that within a few weeks the drain on the monetary reserves of the Sterling Area was so heavy that convertibility had to be suspended. Sterling once again became convertible only among the members of the Sterling Area, and it had become clear that if sterling was to become convertible again this could only be achieved gradually. Convertibility was in due course introduced into the area of the American Account and the area of the Transferable Account. By 1955 sterling had become convertible within each of the two areas, but it was not until 1959 that sterling became freely convertible between members of the different areas. The right to convert sterling into dollars was limited to non-residents.

Convertible Debenture Stock Debenture stock which carries an option to convert into another class of security. See DEBENTURE.

Convertible Preferred Stock (U.S.) Preferred stock (q.v.) which may be exchanged, under certain terms and conditions, for common stock (q.v.). For example, after a stated date each share of the convertible issue may be exchangeable for, say, three shares of common stock.

Co-Operative Movement An organisation consisting of co-operative societies engaged in the manufacture and distribution of consumer goods, run democratically for the mutual benefit of their member customers. The Movement has a long history. It originated in 1844 when a group of unemployed workers belonging to various trades formed a Society in Rochdale "for the pecuniary benefit and improvement of the social and domestic conditions of their members". These twenty-eight men, known as the "Rochdale Pioneers", opened their first store in Toad Lane. Six years later they opened a Wholesale Department for their own use and the use of neighbouring Societies which had been formed and started a corn-mill and a tobacco factory. Control was democratic, each member having one vote. Profits were distributed to members in proportion to their purchases, after payment of interest and collective charges, in the form of a dividend. By 1891, the total membership reached one million. In 1926, the membership stood at five millions, and in 1948 at ten millions. By 1968 the co-operatives had more than thirteen million members and their business accounted for about 9 per cent of all retail trade in Britain.

The most important type of Co-operative Society is the Retail Society, each of which operates one or more stores or shops. The day-to-day control of a Retail Society is carried on by a Committee of Management, which is elected quarterly or half-yearly from and by the members who comprise most of its customers. The Co-operative Wholesale Society provides a merchanting service for the Retail Societies; membership of a Wholesale Society consists of the individual Retail Societies. Both the Retail and Wholesale Societies engage in production. The movement also provides insurance and building society facilities.

Conveyance Legal description for the transfer of property from a seller to a buyer.

Co-Ownership See CO-PARTNERSHIP IN INDUSTRY.

Co-Partnership in Industry Schemes introduced by individual firms to give employees a bigger stake in the prosperity of the firms they work for. Full co-partnership is made up of three main elements:
   (a) machinery for joint-consultation by means of which information and ideas can flow freely between employers and employed;
   (b) the granting to employees of a share of a pre-determined portion of the net profits of the firm, in accordance with a scheme which has secured the prior agreement of all concerned; and,
   (c) the enabling and encouragement of employees to acquire capital in the firm which employs them.
   Besides full co-partnership incorporating all these features, some schemes are confined either to employee-shareholding or profit-sharing.

Co-product One of the principal products of a manufacturing process, in which at least one other product may also be considered a principal product. In conventional coal-gas manufacture, coke, once regarded as a by-product, grew to the status of a co-product. In the manufacture of sulphuric acid by the anhydrite route, portland cement is produced and regarded by the industry as co-product. The difference between a by-product and a co-product appears to be one of degree only.

Corn Exchange A London market and the largest distribution centre in the United Kingdom for cereals, seeds, fertilisers and animal feeding stuffs.

Corner The buying up of the whole or the larger part of the stocks of a commodity with a view to selling later at a higher price from a monopolistic position.

Corporate Planning An approach to top level management problems which emphasises: (a) the need for an organisation to decide exactly what its objectives are; and (b) the need for long-term planning in every part of the organisation to achieve these objectives.

Corporation (U.S.) The United States equivalent of a British limited company.

Corporation Tax *See* COMPANY TAXATION.

Cost The amount of expenditure incurred in obtaining the services of a factor of production (q.v.). Cost was once explained by economists in terms of real effort and sacrifice. The approach to cost is now in terms of the opportunities or alternatives foregone; this approach regards the cost of producing or acquiring certain goods and services as the value of the alternative goods and services that could have been obtained instead. *See* OPPORTUNITY-COST.

Cost-Benefit Analysis A systematic comparison between the cost of carrying out a service or activity and the value of that service or activity, quantifying as far as possible, all costs and benefits whether direct or indirect, financial or social. It is of particular value and relevance where public services are involved, involving both cost and benefit to the general public; thus a public service may be justified in circumstances which a private organisation would regard as "uneconomic". Figure 2 illustrates a general method of making an economic assessment of community air pollution and control; the curves attempt to relate the cost of damage to man, animals, crops and materials, caused by air pollution at varying degrees of control by industry and other emitters; the cost to industry of varying degrees of technical control; and the total cost to the community of damage and control. While the cost of damage is a direct charge to the community, the cost of control is indirect it being assumed that costs incurred by industry will be met by the community through higher prices. Without control, the cost of air pollution to the community is extremely high; with a high degree of control this cost is minimised though not eliminated. The cost of industrial devices and techniques varies from zero up to a point where little or no additional benefit to the community is gained from additional expenditure. The figure suggests that a sensible balance between costs and benefits is achieved when the total costs of damage and control are minimised. Although actual cost curve shapes in any given situation are by no means necessarily as shown, are very difficult to construct and are valid for only a short period of time (say 1 to 5 years), the concept is useful.

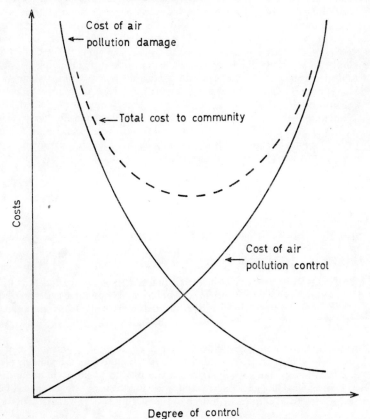

FIGURE 2.—HYPOTHETICAL COST-BENEFIT RELATIONSHIPS

Cost Control The procedure by which the management accountant evaluates the actual cost of a capital project or a manufacturing operation for the purpose of comparison with the authorised estimates or cost standard; in the event of marked deviation, appropriate action can then be taken.

Cost Curve A graph showing by means of a curve the expenses which a firm will incur in achieving any given volume of output.

Cost, Marginal *See* MARGINAL COST.

Cost of Living Index *See* INDEX OF RETAIL PRICES.

Cost of Sales (U.S.) All costs incurred in a factory in converting raw materials into a finished product; such costs include raw materials, labour, and factory overheads.

Cost of Service Principle A basis for charging for services, regard being had to the costs of producing a particular service rather than the value of the service to the consumer. In conditions of perfect competition charges would tend to correspond to costs, including normal profit. In a public utility, the principle may be adopted as a deliberate policy. To apply the cost of service principle accurately is a very difficult matter, however, involving elaborate costing techniques. An initial difficulty is that the phrase itself is ambiguous— it may mean simply the a short-run marginal cost, or it may mean the additional cost plus a fair share of the overhead costs of the undertaking. Assuming the latter, there is still much scope for disagreement as to what is a "fair share" of overhead costs in a particular case. Some have claimed that the system cannot be applied in practice except in a very rough and ready manner. *See* VALUE OF SERVICE PRINCIPLE.

Cost-Plus Contract A contract under which the contractor provides all the necessary material, equipment and labour at actual cost, plus an agreed amount for his services.

Costing The technique and process of ascertaining business costs.

Costs, Fixed *See* FIXED COSTS.

Costs, Long-Run Average The lowest practicable average cost of producing a commodity, within the current state of technical knowledge and managerial ability, after adequate time has been allowed to make all the necessary adjustments.

Costs of Production Expenditure incurred by way of payments for rent, mortgages, interest on loans, dividends, salaries and wages, buildings, plant and machinery and raw materials, in the production of a commodity or a service, including development and marketing costs. Costs are divided into two parts, fixed costs (q.v.) and variable costs (q.v.). *See* SELLING COSTS.

Costs, Private *See* PRIVATE COSTS.

Costs, Selling *See* SELLING COSTS.

Costs, Social *See* SOCIAL COSTS.

Costs, Variable *See* VARIABLE COSTS.

Cottage Industry A system of employment in which craftsmen, aided by their families, work at home either on their own account or on behalf of entrepreneurs, who deliver the raw materials and collect the finished goods.

Council for Mutual Economic Assistance (Comecon) An organisation established in January, 1949, by several eastern European countries for the purpose of centralizing arrangements for trade, credit and technical assistance among the members. The members comprise the Soviet Union, Bulgaria, Czechoslovakia, Hungary, Poland, Rumania, Albania, the German Democratic Republic and the Mongolian People's Republic. The Bank of Socialist Countries, founded under the auspices of Comecon, began to operate on 1st January, 1964. In June, 1962, the Council recommended that the individual development plans of the members should be co-ordinated at the draft stage, envisaging far-reaching economic integration and an end to autarkic tendencies. However, the application of this policy soon met with opposition within the Council, particularly from Rumania.

Council of Economic Advisers (U.S.) An advisory council serving the President of the United States of America, set up under the Employment Act 1946.

Countervailing Duty Or matching duty, a situation achieved when an excise duty (q.v.) on an article produced at home equals the customs duty (q.v.) imposed on a similar article imported from abroad, neither the home-produced or imported product being given an advantage. For example, excise duty on British manufactured beer is matched or "countervailed" by a customs duty of virtually the same level on imported beer.

Coupon Attached to a bearer bond when issued; a coupon is detached and presented for payment of interest when this becomes due. *See* BEARER STOCK OR BOND; BOND

Covered Bear A person, who, believing prices will fall, sells securities with a view to repurchasing them later at a lower price. He does not, however, deliver the securities sold hoping to save expense on repurchasing; if, however, prices rise he is in a position to deliver stock without paying inflated prices.

Craft Union *See* TRADE UNIONS.

Craftsman A skilled worker in a particular occupation, trade or craft, who is able to apply a range of skills to basically non-repetitive work with a minimum of direction and supervision.

Crash Cost The cost associated with the shortest possible completion time for a project. The crash cost is higher than the normal cost due to the expense of using more manpower or more plant and equipment.

Crash Programme   A programme aiming at the shortest possible completion time for a project or projects.

Credit   A loan made either directly, or indirectly through deferred payments for goods received; thus credit may be extended by a creditor (lender) to a debtor (borrower) either through the transfer of cash with the promise of future repayment, or through the sale of goods to be paid for later in an agreed manner.   The creditor may require interest payments over the period of the loan.   The widespread use of credit facilities has provided another avenue for the transfer of purchasing power from savers to investors and consumers.   *See* CREDIT RATING; INSTALMENT CREDIT.

Credit Card   Issued by some banks and other organisations to credit-worthy customers, a card which on production enables the holder to obtain credit in restaurants, shops and other establishments participating in the scheme. The issuing bank or other organisation guarantees to meet the bill, recovering the amount concerned from the card-holder through a single account presented periodically.

Credit Clearing   A system introduced at the London Bankers' Clearing House during 1960/61 which enables money and cheques to be paid in at any clearing bank by a member of the public (whether having a banking account or not) for credit to any banking account at any other clearing bank.

Credit Clubs   *See* INTERNATIONAL CREDIT CLUBS.

Credit Insurance   A type of insurance affording indemnity to merchants and manufacturers against the risk of loss due to the insolvency or protracted default of customers to whom goods are sold on credit. When applied to export credits, the term may embrace facilities outside normal insurance underwriting.   *See* EXPORT CREDITS GUARANTEE DEPARTMENT.

Credit Rating   An evaluation of the soundness of an individual or business firm as a credit risk. It is usually based on the three "C's" of credit: (a) character, or integrity; (b) capacity, or earning power; and (c) capital, or the over-all financial status of the applicant.   *See* CREDIT.

Credit Sale   A procedure for purchasing goods under which the purchaser pays a deposit on receipt of the goods followed by a number of instalments until the debt is cleared.   Generally the goods become the property of the purchaser immediately who may sell or otherwise dispose of them at any time, the liability for the outstanding debt remaining.   If a purchaser defaults on the repayment of his debt he may be taken to court; a court order may then be made requiring him to pay the debt. Interest charges are usually expressed as a flat rate per annum.   *See* HIRE PURCHASE.

Credit Squeeze   The contraction of credit (q.v.) as a result of Government measures.   *See* BANK RATE.

Credit Transfers A simple means of paying money to somebody else, other than by direct payment in cash.

Instead of using a cheque (q.v.) a customer instructs his bank to credit the account of another customer at any branch of his bank, or of any other bank in Great Britain. Anybody who is not a customer can also enter any bank to complete a Credit Transfer in the same way.

It is necessary to obtain the creditor's permission to be paid in this way and to obtain also the name of the account to be credited and the bank and branch.

If a person already has a current account at a bank he need make out only one cheque to pay all his bills. Instead of issuing separate cheques for individual bills, he completes a Credit Transfer form for each account (supplied by the creditor or by the bank), completes a special summary form and hands them to the bank cashier at his own bank with one cheque for the total amount.

A person without an account must, of course, pay the total amount of cash required, plus a small charge for each account paid.

The bank transfers the amounts involved and saves the customer the trouble of sending money through the post or taking it to the creditor by hand.

Credit Union A group of people engaging in organised self-help who save their money together and make low-interest loans to each other. The loans are usually short-term consumer loans, but may extend to loans for farm or small business enterprise purposes. The directors and management committee are chosen by the members from among their own numbers. Credit unions operate under government charters; there appear to be over 28,000 credit unions in existence, located mainly in the United States of America and Canada. *See* CREDIT.

Critical Minimum Effort An expression used by Harvey Leibenstein in his work "Economic Backwardness and Economic Growth" (JohnWiley, 1957) to indicate the effort required not merely to increase the capital available within an economy, but to increase it sufficiently fast so that the increase in output outraces the increase in population. A similar concept is conveyed by the phrase "take-off" used by W. W. Rostow. *See* ECONOMIC GROWTH, STAGES OF.

Critical Path Analysis The analysis of the various work "activities" or time-consuming operations which have to be performed to complete a project from start to finish with a view to establishing the total minimum time needed for the project. The analysis involves the preparation of a network or diagram made up of chains of arrows drawn to represent the various work "activities". The critical path links activities in such a way that the total "float" or free-time is zero; delays in any of these activities delays the completion of the project by the same amount. Critical path planning is a valuable technique of modern management. *See* NETWORK ANALYSIS.

Cross-Booking An unofficial system sometimes adopted by piece-workers who book time saved or "banked" from loose jobs on to tight jobs. The purpose is to conceal loose rates from management and to stabilize effort and earnings. *See* LOOSE TIMES; TIGHT TIMES

Cross-Section Analysis The analysis of a series of records of economic data for different groups of people, firms or countries, at the same moment or in the same period of time.

Crystallised Labour Karl Marx's description of capital; he regarded capital as merely the result of labour which had been expended in the past.

Cum With. *See* CUM ALL; CUM BONUS; CUM DIVIDEND; CUM DRAWING; CUM INTEREST; CUM RIGHTS.

Cum All With all advantages. A description which may be attached to the sale of a security, implying that any dividend, interest, rights, bonus or other benefit, just declared or current is not being withheld. *See* EX-ALL.

Cum Bonus With bonus just declared. A condition which may be attached to the sale of a security.

Cum Dividend With current dividend. A condition which may be attached to the sale of a security.

Cum Drawing With benefit of the current drawing (q.v.). If there is no benefit, it means with the liability for loss of drawing. A condition that may be attached to the sale of a security.

Cum Interest With current interest. A condition which may be attached to the sale of a security.

Cum Rights With "rights" recently issued. A condition which may be attached to the sale of a security.

Cumulative Preference Share A preference share (q.v.) entitling the holder to receive not only the current dividend but also any unpaid arrears, before any dividend is paid to ordinary shareholders.

Cumulative Preferred Stock (U.S.) Preferred stock (q.v.), the dividends on which, if unpaid, continue to accumulate until paid. *See* NON-CUMULATIVE PREFERRED STOCK.

Currency and Bank-Notes Acts 1928-1954 The chief provisions of these Acts were:—

    (a) The Bank of England (q.v.) to take over the Treasury (q.v.) issue of notes (during the period 1914-1928 the Treasury issued notes in denominations of £1 and 10s.);

    (b) The fiduciary issue (q.v.) to be increased by the 1928 Act to £260 million. All notes above this to be backed £1 for £1 by gold. The fiduciary issue to be varied only with the consent of the Treasury;

    (c) Under the 1954 Act the size of the fiduciary issue to depend entirely on the decision of the Government.

See FIDUCIARY ISSUE.

Currency School *See* BANKING AND CURRENCY SCHOOLS.

Currency Swaps Informal arrangements between Governments to supply each other with scarce currencies on a short-term basis, thus avoiding additional pressures in the foreign exchange market. *See* BASLE AGREEMENT.

Current Account (a) An element in the balance of payments (q.v.) account dealing with commercial transactions, i.e. the buying and selling of goods and services. (b) The most commonly used type of banking account, which enables a person to draw cheques against money held to his credit. A Statement, available at any time, gives details of amounts paid in, and out, and the balance standing to the account. *See* DEPOSIT ACCOUNT.

Current Expenditure Expenditure recurrent in nature and not resulting in the acquisition of assets. *See* CAPITAL EXPENDITURE.

Current Ratio Current assets divided by current liabilities.

Current Transactions The receipts and expenditure of income which forms a continuous process, year after year.

Customs and Excise Regulator *See* REGULATOR.

Customs Duty Revenue, protective or preferential duty imposed on goods imported from abroad, e.g. customs duty on leaf tobacco imported into Britain, varying with source and moisture content. The present rates of duty are equivalent to about £0.21 on a packet of 20 cigarettes retailing at £0.27. Imported hydrocarbon oils and beer are also subject to customs duty. *See* EXCISE DUTY.

Customs Union A union of states or countries to form a single customs territory. Tariffs and other trade restrictions between the member states or countries are abolished, but the union maintains a common external tariff wall against other countries. *See* BENELUX; EUROPEAN ECONOMIC COMMUNITY; ZOLLVEREIN.

C.W.O. Cash with order.

Cybernetics The science of communication and control; it is concerned with the basic theory of how to control and manage complex systems of men and machines. It is essentially an inter-disciplinary science drawing upon the sciences of biology, economics and management. The term "cybernetics" was coined by the late Professor Norbet Wiener.

Cyclical Stocks Stocks and shares (q.v.) of those companies which are sharply affected by "feast or famine" swings in their respective industries.

D

Damping In economics, a reducing effect. For example, at low levels of market demand some people may withdraw from the labour market, thus damping the rise in unemployment figures. *See* ACTIVITY RATE.

Day Order An order given by an investor to a stockbroker (q.v.) which holds good for one day only.

Dead Horse Work which has been paid for but has yet to be completed; a procedure observed in some factories, where workers are paid in advance for work which they have yet to complete.

Deadweight Debt That part of the National Debt (q.v.) not covered by real assets, in contrast to Reproductive Debt (q.v.). Most of the National Debt is of this type.

Dealer A person carrying on a business of selling goods, whether by wholesale or by retail, or engaging in the buying and selling of shares. *See* STOCKJOBBER.

Death Duties Duties payable when a property passes at death. Death duties are progressive, increasing in proportion with the value of the estate.

Debentures Long-term fixed interest loans to companies. Interest is payable by a company on these stocks whether a profit is earned or not. Debenture stockholders rank as creditors of the company; if the interest is not forthcoming, the debenture holders can sell up the company and repay themselves (capital and interest due) out of the proceeds. Debenture stocks may be bought or sold in any amounts, subject to any special restrictions imposed by a company. The interests are relatively low, but the capital is usually very secure. There are three main types of debenture:
>   (a) Mortgage debentures. These are secured by the mortgage of a partic-ular fixed property (land or buildings) owned bv the company.
>   (b) Income debentures.
>   (c) Guaranteed debentures, usually incorporating a third party guarantee.

In the case of liquidation of the company, mortgage debentures rank ahead of other types up to the value of the properties on which they are secured. All debenture creditors rank ahead of any shareholder, preferred or ordinary. Debentures may be issued at par (q.v.), at a discount on par, or at a premium on par.

Debt A sum of money, or quantity of goods or services, owed by one individual or body to another. *See* DEADWEIGHT DEBT; FLOATING DEBT; NATIONAL DEBT.

Decimal Currency Metallic and paper currency in which each successive denomination is ten times the value of that next below it; commonly the basic unit of currency is divided into 100 cents. The United States of America was the first country to adopt the decimal system, coining both gold and silver money in 1792; many other countries have adopted the same principle. The system enjoys two main advantages: (a) the ease with which the relationship of the value of the various notes and coins can be computed; and (b) the convenience for arithmetic purposes of stating sums of money as multiples of the unit of account. A decimal system was introduced into Australia from 14th February, 1966, dollars and cents taking the place of pounds, shillings and pence, on the following basis: 10s.=$1, £A1=$2, 6d.=5 cents, 1s.= 10 cents, 2s.=20 cents. New Zealand subsequently followed suit also adopting the dollar and the cent, on the basis of 10s.=$1, £NZ1=$2; the change took effect on 10th July, 1967. In Britain, the Halsbury Committee reported in 1963 on the most convenient and practical form which a decimal coinage might take, if adopted, a majority of the Committee favouring the retention of the pound, the standard unit being divided into 100 sub-units. The Decimal Currency Act 1967 provided for a decimal system based on the pound sterling, the pound being divided into 100 new pence. The new system takes effect from 15th February, 1971. The symbol for the pound will remain £, the present £1, £5, and £10 bank-notes being retained. There will be three new bronze ("copper") coins, the halfpenny, penny and twopence (worth 1.2d., 2.4d. and 4.8d. in the old currency); two new cupronickel ("silver") fivepenny and tenpenny coins (worth 1s. and 2s. in the old currency); and a sixth decimal coin will be for fiftypence, which will replace the old ten shilling note. *See* DECIMAL CURRENCY BOARD; DEMONETISATION.

Decimal Currency Board An advisory body set up in December, 1966, and given statutory functions on 14th July, 1967, under the British Decimal Currency Act 1967. The Board comprises ten part-time members and has a small permanent staff. The functions of the Board are: (a) to examine in detail the problems of the changeover to decimal currency in Britain; (b) to promote the speedy and efficient transition to the use of decimal currency; (c) to organise a programme of guidance to the public; and (d) to examine claims for compensation which might be submitted on special grounds. *See* DECIMAL CURRENCY.

Deduction The method of reasoning from principles to facts, from the general to the particular. It is a method which begins by investigating the principal forces determining a given class of phenomena, and the general laws in accordance with which these forces operate. It then goes on to trace the consequences which ensue from their action and interaction under specified conditions. Alfred Marshall expressed the opinion that in economics, at any rate in dealing with concrete cases, there is no scope for long chains of deductive reasoning.

Nevertheless, he took the view that, "induction and deduction are both needed for scientific thought as the right and left foot are both needed for walking". There is no one method, therefore, which can be properly called the method of economics. *See* INDUCTION.

Deed of Transfer A formal agreement under seal bearing a government revenue stamp and signed by both the buyer and the seller of, for example, shares. Upon the registration of the deed of transfer the holder receives in due course a certificate which, in conjunction with his registration in the company's books, confirms his ownership of shares. *See* BEARER STOCKS OR BONDS.

Deepening Investment *See* INVESTMENT, DEEPENING.

Defence Bonds Issued by the British Government since 1939; from 1952 they were sold for £5 and multiples of £5. The interest, payable half-yearly, was assessable for income tax and surtax; bonuses were free of income tax and surtax. Superseded in 1964 by the National Development Bond (q.v.).

Deferred, Founders' or Management Shares Shares which have to wait for their dividend until all other classes of share have participated in the profits. Often taken by the founder as promoter of the company. These are generally entitled to the whole or a very large portion of the surplus profit after payment of all prior claims.

Deferred Ordinary Share A share which ranks for dividend after the preferred ordinary share (q.v.).

Deferred Rebates Rebates granted on the charge for some service, or on the price of goods, on a deferred basis as a means of encouraging customers to buy exclusively from a particular firm or from members of an association over a period of time. This technique has been employed, for example, by Shipping Conferences (q.v.). Schemes differ in detail, but usually if goods are shipped in Conference ships during a prescribed period (perhaps six or twelve months) a rebate is earned. If, during a further similar period, all goods are again so shipped, the rebate is actually paid or credited. Also called aggregated rebates.

Deficit An excess of liabilities over assets. *See* BALANCE OF PAYMENTS; DEFICIT FINANCING.

Deficit Financing The financing of a budget deficit by the Government by means of borrowing against the issue of Government securities, that is by increasing the National Debt (q.v.). A budget deficit is incurred as a means of stimulating the economy through increased Government expenditure. *See* BUDGET, BRITISH.

Deflation A situation in which prices and money incomes are falling, accompanied by an increase in the value of the monetary unit.

Del Credere Agent An agent who receives goods on consignment selling only to buyers who are able to pay, thus guaranteeing payment to the exporter.

Demand The amount of a commodity or service which will be bought at any given price per unit of time. *See* ELASTICITY OF DEMAND; SUPPLY.

Demand, Cross-Elasticity of The responsiveness of the demand for a commodity or service to changes in the prices of other commodities. It is calculated:

$$\frac{\text{Percentage change in demand for commodity X}}{\text{Percentage change in price of commodity Y}}$$

If commodities are complementary they have negative cross-elasticities, i.e. if X and Y are complementary a fall in the price of Y will lead to an increase in demand for both X and Y. The changes in the quantity of X and the price of Y will have opposite signs. Substitutes have positive cross-elasticities, i.e. a fall in the price of Y will increase the quantity of Y consumed, but will reduce the quantity of X consumed. Changes in the price of Y and the quantity X will have the same sign. *See* COMPLEMENTARY GOODS; ELASTICITY OF DEMAND.

Demand Curve A graphical presentation of a demand function, $x = \phi (p)$, showing how much of a commodity will be bought per unit of time at any given price, providing that the other influences governing demand remain unchanged, i.e. that the incomes of consumers and their tastes remain constant, and that the price level of closely related commodities remains constant. The demand curve is referred to axes OY and OX along which prices and demands are respectively measured. It is an economic convention that demand curves are referred to a vertical price axis. In normal demand curves x decreases as y increases, i.e. the demand function, $x = \phi (p)$, is monotonic decreasing. The shape is generally concave, but the precise form will depend on the commodity and the elasticity of demand. In the case of common salt, for example, a considerable fall in price will not be likely to result in a large increase in sales. The elasticity of demand depends upon a number of parameters such as the number of consumers, their incomes and tastes, and the price of other goods generally and of close substitutes in particular. Figure 3 depicts a normal demand curve. In exceptional circumstances demand curves may be regressive, or backward sloping, indicating that over a limited period the fall in price of a commodity may be followed by a fall in demand, e.g. due to an expectation that price will fall even lower. The terms "expansion" and "contraction" of demand are reserved for changes in demand attributable to changes in the price of the commodity only; the amount demanded at any given price remaining constant. The terms "increase" or "decrease" in demand are reserved for changes in demand attributable to changes in the state of demand; more or fewer goods being demanded at any given price than formerly.

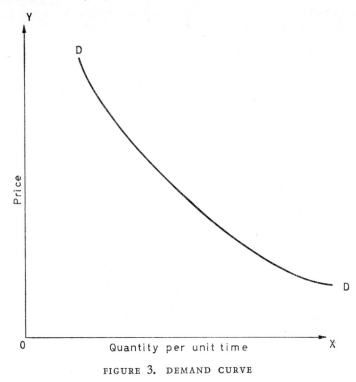

FIGURE 3. DEMAND CURVE

Demand Deposit (U.S.)   A bank deposit withdrawable on demand; not unlike a British current account (q.v.). *See* TIME DEPOSIT.

Demand Schedule   A table giving the demand (q.v.) for a commodity or service at various prices, while all other factors determining demand remain unchanged. *See* SUPPLY SCHEDULE.

Demography   A study in the measurement of certain characteristics of human populations, e.g. the size of a population and its distribution by age, sex, occupation, industry, location, etc., and trends in these characteristics.

Demonetisation   The act of depriving a coin of its status as legal tender; it is authorised in Britain by a Royal Proclamation issued normally a few months before demonetisation is due to occur. After demonetisation the coin concerned may no longer be used as money or exchanged at a bank. *See* DECIMAL CURRENCY; LEGAL TENDER.

Demurrage An additional charge payable to a shipowner by a charterer for failure to load or unload a ship within the time specified.

Deposit *See* BANK DEPOSIT; SPECIAL DEPOSITS.

Deposit Account A banking account for money not likely to be required immediately. Such money is subject to several days' notice of withdrawal. Interest is paid at a rate usually 2 per cent below Bank Rate (q.v.). A Pass Book, available at any time, provides a complete record of the account. *See* CURRENT ACCOUNT.

Deposit Money Money (q.v.) created by the commercial banks (q.v.) constituting the greater proportion of the supply of money.

Deposited Securities Securities in the care of an "authorised depository", e.g. a bank, in order to comply with the requirements of the Exchange Control Act 1947 relating to certain bearer and other securities.

Depreciation The diminution in the original value of an asset due to use and/or obsolescence. Depreciation can be calculated at "historical cost" (the price which was actually paid for the asset at the time of purchase) or at "replacement cost" (the amount that it would take to replace the asset at the present time). Historical cost is the method normally adopted, but economists tend to favour the second method. In "The Financial Obligations of the Nationalised Industries" (Cmnd. 1337) it is stated (para. 19), "depreciation should be on the historic cost basis" but "provision should also be made from revenue for such an amount as may be necessary to cover the excess in depreciation calculated on replacement cost basis over depreciation calculated on historic cost".

In any calculation of depreciation there are three distinct elements:

(a) the length of time over which the asset is depreciated (e.g. houses are depreciated over 60 years, conventional power stations over 30 years, and motor vehicles over 10 years);

(b) the method of depreciating the asset. Several methods are employed. Using the fixed instalment or straight line method a fixed proportion of the original capital outlay is written off annually in order to reduce the asset to zero value at the end of the period; by the diminishing balance method a fixed rate per cent is written off the reducing balance of the asset account each year; using the depreciation fund method the asset is allowed to stand in the books at its original cost, and then a fixed amount, called the "sinking fund instalment", is debited to profit and loss each year and a corresponding amount of cash is invested in securities, the amount being enough to accumulate at compound interest to the sum required to replace the asset.

(c) the difficulty of valuating the asset at present prices when the design and technical capabilities of the asset may have changed considerably.

See DEPRECIATING FUND METHOD; DIMINISHING BALANCE METHOD; FIXED INSTALMENT METHOD; SINKING FUND.

Depreciation Fund Method A method of calculating and allowing for the depreciation of an asset. The asset is allowed to stand in the company's books at its original cost and then a fixed amount, known as the "sinking fund instalment", is debited to the profit and loss account each year and a corresponding amount of cash is invested in securities, the amount being enough to accumulate at compound interest to the sum required to replace the asset. *See* DEPRECIATION; DIMINISHING BALANCE METHOD; FIXED INSTALMENT METHOD; SINKING FUND.

Depression (1929-1935), The Great *See* GREAT DEPRESSION (1929-1935), THE.

Derating A Government technique for reducing the burden of taxation on particular branches of industry and commerce. In 1929 agricultural land and buildings (other than farm-houses) ceased to be assessed for rates; while factories and workshops, mines, docks, canals and railways received relief of 75 per cent of their net annual value. The purpose was to assist agriculture and industry to recover from the depression through a reduction in the overhead costs of production. In 1963, all these derating reliefs, other than agricultural and charitable, came to an end.

Derived Demand The demand for a commodity not required for its own sake, but for its contribution to the manufacture of another commodity.

Devaluation and Revaluation The determination of a new fixed exchange rate (q.v.) for a currency, lower in the former case and higher in the latter.

Devaluation Crises, 1949 and 1967 Crises arising from Britain's adverse balance of payments position associated with a decline of reserves and a speculative movement against sterling, the remedy for which was sought through a substantial devaluation of the pound in relation to the dollar. Since the end of the Second World War there had been growing awareness of the basic weakness of Britain's economy, as revealed by the Convertibility Crisis in 1947, and Britain's balance of payments difficulties. It became gradually accepted that the pound sterling would have to be devalued. This belief led American importers to defer purchases from Britain, thus aggravating the balance of payments position. In September 1949 the decline of Britain's reserves had reached crisis proportions; a speculative movement against sterling forced the Government's hand. The Government decided to reduce the dollar value of the pound from £4.03 to £2.80, a reduction of 30.5 per cent. The twin purpose of this drastic reduction was to bring further expectation of a fall in the value of the pound to an abrupt end and to stimulate exports. During the early post-war years an over-valued pound had kept export earnings high which was advantageous as long as a "sellers' market" existed. However, the return of more competitive conditions meant that Britain must reduce her prices and export a good deal more.

Ralph G. Hawtrey has questioned, however, whether British exporters in general were suffering from excessive costs. He saw devaluation as increasing the demand for British goods while aggravating the difficulties of exporters who were trying to reduce delivery times. Devaluation could only help if the total volume of sales so increased as to bring in more dollars than before. Hawtrey regarded devaluation a failure in this respect because the resources to achieve a greater volume of sales were not at that time available.

As a result of disappointing economic performance, the pound was devalued a second time in November, 1967. Before this devaluation substantial cuts were made in domestic demand and a "freeze" on incomes and prices imposed. Despite these measures the underlying balance of payments position remained weak; the growth of exports was insufficient and imports remained at too high a level, while a large outflow of funds reduced monetary reserves. With the approval of the International Monetary Fund (q.v.) the par value (q.v.) of the pound in terms of gold was lowered on 18th November, 1967, from 2.48828 to 2.13281 grammes, equivalent to a reduction in the exchange rate against the U.S. dollar from 2.80 to 2.40 dollars (a devaluation of 14.3 per cent). New spot dealing limits were set at 2.38 to 2.42. Thus the American penny (cent) became equal to the British penny. Simultaneously the Bank Rate (q.v.) was raised from 6½ to 8 per cent, the highest in 53 years, being lowered to 7½ per cent on 21st March, 1968. In addition limitations on bank advances were imposed except to priority borrowers, minimum hire purchase deposits on cars were raised and maximum repayment periods reduced, corporation tax (q.v.) was to be raised from 40 to 42½ per cent in the next Budget, export rebates were abolished, and the selective employment tax (q.v.) premium was withdrawn from all manufacturers save those in development areas (q.v.). Britain's competitors did not devalue their currencies but some of her food suppliers did—Denmark, Ireland, Spain and New Zealand.

Devaluations, Competitive A situation in which a number of countries devalue their currencies (to stimulate exports and discourage imports) in order to gain, or attempt to gain, a competitive advantage over one another; a self-defeating situation is thus created into which other countries are drawn.

Developing Country A poor or under-developed country which is making economic progress in respect of capital investment, education and training, productivity and general standard of living.

Development Areas Areas in Britain, designated by the Industrial Development Act 1966, in which special measures are necessary to encourage the growth and proper distribution of industry. The development areas comprise five broad areas covering most of Scotland and Wales, all the Northern Region, Merseyside and the Furness peninsula, and most of Cornwall and North Devon. *See* ADVANCE FACTORIES; DEVELOPMENT DISTRICTS; INVESTMENT GRANTS; LOCAL EMPLOYMENT ACTS 1960 TO 1966; REGIONAL EMPLOYMENT PREMIUM; SELECTIVE EMPLOYMENT TAX.

Development Charge The Town and Country Planning Act 1947, nationalised development rights and development charges were imposed on developers of land; compensation was also payable to those who lost development rights. The development charge was subsequently abolished.

Development Districts Compact areas of relatively high unemployment scheduled under the Local Employment Acts of 1960 and 1963. The development districts were replaced in 1966 by the establishment of development areas (q.v.).

Differential Costing *See* MARGINAL COSTING.

Differential Rent *See* ECONOMIC RENT; QUASI-RENT.

Differentiation, Product *See* PRODUCT DIFFERENTIATION.

Diminishing Balance Method A method for calculating and allowing for the depreciation of an asset. In the diminishing, or declining, balance method a constant percentage of the remaining book value of an asset is written off each year. The amount to be written off each year may be calculated from the formula:

$$\frac{P - CD}{n}$$

where P is the initial asset cost; CD the cumulative depreciation charged in previous years; and n the plant life expressed in years. As the method is that of a geometric progression, it cannot provide for the complete depreciation of the plant. It is therefore necessary at a certain point to switch to the fixed instalment, or straight-line, method in order to reach a point where P − CD becomes zero. *See* DEPRECIATION; DEPRECIATION FUND METHOD; FIXED INSTALMENT METHOD; SINKING FUND.

Diminishing Returns, Law of *See* VARIABLE PROPORTIONS, LAW OF.

Direct Costing *See* MARGINAL COSTING.

Direct Taxes *See* TAXES.

Director A member of the governing board of a Company. His duties and responsibilities are defined in the Companies Acts.

Disappreciation A movement of prices which, while downward in direction, was merely a correction of a previously excessive rise.

Discount (a) A reduction in a previously determined price granted to a customer or class of customers; (b) the difference between the price at which a security was issued and the price at which it now stands, if the latter is the lower; (c) to cash a bill before it matures. *See* DEFERRED REBATES; DISCOUNT HOUSE.

Discount House A business institution which will buy acceptances from their owners for less than their face value and hold them to maturity. The difference between the price paid and the face value, expressed as a percentage per annum, is called the "discount rate". Discount houses borrow "at call" from banks and other financial institutions; such funds may be called in by the banks at short notice. Money borrowed is invested in British Government Treasury bills, commercial bills of exchange, British Government securities with a life of up to five years, and to a limited extent local authority bonds. Discount houses also provide an active market in commercial bills; when a bill, bought on the London market, is sold by a discount house it is endorsed, i.e. the discount house adds its name to the bill thus assuming responsibility for the payment of the bill at maturity in the event of default. The twelve members of the London Discount Market Association (q.v.) have a right to borrow from the Bank of England (q.v.) as "lender of last resort" (q.v.) should they become short of money as a result of the calling in of loans by the commercial banks (q.v.). *See* ACCEPTANCE; ACCEPTING HOUSE; BILL OF EXCHANGE; LONDON DISCOUNT MARKET; TREASURY BILLS.

Discount Market *See* LONDON DISCOUNT MARKET

Discount Rate A rate of interest. If a bill promising to pay £100 in three months' time is sold at a discount (q.v.) for £98, then the rate of interest is 2 per cent for three months or 8 per cent per annum.

Discount Rate (U.S.) The rate of interest charged when member banks borrow from Federal Reserve Banks (q.v.). *See* BANK RATE.

Discounted Cash Flow Method A method of comparing the profitability of alternative projects. This method may be sub-divided into (a) yield method, and (b) net present value method. Both of these techniques utilise as a measure of the "rating" of an investment the present cash value of a sum to be received at some future date, discounted at compound interest. The present value or worth of a sum to be received at some future date is such an amount as will, with compound interest at a prescribed rate, equal the sum to be received in the future. The yield method is based upon the assumption that the best investment is that from which the proceeds would yield the highest rate of compound interest in equating the present value of the investment with future proceeds. In the net present value method an appropriate percentage rate is stipulated, the present value of the cash inflow is determined using this percentage, the original cost of the investment is subtracted therefrom, and the resulting surplus is the net present value of the investment. Both the yield and net present value methods give reliable guidance to the profitability of alternative schemes, on the assumptions that may be used. However, errors of a serious nature may occur in the assumptions made regarding capital costs or trading returns.

Discretion The amount by which a broker, on his client's instructions, may vary the price at which his client wishes to deal. The "discretion" may vary from a few pence to a few shillings, depending upon the price of the security.

Dishoarding The desire on the part of individuals to hold fewer assets in the form of money, thus reducing "idle balances". The concepts of "hoarding" and "dishoarding" form part of John Maynard Keynes' liquidity preference theory. *See* LIQUIDITY PREFERENCE.

Disinflation The removal of inflationary pressure from the economy in order to maintain the value of the monetary unit. If Government measures to achieve this go too far, the result may be deflation (q.v.). Disinflation is achieved by direct restriction of consumers' expenditure; methods have included hire purchase controls, the creation of a budget surplus, the raising of interest rates and credit squeezes.

Distribution Branch of economics (q.v.) which examines the determination of payments made to the factors of production for their share in the work of production, these being known as rent, wages, interest and profits.

Distribution, Marginal Theory of A theory seeking to demonstrate that the price of each factor of production depends upon its marginal productivity.

Distribution of Industry Act 1945 An Act transferring to the Board of Trade responsibility for the establishment of trading estates. The pre-war "Special Areas" (q.v.) were renamed "Development Districts". The Act also provided for the issue of Industrial Development Certificates (q.v.), to help to guide industry into the development areas. The Act had its roots in two reports:
  (a) The Report of the Royal Commission on the Distribution of the Industrial Population Cmnd. 6153 H.M.S.O. 1940;
  (b) P.E.P. Report "The Location of Industry", 1939.

Distributor A dealer (q.v.) who has been granted by a company an exclusive or preferential right to buy and sell a specific range of its goods or services in specified markets.

Disutility Opposite of utility (q.v.); it implies that the consumption of a good or service gives rise to dissatisfaction.

Diversification of Risk Often the object of businessmen and investors who seek to produce several products or to invest in different classes of security in different types of business—the distribution of eggs between several baskets.

Diversity Factor The probability of a number of pieces of equipment being in use simultaneously. For example, if 100 electrical appliances of 1 kW each rarely produce a maximum demand in excess of 20 kW, the diversity factor is said to be 1 in 5.

Dividend The portion of a Company's profits which the Directors each year decide to distribute to Ordinary Shareholders. This is usually expressed as a percentage of the nominal value of the shares.

Dividend Cover   The number of times a dividend is covered by a company's earnings.   If the net profits attributable to the ordinary shareholders of a company amount to 40 per cent of the ordinary capital, then a dividend of 10 per cent would be described as "4 times covered".

Dividend Mandate   An order to a company by a shareholder to pay all dividends to a third party.

Dividend Warrant   Payment of a dividend to an investor by means of a cheque. It is accompanied by a tax voucher showing the gross amount of the dividend, and the net amount payable after deduction of income tax.

Division of Labour   The specialisation of labour, which inevitably accompanies agricultural, industrial and commercial development.   Its advantage lies in the fact that individuals gain greater skill and dexterity by doing one job, rather than several.   It permits the exploitation of individual aptitude and encourages the use of machinery.   The result is an increase in productivity and an improvement in quality.   A serious implication of the system is that the community becomes more vulnerable to the strike threats of minorities holding "key" jobs.   In addition, labour through becoming very specialised or "specific" faces difficult problems if suitable forms of employment decline. *See* SPECIALISATION.

Documentary Credits   A method of paying an exporter for goods despatched. Under this arrangement the importer requests his bank to send a letter to the exporter undertaking to pay the exporter as soon as it receives the shipping documents.   In this way, an exporter receives a bank's assurance of payment. A documentary credit is usually irrevocable.

Dollar Area   An area comprising the United States and her dependencies, Canada and what have been known as the "American Account" countries. These American Account countries are those whose sterling in account with banks in the United Kingdom has been freely convertible into dollars— Bolivia, Colombia, Costa Rica, Dominica, Ecquador, Guatemala, Haiti, Honduras, Mexico, Nicuragua, Panama, Salvador and Venezuela.   With the general tendency towards increased convertibility of sterling, the term "dollar area" is losing its former precise meaning.

"Dollar Diplomacy"   A term of denigration, suggesting that the monetary strength of the United States has been used for advancing her political influence.

Dollar Gap   Britain's post-war adverse balance between her receipts from, and payments to, the "dollar area" (q.v.).   The gap has only been closed by a substantial increase in exports to the United States. *See* BALANCE OF PAYMENTS.

Donovan Report   The Report of the Royal Commission on Trade Unions and Employers' Associations (Cmnd. 3623).   The Commission examined the industrial relations problems facing Britain and proposed: (a) the establishment of a Commission on Industrial Relations (q.v.); and (b) the introduction of a comprehensive Industrial Relations Bill.

Double Coincidence of Wants A feature of barter (q.v.) in which A offers x to B, and B offers y to A. For an exchange to take place x must appear more desirable to B than y, and y must appear more desirable to A than x. The wants must coincide. In a money economy, the two sides of a transaction can be separated, i.e. the buying and selling can take place at different times and with different people, and change can readily be given.

Double Entry A technique used in book-keeping whereby two separate entries are made of every transaction.

Double Taxation Relief An arrangement to prevent the same income being taxed twice where, say, a shareholder and company are domiciled in different countries. For example, Australia has separate agreements with the United Kingdom, the U.S.A., Canada and New Zealand for the purpose of relieving the double taxing of incomes flowing between Australia and these other countries.

Dow-Jones Averages—An index of United States security prices. The Dow-Jones railroad and industrial averages have been regarded as significant indicators of both price and business trends. The index has been based upon 30 industrial, 20 railroad, 15 utility and 65 other stocks. *See* DOW THEORY.

Dow Theory A theory of market analysis based upon the performance of the Dow-Jones industrial and railroad stock price averages. According to the theory the market is in a basic upward trend if one of these averages advances above a previously important high, accompanied or followed by a similar advance in the other. When the averages both dip below previously important lows, this is considered an indication of a basic downward trend. The theory does not attempt to predict how long either trend will continue. Dow theory consisted originally of the analysis of the stock market trends by Charles H. Dow (1851–1902), founder with Edward D. Jones of the financial news agency Dow, Jones & Co. and one of the owners of "The Wall Street Journal". *See* DOW-JONES AVERAGES.

Drawback The repayment of certain customs and excise duties in respect of materials, components and goods exported after duty has been paid. For example, cigarettes made from duty-paid tobacco would attract drawback when exported. On 26th October, 1964, the British Government relieved exported goods of the burden of certain other taxes entering into the costs of production, e.g. hydrocarbon oil duty, vehicle excise licence duty and purchase tax.

Drawing A method of determining the order in which creditors are to be paid off. Provisions for the repayment of capital invested in a project may incorporate a scheme for drawing lots to determine the order in which capital is to be paid off. *See* CUM DRAWING; EX-DRAWING.

Dumping The sale of a product on a foreign market at a price below that at which it is being sold on the domestic market.

Duopoly   A market situation in which there are only two sellers, neither seller being able to ignore the actions and reactions of the other. Duopoly is the simplest case of oligopoly (q.v.).

Dynamic Economics   A study of the path by which a set of economic quantities (q.v.) reach equilibrium within a static framework. Dynamic theory is a branch of theoretical economics. *See* EQUILIBRIUM THEORY.

E

Early Warning System Any technique adopted which provides an early indication of an economic problem likely to lie ahead. For example, some members of the Organisation for Economic Co-Operation and Development (q.v.) have developed "early warning systems" for providing advance information on important changes in the demand for labour. Such systems rest upon the study of trends and the analysis of future probabilities. In Britain an arrangement exists whereby employers and trade unions voluntarily notify the Government in respect of all wage and salary claims and proposed settlements which are regarded as significant and, in any case, all those covering 100 or more workers.

Earned Income In the United Kingdom, income arising from the sale of the services of labour, as distinct from "unearned income" (q.v.) arising from the sale of the services of capital, ownership of land and savings. Earned income is taxed more lightly than unearned income.

Econometric Models Mathematical models designed to assist in forecasting (q.v.) the needs and demands of the national economy some years ahead. Models can be constructed for static or dynamic economic situations, and the interaction of forces (i.e. the in-built economic assumptions) can be isolated and studied. A model has been built and developed by the Department of Applied Economics of Cambridge University. It permits the computation for each industry of output, input, investment, manpower, imports and exports, etc., at different rates of projected growth in consumption. Professor Richard Stone has stated that "Such a model takes the form of a system of equations suitable for computing, but its purpose is very similar to that of engineering models of hulls or aerofoils—built to test the reliability of the design before the real ship or aircraft is built".

"Econometrica" The official journal of the Econometric Society. The aim of the Society is the advancement of economic theory in its relation to statistics and mathematics.

Econometrics A branch of economics (q.v.) in which hypotheses are mathematically formulated and statistically tested, and in which economic data are systematically analysed with the aid of a computer (q.v.).

Economic Affairs, Department of A Department set up by the British Government in 1964 with responsibility for making and implementing long-term national economic plans. The economic planning functions of both the Treasury (q.v.) and the National Economic Development Council (q.v.) were transferred to the new Department. The Department was organised into three groups concerned with economic planning, regional planning and industrial policy. Abolished in October, 1969.

Economic and Social Council of France An assembly comprising the heads of employer and worker organisations and Government departmental officers, which stands at the head of the French national planning organisation. The Council's function is to receive and debate draft national Plans prepared by the Commissariat au Plan, the Government making the final decisions in respect of policy. The Commissariat au Plan, set up in 1946, has the principal function of drawing up "indicated targets" for national economic growth; a comprehensive Plan is then prepared and submitted to the Council. The Commissariat has no powers of decision or financial control; nevertheless, in practice, it plays a vital role. The Commissariat employs economists, engineers, educationists and administrators. Each Plan, since the first, covers a period of 4 years ahead. The time-table has been: First Plan, 1947–53; Second Plan, 1954–57; Third Plan, 1958–61; Fourth Plan, 1962–65; Fifth Plan, 1966–69. In addition to the Commissariat, there are some 25 or so Modernisation Commissions each of which is concerned with a particular industry or aspect of policy such as finance, man-power, or regional planning. While French planning is "indicative" only, yet the capital market is so managed as to ensure that funds flow into channels indicated by the Plan. Coupled with the existence of a large public sector, this means that a substantial proportion of total investment in France comes under direct Government influence.

Economic and Social Council of the United Nations Formed in 1945, a Council of eighteen members elected by the General Assembly of the United Nations for the purpose of carrying out that body's responsibilities in respect of economic, social, cultural, educational, health and related matters, and for promoting the observance of human rights and fundamental freedoms. *See* ECONOMIC COMMISSION FOR EUROPE (E.C.E.).

Economic Anthropology The comparative study of the relations between the system of management and allocation of the economic resources of societies of various types, and the structure and values of those societies; a branch of social anthropology.

Economic Appraisal The study of the economic implications of a project, as a first step in assessing its acceptibility.

Economic Behaviour The way in which people pursue their material well-being, individually and collectively. Economic man (q.v.) seeks to bring resources under his control with a minimum of effort, and to redistribute them in a manner which will give him the greatest satisfaction. Thus, economic behaviour consists in the exercise of choice, choice being made in many instances at the margins of expenditure. Equilibrium is reached for the individual when he can find no way by which a shift in expenditure from one thing to another could improve his material well-being.

Economic Commission for Europe (E.C.E.) A commission set up in 1947 by the Economic and Social Council of the United Nations (q.v.) to initiate action to raise the level of European economic activity and for maintaining and strengthening the economic relations of European countries, both among themselves and with other countries. The members consist of the European members of the United Nations and the U.S.A.

Economic Co-operation Administration (U.S.) A U.S. government agency set up by the Economic Co-operation Act 1948, for the purpose of administering the European Recovery Programme (q.v.). It was replaced by the Mutual Security Agency (q.v.) in December 1951.

Economic Council of Canada A Council set up in 1964 with the broad function of advising "how Canada can achieve the highest possible levels of employment and efficient production, in order that the country may enjoy a high and consistent rate of economic growth and that all Canadians may share in rising living standards." The Council comprises 28 members appointed by the Government; the chairman and two directors serve on a full-time basis, the remaining 25 on a part-time basis. The part-time members are broadly representative of different sectors and groups in the economy. Statutory duties require the Council:

"(a) Regularly to assess, on a systematic and comprehensive basis, the medium-term and long-term prospects of the economy, and to compare such prospects with the potentialities of growth of the economy;

(b) To recommend what government policies, in the opinion of the Council, will best help to realise the potentialities of growth of the economy;

(c) To consider means of strengthening and improving Canada's international financial and trade position;

(d) To study means of increasing Canadian participation in the ownership, control and management of industries in Canada;

(e) To study how economic growth, technological change and automation, and international economic changes may affect employment and income in Canada as a whole, in particular areas of Canada and in particular sectors of the economy;

(f) To study and discuss with representatives of the industries concerned and with representatives of labour, farmers and other primary producers, and other occupational groups and organisations, what specific plans for production and investment in major industries in Canada will best contribute to a high and consistent rate of economic growth;

(g) To study how national economic policies can best foster the balanced economic development of all areas of Canada;

(h) To explore and evaluate particular projects of major significance for the expansion of industrial and other economic activities in Canada, whether or not such projects may involve direct governmental participation, and to make recommendations concerning those projects that in the opinion of the Council will contribute to the growth of the Canadian economy;

(i) To encourage maximum consultation and co-operation between labour and management in the fulfilment of the objectives of this Act;

(j) To seek full and regular consultation with appropriate agencies of the Governments of the several provinces;

(k) To conduct, if directed to do so by the Minister, reviews of medium-term or long-term programmes of the Government of Canada that are designed to aid or assist industry, labour or agriculture."

The Council published its first annual review in 1965. This was devoted to a discusion of prospects and policies relating to longer-term economic growth, in the form of a measurement of potentialities rather than a forecast. The review estimated that there should be room for an increase in the real gross national product of 5.5 per cent per annum between 1963 and 1970, of which 3 per cent would result from higher employment and 2.4 per cent from increasing productivity.

Economic Development *See* ECONOMIC GROWTH.

Economic Development Committees ("Little Neddies") Committees set up by the National Economic Development Council (q.v.) to study Britain's major industries, consider ways in which each industry might improve its efficiency and to formulate reports and recommendations. Each of the Committees includes representatives of management, trade unions, the National Economic Development Office, the Government departments concerned with the industry being examined, and up to three independent members. The EDCs have no executive power and no powers of compulsion. Their primary task is to identify the problems within their industries and devise and recommend ways of putting them right. Having agreed on the course of action that should be taken it is up to members of the EDCs to persuade the relevant bodies to take action. Another task of the EDCs is to examine the prospects and plans of the industry, assess from time to time the progress of the industry, and provide information and forecasts to the National Economic Development Council. The creation of the EDCs began in 1964; there are now over twenty at work covering most of Britain's major industries.

Economic Efficiency The efficiency with which scarce resources are used and organised to achieve stipulated economic ends (q.v.). In competitive conditions, the lower the cost per unit of output, without sacrifice of quality, in relation to the value or price of the finished article, the greater the economic efficiency of the productive organisation. *See* PRODUCTIVITY.

Economic Ends The objectives of economic activity. Ends are both quantitative and qualitative, but with the nature of ends economics has no direct concern; economics is concerned only with the number of ends and with their degree of relative intensity.

Economic Friction Influences, natural or deliberate, which tend to impede the full or rapid operation of economic laws. For example, ignorance or habit may inhibit the movement of resources into their most profitable lines of activity; Government measures may be introduced to protect individuals against the harsher aspects of the operation of economic laws in the fixing of minimum wages and in other ways. Conversely, Government measures may be taken to reduce economic friction where this is thought desirable by, for example, making it easier for workers to move between jobs or providing special advisory services to exporters. *See* EXPORT CREDITS GUARANTEE DEPARTMENT; MINIMUM WAGE LEGISLATION.

Economic Geography The study of the production, exchange and transportation of the Earth's products; also known as commercial geography.

Economic Good A scarce good, commanding a price.

Economic Growth The growth per head of the population in the production of goods and services of all kinds available to meet final demands, e.g. goods and services for domestic consumption, capital goods for accumulation, export goods to pay for imports. In the eight years from 1947–55, Britain achieved a rate of growth of 3.1 per cent per annum; in the five years from 1955–60 the rate of growth fell to 2.3 per cent per annum. An acceleration of economic growth requires as much emphasis on such elements as better management, better training of labour and improved education, as on higher capital investment. Furthermore, the quality of investment may count almost as much as the quantity of it. Capital investment, though important, is but one significant factor in the growth rate of an economy. The "growth rate" is the annual growth, usually expressed as a percentage over the previous year, of productive capacity in a community. Figure 4 illustrates the effect on the national income of a range of growth rates from 1 to 10 per cent per annum.

Economic Growth, Stages of Professor W. W. Rostow has distinguished five basic stages of economic growth in society. All societies, in their economic dimensions, lie within one of these five categories; the traditional society, the preconditions for take-off, the take-off, the drive to maturity, and the age of high mass-consumption.

A traditional society is defined as one whose structure is developed within limited production functions, based on pre-Newtonian science and technology, and on pre-Newtonian attitudes towards the physical world. While this concept is in no sense static and would not exclude increases in output, there is a ceiling on the level of attainable output per head. The term embraces the dynasties of China; the civilisation of the Middle East and the Mediterranean; the world of medieval Europe; and post-Newtonian societies which, for a time, remained untouched or unmoved by man's new capability for regularly manipulating his environment to his economic advantage.

The second stage of growth embraces societies in the process of transition; that is, the period when the pre-conditions for take-off are developed. This period witnesses major changes in both the economy itself and in the balance of social values together with the building of an effective centralised national state. The idea spreads not merely that economic progress is possible, but that economic progress is a necessary condition for some other purpose, judged to be good—be it national dignity, private profit, the general welfare, or a better life for the children.

The take-off is the interval when the resistances to steady growth are finally overcome and the forces making for economic progress expand and come to dominate the society. Growth becomes its normal condition. During the take-off, the rate of effective investment and saving may rise from say 5 per cent of the national income to 10 per cent or more, and new industries expand rapidly. The economy exploits hitherto unused natural resources and methods of production; revolutionary changes take place in agricultural productivity.

The drive to maturity takes the form of a long interval of sustained if fluctuating progress, as the now regularly growing economy drives to extend modern technology over the whole front of its economic activity. Some 10–20 per cent of the national income is steadily invested, permitting output regularly to outstrip the increase in population. The make-up of the economy

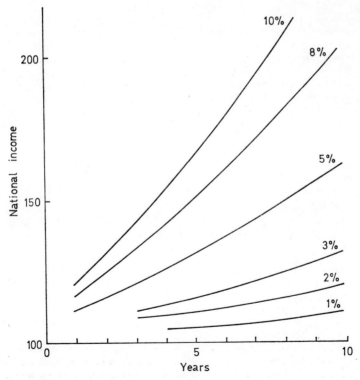

FIGURE 4. RATES OF GROWTH, PER CENT PER ANNUM.

changes unceasingly as technique improves, new industries accelerate, older industries level off; the economy finds its place in the international economy. Maturity is the stage in which the economy demonstrates the capacity to move beyond the original industries which powered its take-off and to absorb and to apply efficiently over a very wide range of its resources the the most advanced fruits of modern technology.

In the age of high mass consumption, the leading sectors of the economy shift towards durable consumers' goods and services; real income per head rises to a point where a large number of persons gain command over consumption which transcends basic food, shelter and clothing. The proportion of urban to total population increases; and also the proportion working in offices or in skilled factory jobs. Society ceases to accept further extensions of modern technology as an overriding objective; the emergence of the welfare state is one manifestation of a society's moving beyond technical maturity.

Economic History The study of the struggle of man to relate scarce resources to competing ends through time; the economic historian hopes to find in the record of history explanations for important economic occurrences and developments.

Economic Indicators Statistics which are sensitive to changes in the state of industry, trade and commerce. United Kingdom economic indicators include the statistics of unemployment and unfilled vacancies; bank advances, gold reserve, basic materials and fuel prices, and retail prices; wage rates, retail sales, H.P. debt; terms of trade and industrial output; imports, exports and imports surplus; output of steel, cars and commercial vehicles, manmade fibres, houses, furniture, bricks, cement, hosiery, radios and television sets, machine tools, petroleum; orders on hand in the engineering, electrical and textile industries; consumer spending. Indicators may be classified into three types; "leaders"—offering advance pointers; "coincidents"—moving in tandem with business conditions; and "laggers"—showing delayed results.

"Economic Journal, The" *See* ROYAL ECONOMIC SOCIETY.

Economic Law A statement of what will occur in the economic world under specified conditions. George J. Stigler, in his "Theory of Price" offers the following statement of an economic law:—

> *If:* (a) An entrepreneur seeks maximum profits;
> (b) His marginal cost curve does not fall so fast as (or more rapidly than) his marginal revenue curve;
> (c) The curves are continuous.
>
> *Then:* He operates at the output where marginal revenue equals marginal cost.

Alfred Marshall's view of economic laws was that "there are no definite and universal propositions in economics which can compare with the Laws of Gravitation and of conservation of Energy in physics. But there are many which rank with the secondary laws of those natural sciences which resemble economics in dealing with the complex actions of many heterogeneous and uncertain causes. The laws of biology, for instance, or, to take an example from a purely physical science, the laws of the tides, like those of economics vary much in definiteness, in range of application—and in certainty. An economic law is then nothing but a general proposition, or statement of uniformity, more or less certain, more or less definite."

As the specified condition for the operation of a law may not be fully complied with in any real-life situation, the law may appear not to operate. In other situations, the operation of a law may be masked by other events. Hence, economic laws are often referred to as "tendencies". For example: "In a free market price *tends* to equate the supply of, and the demand for, an article."

See EQUI-MARGINAL RETURNS, LAW OF; MARGINAL UTILITY, LAW OF DIMINISHING; VARIABLE PROPORTIONS, LAW OF.

Economic Life *See* LIFE.

Economic Man One who is completely rational in satisfying his wants and pays no regard to the interests of others. An abstraction or first approximation useful in economic analysis.

Economic Planning The identification of future economic wants (q.v.) and the marshalling and deployment of scarce resources in the most efficient manner to satisfy those wants. So defined, economic planning is engaged in by the individual, firm, local authority and national government. The means adopted may be described as "economic policy".

Economic Problem A problem of ensuring that all available resources are used to the best possible effect, in the resolving of which decisions must be made as to which ends are to be satisfied first and perhaps which wants will have to be left unsatisfied.

Economic Quantities or Aggregates The subject matter of macro-economics, economic quantities or aggregates include such diverse items as the amount of a commodity produced, stored and consumed; the volume of employment and unemployment; the price of butter; the interest on bank loans; the wages of bricklayers; the price of houses; taxes on tobacco or spirits; the surcharge on imported raw materials, etc. The main task of economic analysis is the explanation of the magnitude of economic quantities.

Economic Rent A payment to a unit of a factor of production (q.v.) which is in excess of the minimum amount necessary to keep that unit in its present occupation. A firm may pay a wage sufficient to retain its present staff. In attempting to increase its staff, however, the firm may find it necessary to raise wages and attract workers from other employment. The increase in wage now enjoyed by the original staff is economic rent. A perfectly elastic supply yields no economic rent as such an assumption implies an unlimited supply available at stable prices; a situation not experienced, or experienced for long, in real life. Economic rent can be enjoyed indefinitely by a factor whose supply is relatively fixed; land enjoys this distinction. *See* QUASI-RENT.

"Economic Review" Journal published by the National Institute of Economic and Social Research (q.v.).

Economic Significance A quality possessed by a good or service when it commands a price and enters into the circle of exchange.

Economic Statistics Data relating to production, prices, wages and employment, etc.; the figures are analysed to find significant trends or inter-relationships. *See* STATISTICAL METHODS.

Economic System, Functions of an The functions of an economic system may be defined as follows:

   (a) generally, to match supply to the effective demand for goods and services in an efficient manner;

   (b) to determine what goods and services are to be produced, and in what quantities;

   (c) to distribute scarce resources among the industries producing goods and services;

   (d) to distribute the products of industry among members of the community;

   (e) to provide for maintenance and expansion of fixed capital investment;

   (f) to fully utilise the resources of society.

In a free enterprise system, the fulfilment of these six economic functions is left to the profit motive (q.v.) and the price mechanism (q.v.) working within a framework of social safeguards. In a socialist society all the operations required are consciously planned by salaried officials; there are no private investors. Britain operates a mixed system, splitting the economy into public and private sectors, the activity of the whole being influenced by direct and indirect planning measures.

"Economic Trends" A monthly publication of the Central Statistical Office containing key statistics of the British economy.

Economic Welfare Defined by A. C. Pigou as "that part of social welfare that can be brought directly or indirectly into relation with the measuring rod of money"; in other words, those aspects of social welfare which are concerned with material as distinct from bodily, moral or spiritual well-being, although obviously these are inter-related in some ways. Pigou stressed that there is no precise line between economic and non-economic satisfactions. Economic or material satisfactions are derived from the consumption of both goods and services; and it is this which is the subject matter of economics. Pigou warned that economic welfare will not serve for a barometer or index of total welfare; this is because an economic cause may affect non-economic welfare in ways that cancel its effects on economic welfare. Non-economic welfare is liable to be modified by the manner in which income is earned and also by the manner in which it is spent—"Of different acts of consumption that yield equal satisfactions, one may exercise a debasing and another an elevating influence."

"Economica" A journal published quarterly by the London School of Economics and Political Science.

Economics A social science concerned with how people, either individually or in groups, attempt to accommodate scarce resources to their wants through the processes of production, substitution and exchange. It is not as a science concerned with the problems of what ought to be, but with the explanation and understanding of what already exists. There have been many definitions of economics in the past. The earliest definitions envisaged economics as the study of wealth. Adam Smith (1723–1790), the founder of modern economics, entitled his great work *An Inquiry into the Nature and Causes of the Wealth of Nations*. Nearly 70 years later, John Stuart Mill (1806–1873) in his *Principles of Political Economy* defined economics as "the practical science of the production and distribution of wealth". The Victorian economist, Alfred Marshall (1842–1924), in his *Principles of Economics* defined economics as "a study of man's actions in the ordinary business of life; it inquires how he gets his income and how he uses it. It is on the one side a study of wealth and on the other part of the study of man". In more recent years, Lionel Robbins, in his *Essay on the Nature and Significance of Economic Science*, has defined the subject more precisely as "the science which studies human behaviour as a relationship between ends and scarce means which have alternative uses".

Formerly treated under three headings "production, consumption and distribution", economic science has become segmented into a number of distinct sciences, reflecting the advantages of a "division of labour". These distinct sciences may be classified as follows:

Theory of Prices	International Trade
Theory of Distribution	Labour Economics
Dynamic Theory	Money and Banking
Social Economics	Public Finance
Demography	Welfare Economics
Theory of Taxation	Theory of Monopolistic
Mathematical Economics	Competition
Statistical Economics	Theory of Determination of National
Descriptive Economics	Income and Employment.

The methods of economics remain the same in the use of inductive and deductive reasoning. Well-observed facts are compared with theoretical constructions wide enough to take account of all the facts. The old name for economics was "political economy". Adam Smith in his *Wealth of Nations* declared that "the object of the political economy of every nation is to increase the riches and power of that country". Today economics is no longer the hand-maiden of government, seeking to justify policy, although one may hope that in fulfilling its role it contributes to successful economic and social policies. John Maynard Keynes (1884–1946) warned, however, "the theory of economics does not furnish a body of settled conclusions immediately applicable to policy. It is a method rather than a doctrine, an apparatus of the mind, a technique of thinking, which helps its possessor to draw correct conclusions."

Economies of Scale The gains by way of reduced costs of production per unit of output often arising from increasing the size of a plant, business or industry. In suitable circumstances, large-scale production leads to important economies in the use of (a) Land—it is most unlikely that a doubling of production requires twice as much land; (b) Labour—persons with specialised knowledge and skill may devote all their time to the tasks they perform most efficiently; (c) Capital—specialised units of equipment may be brought into use and fully employed; (d) Marketing—advertising costs per unit may be less; (e) Buying —raw materials may be bought more cheaply by buying in bulk; (f) Finance— a large firm can usually raise new capital more easily and cheaply than a small firm; (g) Research—development costs are spread over many more units. All forms of production at various periods experience the operation of the laws of increasing, constant and diminishing returns. Firms may attempt to increase profits and spread risks by diversifying activities, producing a wide range of products sometimes of a very contrasting nature. Horizontal and vertical integration of processes may be sought in order to achieve greater economies. *See also* EXTERNAL ECONOMY; VARIABLE PROPORTIONS, LAW OF.

Economist A social scientist who has become an expert in dealing with the economic aspects of social phenomena. He may specialise in theoretical or applied economics. *See* ECONOMICS.

Economist—Extel Index An index of industrial share prices compiled by *The Economist* in association with the Exchange Telegraph Company. It is calculated twice daily. The indicator has the unique feature of combining 50 stocks in an unweighted arithmetic average of their price relatives, rebased each year and then linked back to the original base of the indicator, namely, the average of mid-monthly prices in 1953. Each year end, the constituent shares of the index are reviewed and revised where necessary.

Economy (a) The economic system of a country, or part of a country; (b) The optimum use of resources so that the maximum satisfaction is gained from any given input of resources.

Economy of High Wages A view that if a man is well paid, so that he enjoys a high standard of living, his working efficiency will be raised and with it his productivity.

Economy, Stationary An economy in which there are no changes in the three fundamental sets of data—resources, technology and tastes; an assumption that may be made for the purposes of theoretical economic analysis.

E.C.S. (Export of Commercial Samples) Carnets Carnet documents, issued by Chambers of Commerce, which provide automatic Customs clearance for personally accompanied samples, enabling them to be imported temporarily without duty or deposit of bond.

Effective Demand *See* DEMAND.

Efficiency, Economic *See* ECONOMIC EFFICIENCY.

Efficiency, Technical *See* TECHNICAL EFFICIENCY.

Elasticity of Demand The response of demand to a change in the price of a commodity. It is measured:

$$\frac{\text{Percentage change in quantity demanded}}{\text{Percentage change in price}}$$

If the price is lowered, the amount demanded will normally be increased. Where the percentage increase of the amount demanded is greater than the percentage reduction of price, the demand is described as "elastic"; if it is less, "inelastic". If a given percentage reduction of price leads to an equal percentage increase of the amount demanded, the elasticity of demand is unity.

If a fall of 1 per cent in selling price is accompanied by an increase of 5 per cent in demand, then the elasticity of demand is 5. If a fall of ½ per cent in price expands sales from 100 to 110, the elasticity of demand at the price is 20.

When the elasticity of demand is unity, the total receipts from selling different amounts of a commodity at higher or lower prices remain the same. When demand is elastic a fall in price accompanied by an expansion of demand causes total receipts to increase.   A fall in price when demand is inelastic causes total receipts to fall.   Conversely, a rise in price when demand is elastic causes a fall in receipts.   A rise in price when demand is inelastic causes an increase in receipts.

Many factors influence the elasticity of demand for a commodity.   A commodity having no close substitutes is likely to have an inelastic demand; conversely, a commodity having close substitutes will have an elastic demand.   The demand for a commodity which commands only a small share of consumers' total expenditure is likely to have an inelastic demand. In the case of a durable commodity, the replacement of which can always be readily deferred, demand is likely to be elastic (i.e. to fall sharply) if price rises, and equally elastic (i.e. to increase rapidly) if price falls.   Much depends on the circumstances of the commodity concerned.

It is generally accepted that the elasticity of demand for commodities increases with time.   Thus a 1 per cent increase in price may lead to only ½ per cent fall in demand in the short-term, but later the quantity may decrease by 2 or more per cent.   There are various reasons for this.   A consumer may leave matters for a time to see how other prices change.   For example, if the price of a particular fuel increases by 10 per cent he would need to be sure that this was a permanent relative change in the price of fuels before considering changing any of his heating appliances.   Then again, it may be found that the theoretical saving in running costs may not be sufficient to justify the cost or the upheaval of installing new appliances. A change would be delayed, therefore, until a normal replacement had to be made.

See DEMAND, CROSS-ELASTICITY OF; ELASTICITY OF SUPPLY.

Elasticity of Demand, Income The response of the demand for a commodity to changes in the real income of consumers. Its computation is as follows:

$$\frac{\text{Percentage change in quantity demanded}}{\text{Percentage change in income}}$$

For most commodities, increases in income lead to increases in demand, income elasticity being positive. In respect of "inferior goods" or Giffen goods (q.v.) a rise in income leads to a fall in demand for the commodities concerned, income elasticity being negative.

Elasticity of Substitution A measure of the ease with which a variable factor of production can be substituted for others. Where factors must be employed in fixed proportions, the elasticity of substitution is zero. Where factors are perfect substitutes, the elasticity of substitution is infinite. In the majority of cases, however, the degree of elasticity falls between these two extremes.

Elasticity of Supply The response of supply to a change in the price of a commodity. If the price rises, the amount supplied will normally be increased. The elasticity is calculated as follows:

$$\frac{\text{Percentage change in quantity supplied}}{\text{Percentage change in price}}$$

Thus if a 1 per cent rise in the price of a commodity results in a 2 per cent increase in the quantity supplied, the elasticity of supply is 2. If the price falls, the supply wil normally shrink. There are some important exceptions to the "normal", however, particularly in the international commodity markets (*see* PRICE MECHANISM). The supply of a commodity is likely to be elastic if a given increase in the output of single firms produces only a small increase in the marginal costs of production, and if it is relatively easy for new firms to enter the industry. A supply will tend to be inelastic (elasticity less than unity) for a time in respect of an industry using highly specialised capital or labour, the quantities of which cannot be readily increased. If the proportional change in the quantity supplied equals the proportional change in price, then elasticity is unity. *See* ELASTICITY OF DEMAND; SUPPLY CURVE.

Electricity Council A body set up under the Electricity Act of 1957 to take over the central administration of the electricity supply industry in England and Wales. The Council's statutory duty was "to advise the Minister on questions affecting the electricity supply industry and to promote and assist the maintenance and development by the Electricity Boards of an efficient, co-ordinated and economical system of electricity supply". It also dealt with labour relations, finance and research. The Council's members included representatives of the twelve area electricity boards and the Central Electricity Generating Board (q.v.). Reconstituted as the Electricity Authority in 1970 with new powers to plan and control the policy of the industry as a whole.

Eligible Paper Bills and securities in respect of which the Bank of England is prepared to make an advance to a discount house (q.v.). Eligible paper may consist of Treasury Bills (q.v.), gilt-edged securities with less than five years to run, or first-class commercial bills.

Employers' Association An association of individual employers, providing an organisation capable of negotiating with trade unions (q.v.) and representing employers in discussions with public bodies and the government. The Confederation of British Industry (q.v.) represents, in turn, a large number of individual associations; in many ways it is the counterpart of the Trades Union Congress (q.v.).

Employment and Productivity, Department of A Department with overall responsibility for the British Government's policies on productivity, prices and incomes. It is also concerned with general employment policy, including the distribution of industry and the maintenance of a high and steady level of employment. The Department operates a national system of employment exchanges and other schemes relating to employment. It is also responsible for the provision of services for conciliation, arbitration and investigation in industrial disputes. Through the Factory Inspectorate, it supervises matters relating to the safety, health and welfare of workers in industry and commerce. The Department has responsibilities in relation to the Redundancy Payments Act 1965, Wages Councils Act 1959, and the Industrial Training Act 1964.

Employment, Classical Theory of A theory held by the Classical School (q.v.) of economists, based on two fundamental postulates:

- (a) the wage is equal to the marginal product of labour; and
- (b) the utility of the wage when a given volume of labour is employed is equal to the marginal disutility of that amount of employment, i.e. the real wage is just sufficient to induce the volume of labour actually employed to be forthcoming.

Postulate (a) represents the demand schedule for labour, and postulate (b) the supply schedule for labour. The theory is compatible with frictional or voluntary unemployment; but it is not compatible with involuntary or mass unemployment. The Classical view was that, if workers agreed to a reduction of money-wages, more employment would be forthcoming and involuntary unemployment would disappear. John Maynard Keynes (1884–1946) did not deny the proposition that a reduction in money-wages accompanied by the same aggregate effective demand as before will be associated with an increase in employment. But, a general reduction of wages is ineffective if it results in, and is accompanied by, a fully proportionate reduction in the aggregate effective demand for goods and services. Keynes argued that a reduction in money-wages will have no lasting tendencies to increase employment, except by virtue of its repercussions either on the propensity to consume for the community as a whole or on the schedule or marginal efficiency of capital (q.v.), or on the rate of interest. He recognised

85

that the unemployment which characterises a depression is not due to the refusal of labour to accept a reduction of money wages. Indeed, he recognised that, with wages and prices falling simultaneously, there may exist no expedient by which labour *as a whole* can reduce its *real* wage to a given figure by making revised *money* bargains with the entrepreneurs. He argued that if the propensity to consume and the rate of new investment result in a deficient effective demand, the actual level of employment will fall short of the supply of labour potentially available at the existing real wage, and the equilibrium real wage will be greater than the marginal disutility of the equilibrium level of employment. The insufficiency of effective demand will inhibit the process of production in spite of the fact that the marginal product of labour still exceeds in value the marginal disutility of employment. Keynes rejected the belief, springing from Classical theory, that a flexible wage policy is capable of maintaining a state of continuous full employment. *See* CLASSICAL SCHOOL; EMPLOYMENT POLICY, WHITE PAPER ON; KEYNESIAN REVOLUTION; PROPENSITIES TO CONSUME AND SAVE.

Employment Exchange A local office of the Department of Employment and Productivity which functions as a clearing house for employers seeking particular kinds of workers and individuals seeking employment. These offices were first established in 1909 as Labour Exchanges.

Employment, Full *See* FULL EMPLOYMENT.

"Employment Policy", White Paper On A White Paper (Cmd. 6527) presented to Parliament by the Minister of Reconstruction in May, 1944 outlining the policy which the Government proposed to follow in pursuit of its declared aim to maintain "a high and stable level of employment after the war". The Paper argued that a country will not suffer from mass unemployment so long as the total demand for its goods and services is maintained at a high level. If the necessary expansion of our trade could be assured, the Government believed that widespread unemployment in Britain could be prevented by a policy for maintaining total internal expenditure. It was regarded as an essential part of the Government's employment policy to co-operate actively with other nations, in the first place for the re-establishment of general economic stability after the shocks of the war, and next for the progressive expansion of trade. More specifically, the aims of international co-operation were defined as:

(a) To promote the exchange of goods and services;
(b) To ensure reasonably stable rates of exchange;
(c) To check swings in world commodity prices which alternately inflate and destroy the incomes of the primary producers of foodstuffs and raw materials;
(d) To make arrangements so that countries having temporary difficulties in their balance of payments may receive assistence without recourse to measures which would permanently arrest the flow of international trade.

Among the general conditions necessary for a high and stable level of employment, the White Paper named three essential requirements:

(a) *Total expenditure on goods and services must be prevented from falling to a level where general unemployment appears.* The crucial moment for intervention by the Government is at the first onset of a depression. It was recognised that the main problem was to stop violent fluctuations in public and private capital expenditure, taken together. The possibility of influencing capital expenditure by the variation of interest rates would be kept in view, although it was recognised that high interest rates are more effective in preventing excessive investment in periods of prosperity than are low interest rates in encouraging investment in periods of depression. The Government therefore proposed to supplement monetary policy by encouraging privately-owned enterprises to plan their own capital expenditure in conformity with a general stabilisation policy. Public investment would be used directly as an instrument of employment policy. The trend of public capital expenditure in the past had tended to accentuate the peaks and depressions of the trade cycle (falling in times of slump and rising in times of boom). In the future, Government policy would be directed to correcting this sympathetic movement. Indeed it was desirable that public investment should actually expand when private investment was declining, and should contract in a period of boom. On this latter point, it was fully realised that the demand for housing, schools and hospitals could not be readily postponed. The Government saw in consumption expenditure another field of control. A scheme could be adopted for varying in sympathy with the state of employment the weekly contribution to be paid under the new system of social insurance; the rate of contribution would be less than the standard rate at times when unemployment exceeded the average. Other devices envisaged were variations in the rates of taxation and the incorporation of some system of deferred credits as a permanent feature of national taxation, people being over-taxed in prosperous times. Again, all public authorities could buy for stock when employment flagged and allow stocks to fall in prosperous times. None of these proposals involved deliberate planning for a deficit in the National Budget in years of sub-normal trade activity.

(b) *Stability of Prices and Wages.* This was considered of vital importance to any employment policy. The principle of stability meant that increases in the general level of wage rates should be related to increased productivity due to increased efficiency and effort. In addition, the Government would seek power to inform themselves of the extent and effect of restrictive agreements, and of the activities of combines, and take appropriate action to check practices which might bring advantages to sectional producing interests but work to the detriment of the country as a whole.

(c) *Mobility of Labour.* The White Paper noted that if total expenditure was expanded to cure unemployment of a type due, not to the absence of jobs, but to the failure of workers to move to places and occupations where they are needed, the policy of the Government would be frustrated and a dangerous rise in prices might follow.

The White Paper stressed the need for quick action; in 1920–21 unemployment rose from 5 to 15 per cent in four months. Exact information was also necessary. The problem of local unemployment was not overlooked in the general discussion. This form of unemployment was to be attacked in three ways: (a) By so influencing the location of new enterprise as to diversify the industrial composition of areas which are particularly vulnerable to unemployment, (b) by removing obstacles to the transfer of workers from one area to another, and from one occupation to another, and (c) by providing training facilities to fit workers from declining industries for jobs in expanding industries.

The White Paper conceded that "not long ago, the ideas embodied in the present proposals were unfamiliar to the general public and the subject of controversy among economists". But it was stressed that employment cannot be created by Act of Parliament or by Government action alone. Government policy could only be directed to bringing about conditions favourable to the maintenance of a high level of employment; the success of the policy outlined depended on the understanding and support of the community as a whole—and especially on the efforts of employers and workers in industry; for without a rising standard of industrial efficiency a high level of employment could not be combined with a rising standard of living. The whole productive power of the nation should be employed efficiently; it is not enough that it should be employed.

Lord Beveridge considered the White Paper "a milestone in economic and political history" disposing of the economic fallacy that very little additional employment and no permanent additional employment could, in fact, as a general rule, be created by State borrowing and State expenditure (a dogma that had been attacked as far back as 1929 by Keynes, Henderson, Pigou and Clay). But he criticised the White Paper for offering no serious attack on the instability of private investment. He thought private investment should be stabilised through a National Investment Board which would plan investment as a whole. In addition, Beveridge visualised an expansion of the public sector of business so as to enlarge the area within which investment could be stabilised directly. He also supported the idea of a long-term programme of expanding consumption demand, social and private, which should lead to maintaining investment. He noted the importance attached in the White Paper to balancing the Budget, in the long run, though not in a particular year, thus excluding continuous deficit spending by public authorities; yet, either this or a drastic redistribution of income to increase the propensity to consume was considered in the last resort essential to a permanent policy of full employment.

Employment Rate   The percentage of a body of persons available for employment at any time actually in employment at that time.

Employment Tax, Selective   *See* SELECTIVE EMPLOYMENT TAX

Employment Volume   The number of persons actually in employment at any time in any industry or region.

Endorse Sign on the back (especially of a cheque or bill of exchange).

Endowment Policy An insurance policy entitling the holder to a specified sum on reaching a certain age.

Engel's Law A generalisation that the proportion of income spent on food tends to decline as income grows.

Engineering Economics The application of economic principles to engineering problems, for example in comparing the comparative costs of two alternative capital projects or in determining the optimum engineering course, from the cost aspect.

Engrossing, Forestalling and Regrating Three closely interwoven activities —attempts to "corner" or monopolise a product; buying up produce before it reaches the market; and the buying up of produce in order to resell it within a short time at an enhanced price. Statutes formerly prohibiting these activities proved an impediment to modern trade. An Act of 1844 abolished these offences.

Entrepôt Trade Trade by a country in the products of other countries by way of re-exports.

Entrepreneur A business organiser whose aim is profit. His responsibilities comprise:—

    (a) risk and uncertainty bearing;
    (b) making decisions on what goods and services will be produced, how the factors of production (q.v.) will be combined for this purpose, and the scale of production; and
    (c) marketing of these goods and services.

It is commonly assumed, for the purpose of economic analysis, that an entrepreneur will always seek to maximise his profit. This is a useful generalisation, although business organisers are human and this may modify the concept in practice. Some may be content to sustain a customary standard of living; others may be motivated by thoughts of power and prestige; others may sacrifice profit in the short-run to keep prices low and drive competitors out.

The term "entrepreneur" may be readily applied to the owner-manager of a small enterprise; it is also applied to boards of directors and sometimes to the general body of shareholders.

Equal Pay Equal material reward for men and women doing equal work. The vexed question of equal pay was examined by a Royal Commission, whose findings in the form of majority and minority reports were published in 1946. The Majority Report ascribed the difference in the earnings of men and women to the greater physical strength and greater efficiency of men; the higher sickness rate and more absenteeism among women; and further declared that women generally had less ambition and showed less initiative in a crisis. The Minority Report affirmed that women were equally efficient as men, except where physical strength was required, but that

89

employers were prejudiced against the employment of women in new spheres and afraid of fermenting trouble among their male employees.

The principle of equal pay for men and women has now been accepted in the Civil Service and in the teaching profession. In Canada, eight provinces and the Federal Government have enacted legislation prohibiting discrimination between men and women in rates of pay.

Equilibrium Price *See* PRICE, EQUILIBRIUM.

Equilibrium Theory The study of an economic system as a whole, with its various elements fixed in quantity and so distributed that there is no economic motive for change, thus permitting the effects to be considered when changes in these elements are introduced. It is a state, therefore, which affords the maximum possible economic satisfaction. An individual's expenditure is in equilibrium when the ratio of the prices of any two goods purchased equals the marginal rate of substitution (q.v.) between them. A firm is in equilibrium when the maximum profit is being earned, i.e. when marginal cost equals marginal revenue, and there is no incentive to increase or decrease output. An industry is in equilibrium if there is no tendency for firms to enter or leave the industry. A market is in equilibrium when at the ruling price the amount of commodities being offered for sale is just equal to the amount consumers wish to buy.

Equilibrium may be stable or unstable, partial or general. Stable equilibrium implies that any temporary movement in the factors involved, arising from an outside cause, would be offset after a time by a movement in the opposite direction until the initial situation was restored. In unstable equilibrium any movement in the factors involved will result in the situation departing increasingly from the initial position while showing no tendency to return to it; it will tend to settle down in some quite different position.

A partial equilibrium analysis is one which is based on only a restricted range of data, e.g. the price of a single product, the prices of all other products being held fixed during analysis. The method of partial equilibrium analysis is associated with Alfred Marshall and the Cambridge School (q.v.). General equilibrium analysis is based on all of the data relevant to the problem being studied, e.g. the prices and outputs of all industries. General equilibrium has been associated with Walras and the Lausanne School.

Equi-Marginal Returns, Law of A basic theorem describing the way in which consumers with limited resources divide their expenditure between the innumerable different goods and services they could enjoy, based on the assumptions that consumers wish to obtain the maximum utility (q.v.) from their income and that they act rationally in seeking that end. The theorem asserts that people generally will distribute their expenditure between various commodities so as to ensure that the marginal utility (q.v.) obtained from every commodity purchased is in the same relationship to price, i.e. that the marginal rates of substitution (q.v.) should be everywhere equal to relative prices. As the pattern of prices changes, so the consumer will shift his pattern of expenditure.

Equities The ordinary shares of a limited company. They carry the right to the residue of a company's assets after it has paid all its creditors, and share in the distribution of profits, if any, after interest has been paid to preference share-holders and debenture holders each year. *See* DEBENTURES; PREFERENCE SHARE.

Ergonomics The scientific study of ordinary people in work situations. This knowledge is being increasingly applied to the design of processes and machines, to the lay-out of work places, to methods of work, and to the control of the physical environment, in order to achieve greater efficiency of both men and machines. The object is to make man-plus-machine a more efficient unit.

Estate Duties First imposed in 1894 by Sir William Harcourt, then Chancellor of the Exchequer, duties or taxes payable to the Government imposed on property passing at death. Estates not exceeding £5,000 in value are currently exempt from duty. On estates over £5,000 in value there is a progressive duty ranging from 1 per cent to 80 per cent. The duty extends to gifts made within a specified period before death.

Estate Duties Investment Trust ("Edith") Formed in 1953, an investment trust which buys and holds minority shareholdings in family businesses and small public companies; the facility is used by executors and trustees holding shares in such companies and who are faced with estate duty liability who wish to avoid losing control or selling out.

Euro-Bond Market A European market for long-term capital. *See* EURO-DOLLARS.

Euro-Currency Market A European money market. *See* EURO-DOLLARS.

Euro-Dollars U.S. dollars held by residents outside the United States, serving a dollar market in Europe; hence the term "Euro-dollar market". This international money market was created in 1957 when, as a result of the Suez crisis, restrictions were placed on ordinary sterling credit facilities to finance non-British trade; London bankers sought to overcome the difficulties of meeting traders' demands for credit by tapping the pool of dollars held by residents outside the United States. The market is no longer confined to dollars, but embraces European currencies also; it has become one of the world's largest markets for short-term funds. Outside the direct control of any national central bank it is a free, competitive and flexible market. A wholesale market it deals only in large amounts. Concomitant with the Euro-dollar market is the Euro-bond market, a source of long-term capital.

Euro-Market Another name for the European Economic Community (q.v.) (Common Market).

Euro-Sterling Deposits of sterling held in Europe. *See* EURO-DOLLARS.

European Atomic Energy Community (Euratom) An organisation set up by a Treaty signed in Rome on 25th March, 1967, to co-ordinate the nuclear research and power projects of the European Economic Community (q.v.). Euratom initially had its own Commission and Council of Ministers. It is financed by contributions from member states in proportions set out in the Treaty. *See* EUROPEAN COMMISSION.

European Coal and Steel Community A Community for the creation of a common market for coal and steel established by a Treaty, signed in Paris on behalf of Belgium, France, the German Federal Republic, Italy, Luxemburg and the Netherlands ("the Member Countries") on 18th April 1951, and ratified in all of them with effect from 23rd July 1952. The Treaty is for a period of fifty years. The creation of the Community, to which other European countries may be admitted, was the first step taken by the member countries towards European integration and facilitated the establishment in 1958 of the European Economic Community ("the Common Market") (q.v.) for all products other than coal, steel and nuclear energy, and of the European Atomic Energy Community ("Euratom"). Each of these three communities constitutes a separate entity.

The powers of the Community in respect of the coal and steel enterprises under its jurisdiction were initially vested in the High Authority, subject in certain stipulated circumstances to the concurrence of a Special Council of Ministers and subject to a right of appeal to the Court of Justice of the European Communities ("the Court"). The decisions of the High Authority under the Treaty were binding on the member countries. Twenty-four countries, among them the United Kingdom and the United States of America, have established diplomatic relations with the European Coal and Steel Community. *See* EUROPEAN COMMISSION.

European Commission A single European Commission which on 1st July, 1967, replaced the Coal and Steel High Authority, the Euratom Commission and the Common Market Commission; thus the executives of the three European Communities were merged. See EUROPEAN ATOMIC ENERGY COMMUNITY; EUROPEAN COAL AND STEEL COMMUNITY; EUROPEAN ECONOMIC COMMUNITY.

European Development Fund A fund set up by the European Economic Community (q.v.) to provide aid to the overseas associates of "the Six".

European Economic Community Popularly known as the European Common Market, a free trade organisation created by the Treaty of Rome, 1957 (q.v.). Its members comprise France, West Germany, Italy, Belgium, the Netherlands and Luxembourg, although the Treaty allows for the admission of other countries at a later date. With the signing of the Treaty, the "Six" became combined in three distinct but interlocked functional communities; the European Coal and Steel Community (q.v.) formed in 1952, the European Atomic Energy Community ("Euratom") and the European Economic Community. The total population of the Community, about 180 million, is only slightly less than that of the United States. It is the biggest importer of raw materials in the world and with the United States the biggest exporter of manufactured goods. Its rate of growth has been formidable. From 1958 until 1963 the gross national product of the Common Market countries as a group rose at the compound rate of 5.5 per cent per annum. For the rest of Europe (E.F.T.A.) it was only 3.5 per cent and for the United States 4.0 per cent. In the same period trade grew between the Common Market Countries at a compound rate of 18.3 per cent per annum—a remarkable achievement.

The Common Market idea had its roots in the aftermath of the Second World War. Western Europe felt menaced by the Soviet Union and there was the problem of Germany; it felt too the need to strengthen its bargaining position with the United States. In addition, as a result of the War and its aftermath, the European countries lost many of their safe colonial markets; alternative outlets lay in Western Europe itself providing the pre-war structure of high tariff barriers was not re-created. French economists visualised a Common Market as a third force in world affairs. Before the signing of the Treaty of Rome, the desire for European Unity had already found expression in several international European organisations, the most notable of which have been the Economic Commission for Europe (q.v.); the Organisation for European Economic Co-operation (q.v.); the Council of Europe; the North Atlantic Treaty Organisation; Western European Union; and the European Coal and Steel Community (q.v.).

The purpose of the Treaty is to permit goods to travel freely, without custom duties or quota restrictions, throughout the area of the Six, and thus to permit manufacturers to invest on the scale that modern technology makes possible and necessary: to permit workpeople to move wherever wages and conditions are best for them; and to permit free competition to eradicate waste and inefficiency. Progress has been rapid. Between the date of inception, 1st January 1958, and 1st July 1963, the members of the Community eliminated 60 per cent of internal tariffs on manufactures. Additional 10 per cent reductions were scheduled for 1st January 1965, and 1st January 1966. By 1st July, 1968, virtually all remaining customs duties between members were abolished and a common external tariff completed. The common tariff raises Benelux and German tariffs, greatly reduces French and Italian. A considerable degree of mobility of labour and capital among members has been achieved. *See* EUROPEAN COMMISSION; TREATY OF ROME, 1957.

European Free Trade Area A free trade area to comprise the European Economic Community (q.v.), the United Kingdom and other members of the Organisation for European Economic Co-operation (q.v.); the proposal was the subject of two years of negotiations which finally broke down in 1958. Subsequently, seven of the non E.E.C. members formed the European Free Trade Association (E.F.T.A.) (q.v.).

European Free Trade Association (E.F.T.A.) An association of seven western European states (Austria, Denmark, Norway, Portugal, Sweden, Switzerland and the United Kingdom), who have agreed to gradually eliminate tariffs and restrictions on trade with each other. Proposals for such a free trade area were first made in July 1956 at the Council of Ministers of the Organisation for European Economic Co-operation (q.v.). Subsequently, an O.E.E.C. committee reported that such an Association was technically feasible. The United Kingdom supported the proposals with the proviso that foodstuffs should be excluded from their scope. The Association was formed in 1960. It is often referred to as "the outer seven", a description arising from the geographical position of the members in relation to the Common Market "Six". Finland is now an associate member of E.F.T.A. Industrial Trade between the E.F.T.A. countries was substantially freed from protective customs and tariffs from January, 1967. The Association represents a free market of nearly 100 million people.

European Fund *See* EUROPEAN MONETARY AGREEMENT (E.M.A.).

European Investment Bank (E.I.B.)   A bank established by the European Economic Community (q.v.) in 1958 to assist economic development within the Community.

European Monetary Agreement (E.M.A.)   An Agreement concluded in August, 1955, by the members of the Organisation for European Economic Co-operation (O.E.E.C.) (q.v.). The E.M.A. came into operation in 1958, replacing the European Payments Union (E.P.U.) (q.v.) which had been in operation since 1950. The general objective of the Agreement is to foster the achievement and maintenance of full multilateral trade and convertibility in Europe by providing a framework for monetary co-operation between governments and between central banks. Its more specific objectives are:

(a) To lay down certain basic rules concerning the foreign exchange transactions of Member countries;

(b) To discourage any relapse into bilateralism in international relations between Member countries; and

(c) To provide a source of financial assistance for the purpose of helping Member countries to overcome temporary balance-of-payments difficulties.

The E.M.A. has two main parts: (a) the European Fund, to which Members contribute, which can grant credit to Member countries additional to credit facilities they could obtain from the International Monetary Fund (q.v.), and (b) the Multilateral System of Settlements, under which each Member country's central bank is assured of obtaining settlement in dollars, at an exchange rate known in advance, of its holdings in other Members' currencies. This arrangement is designed to back-up the efficient operation of the foreign exchange markets. The Execution of the Agreement is supervised by the Board of Management of the E.M.A., which consists of a small group of financial experts nominated by Member countries and appointed by the Council of the Organisation for Economic Co-operation and Development (O.E.C.D.) (q.v.). The E.M.A. is the only financial institution linking three groups of European Member countries—the European Economic Community (q.v.), the European Free Trade Association (E.F.T.A.) (q.v.) and the remaining countries. As such it can be used for mutual support between, as well as within, these three groups.

European Nuclear Energy Agency An agency set up in December, 1957, as part of the Organisation for European Economic Co-operation (O.E.E.C.) (q.v.) to develop collaboration in the use of nuclear energy for peaceful purposes by the countries of Western Europe. There are eighteen members; the United States, Canada and Japan are associate members. The European Atomic Energy Community (Euratom) (q.v.) also takes part in its work.

European Payments Union (E.P.U.) A payments system which operated between member countries of the Organisation for European Economic Co-operation (q.v.) between 1950 and 1958, taking the place of the system previously operating under the Intra-European Payments Agreement (q.v.). The object of the E.P.U. was to encourage European trade by facilitating payments from one European country to another. European currencies became freely convertible into each other, but not into dollars. The detailed operation of the scheme was carried out by the Bank for International Settlements (q.v.). In 1958 new arrangements came into force under the European Monetary Agreement (q.v.).

European Productivity Agency An agency established by the Organisation for European Economic Co-operation (q.v.) to examine methods of raising productivity in Western Europe.

European Recovery Programme (The "Marshall Plan") Named after the U.S. Secretary of State, General G. C. Marshall, a plan to provide aid ("Marshall Aid") to countries, mainly in Europe, whose economies had been seriously impaired by the Second World War, for the purpose of speeding recovery. The plan, which operated from 1948 to 1951, was administered by the Economic Co-operation Administration (q.v.) and the Organisation for European Economic Co-operation (q.v.). The plan, generous in scope, greatly speeded up the recovery of western Europe. Under the Plan Britain received goods to the value of nearly £1,500 millions. The plan was superseded by Defence Aid to help with the re-armament of western Europe.

European Social Fund A fund set up under the Treaty of Rome, 1957 (q.v.) to help workers within the European Economic Community (q.v.) to move to new types of work or to new areas of work, particularly workers in areas dependent on a local industry adversely affected by increased competition within the Community as tariff barriers were lowered. The fund came into operation in 1961.

Ex Without or minus.

Ex-All Without everything that has just been declared payable or detachable from a security.

Ex Ante "From beforehand"; thus an ex ante definition of saving means saving as it is expected to be in the future in the light of present plans. Ex post or actually realised saving may diverge from that expected for a variety of reasons. Ex ante and ex post savings and investments are important in determining changes in the level of national income (q.v.).

Ex-Bonus Without the bonus just declared. Shares are sold either ex-bonus or cum-bonus (q.v.).

Ex-Capitalisation (Ex-Cap.) Description of a share when the buyer is not entitled to the "capitalisation issue" attaching to the share. *See* SCRIP OR BONUS ISSUE.

Ex-Coupon Without the coupon (q.v.) just paid.

Ex-Dividend Without the current dividend; a term used with the price of a share to indicate that the seller will take the current dividend.

Ex-Drawing Without the benefit of the current drawing (q.v.). If there is no benefit but a loss on drawing, it is without the loss. A term used in connection with the sale of securities.

Ex-Interest Without the current interest. A term used in connection with the sale of securities.

Ex-New *See* EX-RIGHTS.

Ex Post *See* EX ANTE.

Ex-Rights Description of a share when the buyer is not entitled to the "rights issue" (q.v.) attaching to the share.

Excess Capacity Productive capacity not in use.

Excess Profits Duty Tax imposed during the First World War on the excessive profits being made by industry out of the war, particularly by the armaments industry.

Exchange The act of accepting one thing for another, e.g. as in barter (q.v.) or in a transaction involving money (q.v.).

Exchange Control Control of rates of exchange of currencies by a Government. Exchange control may be utilised in support of any of the following objectives:
    (a) to keep exchange rates stable;
    (b) to keep the currency undervalued to stimulate exports;
    (c) to keep the currency overvalued to handicap exports and encourage imports.
    In Britain, exchange control arose out of the circumstances of the Second World War with the need to restrict the movement out of the country of money and assets. Varying degrees of control have been exercised continuously since then, the Treasury (q.v.) having powers bestowed upon it by the Exchange Control Act 1947. Under this Act certain transactions are prohibited without the permission of the Bank of England acting on behalf of the Treasury. Most banks have been appointed "Authorised Banks" to undertake the day-to-day work of applying the regulations.

Under the Exchange Control Act, bank accounts held in Britain are classified according to the residence of the account-holder. Accounts are classified as either "resident" or "non-resident". A resident account is an account of which the account-holder is permanently resident in the Sterling Area (q.v.). A non-resident account is an account of someone who resides permanently outside the Sterling Area. Accounts are of two main types—"external accounts" which can be used freely and "blocked accounts" (q.v.) which cannot. The payment of funds out of a resident account into a non-resident account requires Treasury permission. The regulations also forbid any resident of the United Kingdom to hold certain specified foreign currencies, or gold, without special authority. Exchange control, while playing its part since 1947 in protecting the value of the pound, has nevertheless been progressively relaxed.

Exchange Equalisation Account An Account set up by the Finance Act 1932 to provide a fund which could be used, under the control of the Treasury, for the purchase and sale of gold and foreign currencies with the purpose of preventing excessive fluctuations from day to day in the exchange value of sterling. The Finance Act 1946 extended the purposes for which the Account might be used to include, "the conservation or disposition in the national interest of the means of making payments abroad". The Radcliffe Committee (q.v.) described the Account as "the custodian of the country's reserves of gold and foreign currencies". The Bank of England (q.v.) manages the Account, on behalf of the Treasury (q.v.).

Exchange Rate Parity The fixed rate of exchange between one currency and another, e.g. £1 = $2.40. If a currency has no parity then it is described as having a floating exchange rate.

Exchequer The central account of the Government, kept by the Treasury (q.v.) at the Bank of England (q.v.). The Exchequer and Audit Departments Act 1866 provides that all moneys received by the central Government must be paid into, and all payments authorised by Parliament must come out of, the Exchequer.

Exchequer Return A weekly Treasury statement showing the ordinary revenue and expenditure for the week in respect of the Exchequer (q.v.) together with cumulative figures for the financial year.

Excise Duty A revenue duty imposed on goods and services produced in Britain, e.g. excise duty on whisky and beer made in Britain, and on betting and gaming. *See* CUSTOMS DUTY.

Exclusive Dealing Agreement An agreement between two or more firms to deal exclusively with each other and refuse to deal with other parties in respect of a commodity or service, or class of commodities or services, or in respect of a specified technology or class of technology.

Execution On the Stock Exchange (q.v.), the completion of a bargain (q.v.).

Expanded Programme of Technical Assistance (E.P.T.A.) A programme launched by the United Nations in 1950 to help under-developed countries.

Expenditure-dampening Policies Government measures designed to reduce the aggregate demand for goods and services in the community. The measures may consist of raising taxes (q.v.), lowering government expenditure, or curtailing hire-purchase or other credit facilities. *See* EXPENDITURE-SWITCHING POLICIES.

Expenditure-switching Policies Government measures designed to influence the pattern of expenditure by the community. For example, the taxing of imported goods may effect a switch of expenditure from imported to home-produced goods; devaluation of the nation's currency may have the same effect as imports become more expensive. *See* EXPENDITURE-DAMPENING POLICIES.

Export Bounty A premium or subsidy paid by the State to encourage exports.

Export Councils Councils whose task is to do everything possible to promote exports from Britain to their respective markets. These Councils include the Western Hemisphere Exports Council (formerly known as the Dollar Exports Council), the Export Council for Europe, the Council for Middle East Trade and the Commonwealth Exports Council. The Commonwealth Exports Council has separate committees for Canada, Australia, New Zealand, Africa, Asia and the Caribbean. The activities of all these councils are co-ordinated with those of the British National Export Council (q.v.).

Export Credits Guarantee Department A British Government department which gives insurance against a wide range of losses that an exporter might incur, such as losses due to the insolvency of a buyer; a buyer's failure to pay, within six months of the stipulated date for goods which he has accepted; a buyer's default on a contract; action by a Government which prevents or interferes with payments; the cancellation of licences or the introduction of new licensing systems; war or civil disturbance; and losses due to any other cause, not within the control of importer or exporter, which is not normally insurable with commercial insurers. The E.C.G.D. is responsible to the Board of Trade (q.v.).

Export Duties Duties or taxes imposed on goods exported from a country· Such duties tend to check exports and are rarely imposed today. Duties on exports from Britain were abolished by Huskisson in 1828.

Export Finance Corporation of Canada A body which assists in financing for medium terms (1 to 5 years) of exports which have been insured by the Export Credits Insurance Corporation, a Crown Company.

Export Finance House Business house whose main role is in providing short-term finance for components and consumer goods, and medium-term finance for capital goods; credit is extended mainly to the buyer.

Export Licence A Board of Trade licence required for the export of certain items, such as works of art and articles of historical value, from Britain. Export licensing has also been applied to "strategic" goods to prevent their sale to certain countries.

Export Merchant A merchant who buys goods from a producer, seeks out a demand in an overseas market and sees to the entire sale transaction from the time the goods arrive at the port for shipment, including finance and documentation.

Export Multiplier The net effect on a country's national income of an increase or decrease in its receipts from exports arising from a shift in world demand from or to the goods of other countries.

Export Rebate *See* DRAWBACK.

Exports Goods and services sold abroad.

Exports, Unrequited *See* UNREQUITED EXPORTS.

External Accounts With certain exceptions, the sterling accounts of non-residents, i.e. those of residents of countries outside the Sterling Area (q.v.).

External Economy A fall in the cost of any of the materials and services which a firm requires, which are obtained from outside sources. These materials and services comprise raw materials, labour, fuel and power, transport services, and the services of specialised firms and selling agencies. Where large quantities of, say, fuel and ores are used then any change in their prices may have a marked effect on costs of production without any change in the internal economy of a firm. *See* ECONOMIES OF SCALE.

External Sterling Sterling currency held by non-residents of the Sterling Area (q.v.). *See* EXTERNAL ACCOUNTS.

Extractive Industry Primary industry (e.g. agriculture, mining, quarrying, fisheries) concerned with extracting natural products.

F

Factor Cost What producers receive for the sale of their products and services. This is not synonymous with market prices (q.v.) but the net amount after the state has taken indirect taxes or similar charges.

Factor Incomes Incomes accruing to the factors of production (q.v.); wages, salaries, profits, interest and rent.

Factories Acts Acts of Parliament intended to protect and improve the position of the worker and to prevent the employment of women and children in unsuitable work. The provisions of the Acts are enforced by a Factory Inspectorate.

Factoring A system designed to eliminate payment risks in overseas sales and to ensure that the seller receives prompt settlement. The exporter attends to the selling and shipment of goods, invoices being sent to both the buyer and the factor. The factor pays the exporter and in due course the buyer pays the factor.

Factors, Non-Specific Factors of production which are not specialised and can be put to alternative uses, e.g. most land, unskilled labour, raw materials.

Factors of Production The various agents which combine to produce goods and services. Land, labour and capital are the traditional categories; organisation or enterprise is sometimes added as a fourth category. There are many types of each factor; although not perfect substitutes for each other one factor can often be substituted to a large extent for another, e.g. capital for labour. The tendency today is to classify factors as specific and non-specific. *See* FACTORS, NON-SPECIFIC; FACTORS, SPECIFIC.

Factors, Specific Factors of production of a specialised kind which cannot easily be adjusted to serve an alternative purpose, e.g. skilled labour, intricate machinery.

Factory System The system of employment established by the Industrial Revolution (q.v.) when work was conducted under supervision in factories.

Family Allowances An aspect of British social insurance in which a weekly allowance is paid to the mother for each child, except the first, up to a specified age limit. This age limit is in general the normal school leaving age of 15 years, but if a child continues at school or is an apprentice the allowance is paid until the 19th birthday. Family allowances were introduced as a result of an Act passed in 1946. *See* SOCIAL INSURANCE.

Family Expenditure Survey *See* INDEX OF RETAIL PRICES.

F.A.S. Free alongside (cf. F.O.B., F.O.R.).

Feasibility Study The study of a proposed project in its technical and economic aspects to ascertain the possibility of commercial exploitation; such a study usually precedes the construction of a pilot plant or prototype.

Federal Advisory Council (U.S.) A Council composed of twelve representatives of the Federal Reserve Banks (q.v.), which advises the Board of Governors of the Federal Reserve System on the views of member bankers.

Federal Open Market Committee (U.S.) A Committee of the Federal Reserve System which controls the purchases and sales of Federal Government securities. The Committee consists of the seven members of the Board of Governors, together with the heads of five of the twelve Federal Reserve Banks (q.v.) including the head of the New York Reserve Bank which is always represented. The Committee meets every three weeks; at these meetings decisions are made in respect of open market operations and executed by the Securities Department of the New York Reserve Bank. A purchase of securities by the Reserve Bank adds to the cash reserves of member banks; a sale of securities reduces the cash reserves of member banks.

Federal Reserve Banks (U.S.) The equivalent in the United States of the central banks of other countries. The Federal Reserve Act of 1913 divided the United States into twelve regions or Federal Reserve Districts, each of which has a Federal Reserve Bank. The most important is the Federal Reserve Bank of New York. The Federal Reserve Banks hold the cash reserves of the member banks, rediscount bills for them and provide clearing facilities.

The activities of the twelve Banks are controlled and co-ordinated by a Federal Reserve Board. The Board can prescribe the minimum reserve ratio to be preserved between the cash deposits of the member banks at the Reserve Bank and customers deposits at the member banks; fix maximum rates of interest on deposits; and also fix discount and other interest rates charged by the Reserve Banks. *See* FEDERAL ADVISORY COUNCIL; FEDERAL OPEN MARKET COMMITTEE.

Federal Reserve Board (U.S.) *See* FEDERAL RESERVE BANKS.

Federation of British Industries A national organisation incorporated by Royal Charter and founded in 1916 "for the encouragement, promotion and protection of industries of all kinds". Its membership included over 9,000 individual firms and nearly 300 Trade Associations collectively representing some 40,000 other firms. In August, 1965, its functions were taken over by the new Confederation of British Industry (q.v.).

Feedback A characteristic of interrelated markets in that a change in one market may affect many other markets, and the changes in these other markets may in turn affect (feed back onto) the original market.

Fiat Money Money which the State declares to be legal tender, although its content value may be little or nothing. Most of fiat money consists of notes, although token money may also be included in the term.

Fiduciary Issue That portion of the bank-note issue which is not backed by gold; nearly the whole of the bank note issue of the United Kingdom has become fiduciary. Originally, under the Bank Charter Act, 1844 (q.v.), all notes except for a very limited amount were to be backed £1 for £1 by gold. The amount not covered amounted to £14 m. and was known as the "fiduciary issue"; these notes were backed by Government securities. In 1928, the fiduciary issue was increased to £260 m. Today the size of the fiduciary issue depends entirely on the decision of the Government acting within the terms of the Currency and Bank Notes Act 1954; by the late 1960s the fiduciary issue stood at over £3,000m.

Final Utility Term used by Alfred Marshall and William Stanley Jevons to describe marginal utility (q.v.). *See* MARGINAL REVOLUTION.

Finance The provision of money at the time it is wanted. It provides the means by which people are enabled to consume more than they produce in certain periods of time. This lack of identity between payments and receipts is particularly acute during the setting up of a business when there may be no receipts for a considerable period of time. For example, an industrialist may pay others to build a factory for him over many months, or even years, before he is able to earn an income from it. In the nationalised sector, the construction of a power station may take 5/6 years and involve an outlay of up to £100 m. (depending on size and type) before it supplies electricity to the Grid. An arable farmer may work himself and pay wages to those whom he employs, for many months before receiving a return; it is only when his crop is grown, harvested and sold that he is repaid for his own work and for the wages and expenses he has incurred.

Many British firms borrow their short-term capital requirements from the banks, loans being generally for periods of 3 to 6 months, though renewable. Long-term capital is obtained from the "capital market". Original fixed capital is usually financed by the issue of shares. For the renewal of fixed capital, industry depends mainly on itself; reserves are built up out of undistributed profits and then used to purchase new machinery or other capital equipment that has either worn out or become obsolete. Expansion too may be financed from profits; the majority of new capital is provided in this way.

Short-Term Finance

Sources are:
  (a) The banks;
  (b) Trade creditors;
  (c) Hire Purchase;

(d) Inter-company loans where there are several companies in a group;
(e) Provision for taxation—tax payments are made much in arrears and in the meanwhile the money for this purpose may be used;
(f) Bills of Exchange (for international trade).

Long-Term Finance

Sources are:

(a) *Issue of debenture stocks.*—These are long-term fixed interest loans raised on the capital market (repayment periods may be ten to forty years or longer). If a company fails to meet its obligations to pay interest on these stocks, the stockholders (as creditors) have the right to put the company into liquidation and to pay themselves both principal and interest on their loans out of the sale of assets.

(b) *Issue of shares.*—This may be done in several ways:
    (i) Public Issue;
    (ii) A "Rights Issue"—issue to existing shareholders only;
    (iii) A "Pink Form" issue—a compromise between (i) and (ii);
    (iv) A "Placing" or Stock Exchange Introduction—a limited amount of new shares may be sold direct on the Stock Exchange (with, of course, Stock Exchange permission).

(c) *Industrial and Commercial Finance Corporation Ltd.*—Established in 1945 by the English and Scottish Banks (with the approval of the Bank of England and the Government). Exists to help small and medium-sized companies with amounts ranging from £5,000 to £200,000 on a first application.

(d) *Finance Corporation for Industry Ltd.* Also set up in 1945 by the Bank of England, big insurance companies and investment trusts, to make loans to large basic industries (such as steel and textiles).

(e) *Exchequer*—the nationalised industries invest over £800 m. a year, about half of which comes from earnings and the remainder by way of loan from the Exchequer. The Exchequer charges interest on such loans.

(f) *Mortgage borrowings.*

(g) *Sale/lease-back arrangements.*

Finance Bill A bill not involving goods, simply promising to pay a specified sum of money on a specified date. *See* TREASURY BILLS.

Finance Corporation for Industry Ltd. (F.C.I.) A corporation set up in 1945 by the insurance companies, investment trust companies and the Bank of England (q.v.) to provide capital for the rationalisation (q.v.) and the re-equipment of industries in cases where the existing financial facilities are inadequate. The corporation only lends if: (a) the funds required exceed £200,000; (b) it can be shown that these funds cannot be obtained on reasonable terms from any other source; and (c) the project appears to be important for the national economic interest. Industries assisted include shipping, steel, aircraft, diesel engines, chemicals and oil. *See* FINANCE

CORPORATIONS; INDUSTRIAL AND COMMERCIAL FINANCE
CORPORATION LTD.

Finance Corporations Specialised financial institutions established to provide
medium- and long-term finance (q.v.) where it cannot be provided easily
from traditional sources. *See* AGRICULTURAL MORTGAGE CORPORATION;
BANKERS' INDUSTRIAL DEVELOPMENT COMPANY; COMMONWEALTH
DEVELOPMENT FINANCE COMPANY LTD.; FINANCE CORPORATION FOR
INDUSTRY LTD.; INDUSTRIAL AND COMMERCIAL FINANCE CORPORA-
TION LTD.; INDUSTRIAL RE-ORGANISATION CORPORATION; SCOTTISH
AGRICULTURAL SECURITIES CORPORATION; SECURITIES MANAGEMENT
TRUST; SHIP MORTGAGE FINANCE COMPANY LTD.; TECHNICAL
DEVELOPMENT CAPITAL LTD.

"Financial and Economic Obligations of the Nationalised Industries" A
White Paper, published in 1961, in which the Government reviewed the past
financial results of the nationalised industries in the context of statutory
requirements and set out general criteria on which financial performance
should be assessed for the future. The general outcome was a planned improvement in the self-financing ratios (q.v.) of the nationalised industries.

Financial and Fiscal Years In the United Kingdom, the financial year begins
on the 1st April of one year and ends on the 31st March of the next. For fiscal
purposes, however, the year runs from the 6th April of one year to the 5th
April on the next; on the last day the Chancellor of the Exchequer presents
his Budget to the House of Commons. In the United States the fiscal year
starts on the 1st July and ends on 30th June of the following year.

Financial Inter-relations Ratio (F.I.R.) The ratio between the value of the
total financial assets and the value of all real assets, or national wealth, of a
country. It is a measure of the relative size of a country's financial super-
structure at a given point in its economic development. Research suggests
that, broadly speaking, the higher the F.I.R. the more developed financially
is a country and the greater is the importance of the financial instruments and
financial institutions within it.

Financial Ratios Ratios indicating the financial position of a business. Examples
of financial ratios are:

$$\frac{\text{Profit}}{\text{Sales Invoiced}} \quad \text{(Profit margin)}$$

$$\frac{\text{Sales Invoiced}}{\text{Capital}} \quad \text{(Capital turnover)}$$

$$\frac{\text{Total Capital Employed}}{\text{Liquid Assets}} \quad \text{(A measure of the degree of employment of liquid assets).}$$

Financial Statement A statement presented on Budget Day by the British
Chancellor of the Exchequer which besides detailing the changes in taxation
proposed in the Budget Speech, forecasts Exchequer (q.v.) receipts and

payments in the year to come and compares the achievements for the past twelve months (1st April to 31st March) with the previous Budget estimates. *See* BUDGET, BRITISH.

Financial Times—Actuaries Share Indices *See* INDICES, FINANCIAL TIMES—ACTUARIES SHARE.

Financial Times Industrial Ordinary Share Index *See* INDEX, FINANCIAL TIMES INDUSTRIAL ORDINARY SHARE.

Fine Bank Bills The best class of acceptances. *See* ACCEPTANCE.

Finest Rate of Discount Lowest rate of discount.

Firm A unit of management operating under a trade name organised either to extract minerals, produce or manufacture goods, or to sell goods or services, or to engage in two or three of these activities simultaneously. A firm may be a sole proprietorship, a partnership, a private or public limited company, or a state-owned enterprise.

Firm, Theory of the The theory of the ways in which prices are determined and resources allocated among different uses in respect of the products of the individual firm. *See* EQUILIBRIUM THEORY; FIRM; OPTIMUM FIRM; PROFIT MOTIVE.

First Call The first demand for payment of the initial instalment due on shares after allotment.

First Mortgage Bond (U.S.) A fixed interest loan repayable on a given date; similar to debenture (q.v.). The term "first mortgage" means that the bond holders have a claim before other creditors on the assets of the corporation (q.v.).

Fiscal Policy The policy adopted by a Government for raising revenue to meet expenditure and for influencing the level of business activity. Fiscal policy finds expression in the annual Budget. *See* BUDGET, BRITISH.

Fisher's Ideal Index An index based on a formula devised by the American economist Irving Fisher (1867-1947). It is intended to be a "true" index, the Laspeyres' index (q.v.) giving an upper limit and the Paasche index (q.v.) a lower limit to this "true" index; it is in fact an index of the geometric mean of the Laspeyres' and Paasche indices. The formula is:

$$\left[\frac{\Sigma P_n q_o}{\Sigma P_o q_o} \times \frac{\Sigma P_n q_n}{\Sigma P_o q_n} \right]^{\frac{1}{2}}$$

where, P_o = price in the base-year; q_o = quantity in the base-year; P_n = price in the year being considered; and q_n = quantity in the year being considered. *See* INDEX NUMBERS.

Fixed Costs Production costs which tend to be unaffected by variations in the volume of output. Once the Central Electricity Generating Board (q.v.) has constructed a power station, it incurs considerable annual fixed capital charges (q.v.), irrespective of the amount of electricity generated. Also known as "supplementary costs" or "overhead costs".

Fixed Instalment Method A method for calculating and allowing for the depreciation of an asset. The fixed instalment, or straight-line, method distributes the cost of an asset uniformly over its depreciable life. The amount to be set aside each year may be calculated from the formula:

$$\frac{P - L}{n}$$

where P is the initial asset cost; L the expected salvage value at the end of the useful life of the asset; and n the plant life expressed in years. *See* DE-PRECIATION; DEPRECIATION FUND METHOD; DIMINISHING BALANCE METHOD; SINKING FUND.

Fixed Trust A type of Unit Trust (q.v.) whose trust deed specifies a portfolio of securities for the investment of trust monies.

Flat A description of bonds being sold in default, since no interest is being paid.

Flat-Rate Tariff A tariff for the supply of electricity consisting solely of a single-unit charge; used chiefly by very small users of electricity for lighting and power.

Floaters First-class bearer securities.

Floating Capital Capital which circulates, leaving a business by way of expenditure on materials and wages, and returning by way of receipts from sales.

Floating Debt That part of the National Debt (q.v.) which involves short-term borrowing; it consists of Ways and Means Advances (q.v.) and Treasury Bills (q.v.). It amounts to about one-fifth of the internally held National Debt.

Floating Exchange Rate An exchange rate of any currency free to float to any level which supply and demand may determine; exchange rate with no fixed parity.

Flotation The raising of new capital by public subscription.

Flow Chart Depicts a sequence of events in diagrammatic form.

F.O.B. Free on Board. Term used of goods shipped where the price does not include shipping or insurance charges; opposite to C.I.F. (q.v.). An F.O.B. quotation means that the exporter will deliver the goods free on board a ship in accordance with the contract at the port named; he pays all expenses up to that point. From then on the buyer must take responsibility, paying for freight, insurance, and all subsequent expenses.

F.O.Q. Free on quay. A quotation term where goods are to be delivered to a quay, but the loading expenses are to be borne separately by the buyer.

F.O.R. Free on rail (cf. F.O.B. and F.A.S.).

F.O.T. Free of tax.

Food and Agriculture Organisation of the United Nations (F.A.O.) An organisation whose task is to find a way of increasing world agricultural productivity at a rate at least equal to the rate of expansion of the world's population. F.A.O. works on three levels in the fields of agriculture, fisheries, forestry, nutrition and economics. On the first level, F.A.O. carries out a "world intelligence service" to find out what the world is producing and to estimate future needs. On a second level, F.A.O. encourages governments to join forces to meet specific needs. On the third level, F.A.O. offers direct technical assistance to governments. One of F.A.O.'s chief concerns has been a "Freedom from Hunger" campaign to enlist the interest of governments and non-governmental organisations, of industry and commerce, and of individual citizens in all countries in eradicating hunger in the under-developed countries.

"For the Account" On the stock exchange (q.v.), implies that the bargain will be completed (i.e. the stock or shares handed over and paid for) on the next account day (q.v.). Most dealing is "for the Account".

Forced-Draught Expansion Economic expansion accelerated by special government measures or strong external influences.

Forced Saving Saving achieved through an enforced reduction in the consumption of consumers' goods by the community. A Government may achieve this by raising additional finance for investment purposes through increased taxation. On the other hand the same result may be achieved, though through an inflationary process, by the Government creating money to finance investment.

Forecasting, Economic The use of collected and analysed data derived from the present and the past to predict future economic, business or sales developments. In recent years the services of the economist have been increasingly used for this purpose by national and business organisations. The art of economic and business forecasting, in the long-term as well as in the short-term, enhances the background of information against which realistic budgets and the most advantageous plans can be prepared. While it has, on the whole, proved a valuable aid to policy-making and business management, it cannot be a substitute for sound judgment based on past experience. Henry Fayol, an early pioneer of scientific management, said that "forecasts are not prophecies, their function is to minimise the unknown factor."

Some forecasts cover only one aspect of the activities of a business, industry or economy, while others are comprehensive in scope; some are concerned with the immediate future or at the most a few months ahead, while others attempt predictions of conditions several years ahead.

The Institute of Cost and Works Accountants in their publication "An Introduction to Business Forecasting" (1960) has recommended that when a forecast is to cover all the activities of a business, the most convenient method is to sub-divide the work according to the main functions of the business and to prepare separate but inter-related forecasts for each:

(a) Forecast of sales;

(b) Forecast of output;

(c) Forecast of capital expenditure;

(d) Forecast of trading results;

(e) Forecast of cash position.

Forecasting is now an indispensable tool for governments and an account of the various methods used is given in the O.E.C.D. publication "Techniques of Economic Forecasting" (1965).

Some of the more important forecasting techniques used by industry and governments are summarised below:

(a) *Very Short-Term Forecasting* Forecasts perhaps on a weekly or monthy basis for three months ahead, or even daily for a month ahead. A common technique is that of "exponential smoothing". In its simplest form, the exponential system can be used to forecast expected sales in the next period by using a weighted average of actual sales in the current period together with the forecast of sales for the current period made in the previous period. Trend and seasonal factors can be taken into account. A discussion of this method can be found in the I.C.I. Monograph No. 2 "Short-term Forecasting" (1964). Extensions of this technique have been developed.

(b) *Short-Term Forecasting* Forecasts made up to a period of perhaps two years ahead either on a monthly, quarterly, or an annual basis. The econometric approach to the problem consists essentially in building an economic model with either one or more relationships as is necessary and estimating these using a single-equation or a multiple-equation approach. This method for making general economic forecasts using the econometric model has been used extensively by the Netherlands Statistical Office. Similar models have been developed for the economies of various countries. A second approach is to use iterative procedures which make use of certain behavioural relationships to build a model, which is then checked for internal consistency, and then used for forecasting. This method has been used for making economic forecasts in the United Kingdom. A third approach is to use an analysis of consumer behaviour. In such surveys, widely employed in the United States, data on psychological variables (e.g. motives, attitudes, expectations), demographic variables (e.g education, family size) and financial economic variables (e.g. income, assets) are collected. A study of the inter-relationships between the different variables is then attempted using principally the tool of regression analysis. Through repeated sampling, it is claimed that changes in motives and attitudes over time can be determined.

(c) *Long-Term Forecasting* One technique is known as "mathematical curve fitting". This may be applied to a single time-series, a smooth mathematical curve being plotted through the points and extrapolated into the future. This technique is discussed in the I.C.I. Monograph No. 1 "Mathematical Trend Curves—An Aid to Forecasting" (1964). The econometric approach to long-term forecasting involves the two steps of specifying the major determinants of the system and then estimating the various relationships between them. These estimations may involve a single-equation approach or a multiple-equation approach.

Foreign Currency Accounts A bank account consisting of foreign currencies; subject to exchange control regulations, certain U.K. residents and most foreign residents are entitled to maintain accounts in foreign currencies.

Foreign Exchange Broker A broker who deals in foreign currencies, acting as an intermediary between banks.

Foreign Exchange Market A market in which foreign money can be bought and sold. Such a market consists of foreign exchange dealers and brokers who are in touch with each other and with other similar markets elsewhere in the world. The rates charged for foreign currency fluctuate with changes in supply and demand. Movements are usually kept within reasonable limits, however, by Government intervention. Under British Exchange Control Regulations banks are authorised to buy and sell currencies on behalf of their customers.

Foreign Investment The acquisition by the Government or inhabitants of a country of assets abroad. These assets may take the form of titles to land, buildings and capital equipment; foreign Government or industrial securities; foreign Government bills or bank deposits.

Foreign Operations Administration A U.S. government agency which replaced the Mutual Security Agency (q.v.) on 1st August 1953, and assumed the responsibility for co-ordinating all the programmes through which the U.S.A. gave assistance to foreign countries. The F.O.A. was abolished on 30th June 1955, and replaced by the International Co-operation Administration (q.v.).

Foreign Trade Multiplier The net effect on a country's foreign trade following an increase in spending at home after taking into consideration (a) the additional spending on imports to serve the increase in home demand, and (b) the effect of the increase in imports on the income of the exporting countries and the influence this increase in income may have on the demand for the exports of the country concerned.

Forestalling Policies Government measures to correct disturbing trends in the economy which might otherwise lead to a disruption of declared objectives, e.g. full employment, steady growth or stable prices.

Forward Exchange The purchase or sale of amounts of a foreign currency for delivery at a specified future date.

Free Depreciation An arrangement whereby an industrialist who goes to the expense of putting in modern plant and machinery is not liable to pay any tax until he has written off the entire investment. This arrangement was introduced by the Local Employment Acts of 1960 and 1963 to encourage the development of industry in the Development Districts (q.v.).

Free Exchange Rates Exchange rates which depend upon the supply and demand for a currency on the foreign exchange market.

Free Goods In economics, those goods which are not scarce in relation to demand and therefore do not command, or could not command, a price or exchange value. Such non-economic goods may still yield utility in use.

"Free of Particular Average" A type of marine insurance policy which covers complete loss through marine risks. This type of policy is cheaper than the more comprehensive cover provided by "With Particular Average" (q.v.).

Free Overside A quotation term implying that the seller of the goods involved will pay all expenses up to the port of discharge, subsequent expenses, including lighterage, being borne by the buyer.

Free Ports Ports at which imports may be landed without paying duties. The system permits an "entrepôt trade" (q.v.) without having to pay and reclaim Customs Duties.

Free Trade Trade which is unimpeded by tariffs, import and export quotas and other devices which obstruct the free movement of goods and services between countries. The formation of a free trade area by two or more countries, however, does not preclude the retention by those participating countries of tariffs against non-member countries.

Fringe Benefits Payments and benefits given to an employee by his employer in addition to his normal earnings; such benefits may include holidays with pay, paid sick leave, redundancy awards, subsidised canteens, travel concessions, free fuel or housing, etc.

Fuels, Primary and Secondary Primary fuels are those obtained directly from the ground, e.g. coal, oil and natural gas. Secondary fuels are those derived from primary fuels, e.g. electricity, coke and town gas.

Full Cost Pricing The fixing of the prices of goods by a manufacturer on the basis of average direct costs in labour and materials plus an allowance for overheads. The overheads, or average fixed costs, are calculated on the assumption of less than full capacity operation of the plant to allow for fluctuations in production activity; this calculated figure then becomes the normal or standard for the purpose of costing. Firms may adopt an even simpler procedure by adding a uniform percentage mark-up above direct costs to a wide variety of products without any careful assessment of the fixed costs properly attributable to each line.

Full Employment A situation in which all those persons seeking work in a community are able to find suitable work fairly readily, with the consequence that a very high proportion of the working population is actually in work at any one time. To achieve this in practice, the number of unfilled vacancies must exceed the number of persons seeking work as in any locality some vacancies may not be suitable for local applicants. Furthermore, the number of vacancies in a country should be distributed according to local needs, otherwise an excess of vacancies may occur in one locality and a deficiency in another.

Lord Beveridge defined full employment as a situation in which the number of those unemployed did not exceed three per cent of the total working population. Since the end of the Second World War, the British Government have accepted responsibility for the maintenance of a "high and stable level of employment". The general level of unemployment throughout Britain has rarely exceeded 2 per cent since the end of the War, and it is this percentage, rather than 3 per cent, which represents today perhaps the upper limit of political acceptability. An employment rate of 2 per cent in Britain represents nearly half a million persons unemployed. Most attention since the War has been devoted to the problems of areas where the unemployment level has risen well above the national average; as, for example, in Scotland, Northern Ireland, South Wales, North East and North West England. The rate of unemployment in the South-East of England has remained steadily well below the national average. A situation in which the numbers of unfilled vacancies, greatly exceeds the number of persons seeking work is described as one of "over-full" employment; this is an important factor in causing wage-push or cost-push inflation and wage drift (q.v.). *See* DISTRIBUTION OF INDUSTRY ACT 1945; EMPLOYMENT, CLASSICAL THEORY OF; "EMPLOYMENT POLICY", WHITE PAPER ON; LOCAL EMPLOYMENT ACTS 1960 TO 1966; OVER-FULL EMPLOYMENT; WAGE DRIFT.

Full Gold Standard *See* GOLD STANDARD.

"Full Line Forcing" A situation in which a company will not supply certain types of goods or machinery (in which it may have an important monopoly) to dealers who do not order also certain other specified types of goods or machinery which the company manufactures. The company thus ensures the sale of its full line of products.

Function, Output Response *See* OUTPUT RESPONSE FUNCTION.

Funded Debt *See* NATIONAL DEBT.

Funding The conversion of short-term debts into long-term debts.

Futures Contract Contract for sale or purchase of a specified grade of a commodity at an agreed price on a certain future date.

Futures Market A market in which goods are sold for delivery at some future date, say, in three months' time.

G

Games, Theory of A branch of mathematics concerned with the analysis of various problems of conflict, abstracting common strategic features for study in theoretical models or games. Games and economic situations have several common factors such as conflicting interests between those participating, incomplete information and the interplay of rational decision and chance. John von Neumann and Oskar Morgenstern, in their joint work "Theory of Games and Economic Behaviour" (1944), developed the analogy between business competition and rivalry in games, exploiting it as an analytical tool.

Gantt Chart A chart widely used in industry for production planning and plant utilisation. It is a form of bar chart, except that the bars are plotted horizontally instead of vertically. The bar length can represent any unit of measurement, e.g. quantity, value or time.

Gas Council A central body set up under the Gas Act of 1949. The Council comprises the chairmen of the twelve regional gas boards. It is responsible for finance and general policy in respect of the industry.

Gearing *See* CAPITAL GEARING.

General Agreement on Tariffs and Trade (G.A.T.T.) An international commercial treaty which came into force on 1st January 1948. Some forty governments, accounting for well over four-fifths of the world's trade, are now contracting parties to the Agreement. The staff originally appointed to work for the International Trade Organisation (q.v.) became the G.A.T.T. secretariat.

G.A.T.T. provides a code of conduct for international trade and, in addition, seeks to help raise living standards, to develop the world's resources, to promote economic development, to expand production and exchange of goods and to bring about full employment. In becoming parties, governments are pledged to work together towards those goals.

The code of conduct for international trade includes in its principles that trade should be conducted on the basis of non-discrimination, and existing preferential arrangements should be gradually reduced through negotiation and finally eliminated. As a result of a series of tariff bargaining conferences, customs duties have been lowered on products accounting for about half of the world's trade. In addition, the G.A.T.T. parties have worked with the International Monetary Fund (q.v.) to break down restrictions barring the natural flow of imports and exports. *See* KENNEDY ROUND.

112

General Grant A central government grant to local authorities to help pay for education and local welfare services. Superseded in 1968 by a rate support grant (q.v.).

General Partnership (Can.) A business partnership in which members are not only jointly liable for debt, but also severally liable.

General Strike A strike of workers simultaneously in several trades and industries. A general strike involving workers in several key industries and services occurred in Britain in 1926. The strike failed and in 1927 the Trades Disputes Act was passed to make this type of strike illegal. This Act was repealed in 1946.

Geometric Progression A series of quantities taken in order which increase or decrease by a constant ratio, called the common ratio, e.g. 2, 4, 8, 16, 32, 64, ... in which the common ratio is 2.

$$\text{The } n^{th} \text{ term} = ar^{n-1}$$

where a is the first term and r the common ratio. The sum of the terms, S

$$= a(r^n - 1) \qquad \text{if } r > 1 \text{ and positive}$$
$$= \frac{a(1 - r^n)}{1 - r} \qquad \text{if } r < 1 \text{ or negative}$$

Giffen Goods Sometimes known as "inferior goods", commodities of relatively low quality which form an important element in the diet of poor people, e.g. bread and potatoes. Sir Robert Giffen is thought to have been the first to draw public attention to the fact that the poor of his time consumed more bread when it was dear than when it was cheap. The explanation probably lay in the fact that a rise in the price of bread caused a fall in real income. Thus after paying for bread, the family was left with less to spend on more expensive things. Thus expenditure on such items as meat and cakes would be reduced. The reduction of these items would, however, leave a nutritional gap which would then be filled by buying more bread.

Gilt-Edged Securities British Government securities generally. The rate of interest is fixed and generally these securities are repayable at par at a definite date or dates, which may be anything from one to thirty or more years ahead. These securities are considered to be very safe. A gilt-edged security is classified as "short-dated" if it has five years or less to run to the final maturity or repayment date; if it has more than five years but less than ten years to run it is classified as "medium-dated"; if it has ten years or more to run it is classified as "long-dated". *See* CONSOLS.

Giro System A mechanism for the transfer of payments operated by the post-office in many European countries and in Japan. Any concern or person may open an account with the "giro" by paying cash or a cheque into the post office. Transfers from one account to another are made by a written instruction to the post-office to debit the "giro" account of the payer and credit that of the payee. Several payments can be made on a single instruction.

A National Giro was opened in Britain on 18th October, 1968. All accounts are held at a single centre at Bootle, Lancashire; payments between account holders can be made by sending transfer instructions to the centre following which both payer and payee are informed that the transfer has been made, a full statement of account being sent to each. Deposits in an account carry no interest and no overdraft facilities are available. Payments in cash are obtainable at any post office by way of withdrawals by an account holder; third parties may also cash Giro cheques. The National Giro offers a simple, cheap and rapid means of transferring money. Deposits are invested in the London money market and elsewhere; the interest earned pays for the many free services offered by the Giro. *See* CREDIT TRANSFERS.

Global Marketing Marketing in which all markets are served which offer scope for sales, there being no rigid distinction in thought between home and export markets. Global marketing offers an opportunity for a larger volume of production in which lower costs of production per unit of output may be achieved. The prospects of increased profitability in the home market are improved while there are greater opportunities to counter falling demand in one area by increasing demand in others.

Glut The supply of a commodity greatly in excess of the previous demand for it, leading in consequence to a considerable fall in price.

"Gnomes of Zurich" Appellation, not unfriendly, for central European bankers notably members of the Swiss Banking Association.

Going Long In the commodity markets, buying first and selling later. *See* GOING SHORT.

Going Short In the commodity markets, selling first and buying later. *See* GOING LONG.

Gold Bullion Standard *See* GOLD STANDARD.

"Golden Triangle", The A geographical area of exceptional economic growth. It has its apex in the Midlands and stretches on the one side to the Ruhr and on the other to Greater Paris. Among other prosperous regions, this triangle encloses South-East England and the Benelux countries.

Gold Exchange Standard. *See* GOLD STANDARD.

Gold Market, London *See* LONDON GOLD MARKET.

Gold Pool *See* INTERNATIONAL GOLD POOL

Gold Standard A monetary system in which each unit of currency is worth a fixed amount of gold. The rules of a gold standard are:
   (a) All paper currency must be convertible at its face value into gold;
   (b) There must be no restrictions on the import or export of gold;
   (c) A gold reserve must be maintained, fully sufficient to meet all demands made upon it.

One of the advantages of a Gold Standard is that it maintains stable exchange rates "automatically" between countries operating the system. This depends on the "mint par of exchange" (q.v.). Balance of payments (q.v.) crises do not arise. However, a marked disadvantage is that changes in the stocks of gold cause fluctuations in production and employment. If imports exceed exports, the deficit is met by the export of gold. This reduces the amount of money in the country leading to restriction of credit and falling prices and incomes. As wages generally resist reduction, the effect of deflation is to cause unemployment. A surplus, exports exceeding imports, has an opposite effect. The "full Gold Standard" described above was operated in Britain until 1914. The gold sovereign, then in circulation, consisted of gold 11/12 fine at £3 17s. 9d. per fine ounce. Between 1925 and 1931, Britain operated a modified system known as the "Gold Bullion Standard". Under this modified system, individual bank-notes were no longer convertible into gold on demand; the Bank of England would, however, exchange gold bars of 400 ounces each for an equivalent value in notes.

During the same period, 1925–1931, the Scandinavian countries adopted a "Gold Exchange Standard". Under this system, the Central Bank would exchange on demand the currency of its country, not for gold, but for the currency of some other country on the Gold Standard. Following the Crisis of 1931, the Gold Standard was generally abandoned, although gold is still used in the settlement of international debts.

Good A tangible commodity such as a house, car, refrigerator or foodstuff. *See* SERVICE.

Goodwill The commercial benefit arising from a firm's reputation or business connections.

Government Broker The representative of a firm of stockbrokers which conducts operations in the gilt-edged market on behalf of the Bank of England (q.v.). The Bank does not itself enter the Stock Exchange.

Government Stock Government issued securities which include Consols (q.v.), Annuities, Savings Bonds, Treasury Stock, Guaranteed Stock, Funding Stock, Redemption Stock, War Stock, Conversion Stock, Victory Bonds, Exchequer Stock. The stock carries a fixed rate of interest but the price at which stock may be bought or sold varies with the market. Government stock may be bought and sold through the Post Office Savings Department, as well as through stock exchanges.

Government Training Centre Training centres which enable men who have missed the opportunity of acquiring a skill by apprenticeship, or whose skill has been displaced by technological advance, to acquire quickly a new skill which is in demand. Over fifty centres have been established within easy reach of the main industrial centres of Britain. The aim of the centres is to reduce the shortages of skilled workers, particularly in the construction and engineering industries.

Grants-in-Aid A central government grant to local authorities to help pay for houses, roads, police and other services not covered by the general grant (q.v.). These grants have to be approved and paid through the Ministries responsible.

Grants to Local Authorities *See* GENERAL GRANT; GRANTS-IN-AID; RATE DEFICIENCY GRANT; RATE SUPPORT GRANT.

Gravy Jobs Jobs on which it is easy to make money; opposite to "stinkers".

Great Depression (1929-1935), The In October 1929 the New York stock market crash occurred followed by innumerable bankruptcies of banks, factories and mines. The economic distress extended to Europe, Asia, Africa, Australia and South America. About 25 million workers throughout the world were unemployed. Between 1929 and 1932 world wholesale prices fell by about one-third. Cotton was ploughed under in the United States; Canada burned some of her wheat crops; Brazil dumped coffee into the sea. An increased tariff schedule was immediately prescribed by statesmen throughout the world, but the general effect of these tariffs was to hinder international trade and to aggravate the world economic depression. By 1935, only France, Holland, Belgium, Switzerland and Poland remained on the gold standard. Recovery was slow, and not completed by the outbreak of the Second World War.

Green Belts Belts of land of irregular shape, usually several miles wide, around urban areas. Their purpose is to prevent further expansion; prevent the coalescence of neighbouring conurbations; and perhaps to channel the growth of a conurbation in a certain direction or to preserve the special character of some historic cities. The London Green Belt was approved in 1959.

Gresham's Law A generalisation embodied in the maxim "bad money drives out good." When the value of money depends upon its value as metal, debasement of the coinage by the issuing authority leads to a fall in the value of such money. The British sovereign and half-sovereign when in circulation were worth their face value in terms of the metal they contained and debasement did not occur. Coins today have only token value, their value as metal being much less than their face value; but they are legal tender (q.v.) and their value is determined by other factors.

Gross and Net Output The gross output of a firm or industry is the total selling value of production of that firm or industry within a given time-period. Gross output includes the value of materials, fuel and other supplies bought from firms outside the industry. To establish the "net output", or the value of the contribution made by the industry itself, it is necessary to deduct from the gross output what has been spent on incoming supplies. Net output is therefore the value added by a firm or industry in the productive process in a given time-period. Net output is a useful indicator of an industry's importance in the economy.

Gross Domestic Fixed Capital Formation Investment (q.v.) in fixed assets, e.g. expenditure on buildings, vehicles, plant and machinery for replacing or adding to the stock of existing fixed assets, expenditure on maintenance and repairs being excluded. *See* CAPITAL FORMATION AND DEPRECIATION; DEPRECIATION.

Gross Domestic Product at Constant Prices The Gross Domestic Product at Factor Cost (q.v.) or the Gross Domestic Product at Market Prices (q.v.) taken over a series of years and adjusted to discount changes in the value of money. Thus the Gross Domestic Product in 1970 may be adjusted to 1963 prices to give a measure of the real change in national income (q.v.) over the seven year period.

Gross Domestic Product at Factor Cost The value of goods and services produced within the nation, representing only the sum of the incomes of the factors of production (q.v.). It is equal to the Gross Domestic Product at Market Prices (q.v.), *minus* indirect taxes *plus* subsidies. Valuation at factor cost displays the composition of the gross domestic product in terms of the factors of production employed, the contributions of the factors being measured by the incomes they receive. *See* FACTOR INCOMES; GROSS NATIONAL PRODUCT AT FACTOR COST.

Gross Domestic Product at Market Prices The value of goods and services produced within the nation, charged at ruling prices. Prices include all taxes on expenditure, subsidies being regarded as negative taxes. The Report of the National Economic Development Council entitled " The Growth of the Economy " (1964) gives a more precise definition:
"the gross domestic product is taken to mean the output of goods and services valued at market prices. It equals total domestic factor incomes (gross domestic product at factor cost) plus *indirect* taxes *less* subsidies. Gross domestic product does not include net property income from abroad."
This definition follows international practice. *See* GROSS DOMESTIC PRODUCT AT FACTOR COST; GROSS NATIONAL PRODUCT AT MARKET PRICES.

Gross Investment The value of investment (q.v.) before allowance is made for the wearing-out or depreciation (q.v.) of existing assets. *See* NET INVESTMENT.

Gross National Product at Factor Cost The Gross Domestic Product at Factor Cost (q.v.) plus net income from abroad. *See* GROSS NATIONAL PRODUCT AT MARKET PRICES; NATIONAL INCOME; NET NATIONAL PRODUCT AT FACTOR COST.

Gross National Product at Market Prices The Gross Domestic Product at Market Prices (q.v.) *plus* net income from abroad (i.e. exports minus imports). *See* GROSS NATIONAL PRODUCT AT FACTOR COST; NATIONAL INCOME.

Gross Return on Net Assets Gross profits (before payment of interest and depreciation) earned from the employment of fixed assets, expressed as a percentage of the cost of those assets. The gross return obtained on investment, therefore, depends upon the difference between costs (other than capital charges) and selling price. The gross return in private industry is generally about 15 per cent.

Gross Trading Profits Profits before providing for depreciation and stock appreciation.

Group of Ten A group of ten countries consisting of the United States, United Kingdom, Canada, France, West Germany, Sweden, Netherlands, Belgium, Italy and Japan, which has agreed to lend if requested to the International Monetary Fund for the purpose of increasing the lending resources of that body. The agreement is embodied in a document entitled "General Agreements to Borrow". The agreement was reached following Britain's 1961 crisis, but was not invoked by Britain until 1964.

Growth *See* ECONOMIC GROWTH.

Growth Areas Areas within regions considered to have the best growth prospects which can be used to raise the level of economic activity and employment within the region as a whole. Growth areas in Britain are given priority for increased public service investment to provide roads and services to industry, housing and amenities.

Growth Rate The annual growth, usually expressed as a percentage over the previous year, of productive capacity in a community. *See* ECONOMIC GROWTH.

Growth Shares Shares which are expected, as a consequence of higher productivity and increased returns on assets within the companies concerned, to become more valuable. *See* SHARE.

Guarantee Fund A fund maintained by the London Stock Exchange which guarantees members of the public against loss, at the discretion of the Stock Exchange Council, in the event of the failure of a member or member firm. *See* HAMMERING; STOCK EXCHANGE.

Guaranteed Prices In Britain, a term associated with the agricultural industry in which the Government has guaranteed prices to farmers by means of subsidies in respect of cereals, eggs, fatstock, milk, wool and potatoes.

Guillebaud Committee A committee which reported in 1960 on the subject of acceptable scales of wages for railwaymen.

H

Hammering Formal announcement that a member of the Stock Exchange (q.v.) cannot meet his obligations. *See* GUARANTEE FUND.

Hard Currency Currency which enjoys a relatively stable value in international exchange and tends to maintain its value, at least in comparison with other currencies. In the first ten to fifteen years after the Second World War the United States dollar was a hard currency, while sterling and other continental currencies tended to be soft. *See* SOFT CURRENCY.

Hardware and Software The constituents of a computing system; the hardware of a system consists of the physical devices such as paper tape punches, readers, card punches, printers, core storage and all electronic circuitry making up the equipment; the software consists of the programming systems and programs which are necessary to make use of the hardware. *See* PROGRAM.

Hatry Crash, 1929 Crisis on the Stock Exchange (q.v.) in 1929, precipitated by fraud. Members of the House raised a guarantee fund of £1 million in an attempt to prevent the failure of those members who were actually victims of the fraud. Nevertheless, some members failed and the public lost a good deal of money. This crisis was not the cause of the Great Depression, 1929–35 (q.v.), which ensued in the same year as a consequence of a crash on Wall Street, the New York Stock Exchange. *See* GUARANTEE FUND.

Health, Ministry of Established initially in 1919 as the Local Government Board, a Ministry today responsible for the administration of the general practitioner services; nursing; general relations with the health professions; local authority health and welfare services; hospitals and specialist services; mental health services; nutrition, and international health matters. Merged with Ministry of Social Security in 1968.

Heckscher-Ohlin Law A "law" of factor price equalisation—the tendency towards the international equalisation of the prices of the factors of production (q.v.) under free trade. Ohlin has claimed that actually only a partial equalisation of factor prices will take place; with the exception of special cases, complete equalisation of factor prices could occur only if the factors of production themselves were freely mobile internationally.

Hedging A technique of insurance against fluctuations in the prices of raw materials or goods scheduled for future delivery by dealing in "futures". The two basic types of hedge operation are the "buying hedge" and the

119

"selling hedge". As an example of a buying hedge, suppose a processor contracts to sell a quantity of concentrated orange juice at an agreed price, to be delivered two months after the date of the sale. However he does not have the concentrate in stock to meet the order, nor does he have the space to store the fruit. In consequence, he decides to defer buying the oranges until shortly before the delivery date. Since the price of box oranges could go up before he is ready to buy them, he buys enough "futures contracts" to cover the amount of concentrate he will need. Now fully hedged, he is protected against a rise in price. If the price of box oranges does go up before he is ready to concentrate them he must buy his box oranges in the cash market at the increased price but at the same time he will sell his futures at an increased price; he then uses his futures profits to offset the higher price paid for the oranges. The result would be the same if the price of box oranges went down; losses on futures would be balanced by the additional profit arising from the lower cost of box oranges. As an example of a selling hedge, suppose a processor buys a quantity of fruit from the growers during the harvest season. He converts it into concentrate, stores it and then proceeds to sell it periodically to consumer outlets. To hedge himself during the period of his ownership of the concentrate he would have to sell an equal value of futures contracts on the Exchange. If the market price of the cash commodity falls, he will show a loss on the concentrate sold to consumer outlets, but he can buy back his futures contracts at a lower price and thereby show a profit. If the price of the concentrate had gone up instead, the net result would have been the same. The processor would have gained on the sale of concentrate but lost on his futures transactions. *See* FUTURES CONTRACT.

Higgling The process by which price is determined in the market place where there is direct negotiation between buyer and seller. The seller usually begins by asking a price he is prepared to lower, while the buyer tends to offer a price he is prepared to raise. Through the process of higgling a price is reached mutually satisfactory to both parties.

High Finance Finance (q.v.) concerned with large sums of money.

Hire Purchase A procedure for purchasing goods under which the purchaser pays a deposit on receipt of the goods followed by a number of instalments until the debt is cleared. The goods do not become the property of the purchaser until the last instalment has been paid. In the event of the default of the purchaser in respect of the instalments, the firm can resume possession of the goods in question. However this right cannot be enforced without an order of a County Court if more than one-third of the total price has been paid, unless the purchaser wishes to give the goods up. The rate of interest charged is normally higher than that charged for personal loans from banks (q.v.). *See* HIRE PURCHASE FINANCE HOUSES.

Hire Purchase Finance Houses Finance houses concerned with the granting of credit for the purchase of certain classes of goods on the condition that their advances are repaid by regular instalments over a fairly short period of time, together with interest charged on the amount borrowed. Credit is extended to private persons for the purchase of consumer durables, and to industry and agriculture for the purchase of motor vehicles and machinery. *See* HIRE PURCHASE.

Hoarding The act of holding money. If the desire to hoard increases the result will be (assuming that no new money is created) that money incomes will fall. Conversely, if there is a fall in the desire to hold money, incomes will rise. If an increase in the quantity of money circulating brings about a fall in the velocity of circulation or an increase in the volume of trade, then the increased quantity of money need not be accompanied by any rise in the price level. The holding or hoarding of money must be distinguished from money used for investment in capital assets; in the latter case, the money returns to the economic system as income. The term "hoarding" was used by John Maynard Keynes (1884–1946) to denote liquidity preference (q.v.) as distinct from saving proper.

Holding Company A company which holds a majority or the whole of the equity capital of one or more other companies. These other companies are known as subsidiaries, and while they continue to exist their general policy is controlled by the holding company.

A holding company may serve a useful purpose where the optimum size of the financial unit, the managerial unit, or the marketing unit is larger than the optimum size of the production unit: the holding company may undertake one or more of these functions, and others, on behalf of the whole group.

On the other hand, the extension of control over the price and output policies of a number of potentially competitive producers may create monopoly conditions not necessarily serving the national interest.

Holding companies (unless specially exempted) are required by the Companies Act of 1948 to publish either separate accounts for all the companies in the group or consolidated accounts for the whole group together.

Homogeneous Products Identical products.

Horizontal Integration The amalgamation of firms engaged in the same stage of production of the same commodity to achieve greater economic strength and profitability. An example is the Bradford Dyers' Association which is a combination of all firms engaged in dyeing. Also known as "horizontal combination". *See* VERTICAL INTEGRATION.

Hot Money Money which is transferred rapidly from one financial centre to another to take advantage of differences in short term interest rates or to escape the financial penalties of devaluation.

Household An economic unit consisting of a single person living alone, a married couple or a complete family, each unit with a source of income and responsibility for its disposal.

Housing and Local Government, Ministry of A Ministry set up in 1951 (under the initial title of Ministry of Local Government and Planning) it took over the housing and local government functions of the Ministry of Health and the functions of the Ministry of Town and Country Planning. The Ministry was responsible for the administration of Government housing policy, in respect of both new housing and slum clearance; the administration of the planning acts, including development plans, green belts, overspill, development control and national parks; the supervision of local government affairs generally, including re-organisation, public health Bills, clean air and noise abatement; the administration of Government policy in respect of water, sewerage, River Boards and river pollution; the development of new towns; and had duties in respect of minerals and alkali works. Absorbed in October, 1969, into the Department of Local Government and Regional Planning.

Hyperinflation Inflation (q.v.) which has got out of control; runaway inflation. A particularly outstanding example of this occurred in Germany in the 1920's when savings were destroyed in value by an astronomical rise in prices; to the middle classes the effect was disastrous.

I

Imperfect Competition A market situation in which neither absolute monopoly (q.v.) nor perfect competition (q.v.) prevails; a situation closest to real life in most circumstances. It is characterised by the ability of sellers to influence demand by product differentiation (q.v.), branding (q.v.) and advertising (q.v.); restriction of entry of competitors into various lines of production either because of the size of the initial investment required or because of restrictive practices; the existence of uncertainty (q.v.) with imperfect knowledge of profits earned in similar or other lines of production; and the absence of price competition in varying degrees.

Imperfect Market A market in which conditions do not correspond to the conditions for a perfect market (q.v.). All markets are, therefore, imperfect, the most imperfect being monopolistic.

Import Deposit A deposit of 50 per cent of the value of the goods which has to be paid on most goods imported into Britain other than basic foods, feeding stuffs, fuel and raw materials, before the Customs will release them. The goods affected are mainly manufactured goods. Customs retain the deposit for six months; it is then repaid automatically to the original payer of the deposit. The deposits do not bear interest. The measure was introduced on 27th November, 1968, as an additional measure to discourage imports. *See* IMPORT SURCHARGE.

Import Duties Act 1932 An Act introducing a full system of tariff protection for Britain, with the object of reducing imports as a whole. The Act imposed a general tariff of 10 per cent on all imports; at the same time it provided for exemptions for goods included in a Free List, and for the imposition of even higher duties on specific goods if recommended by an Import Duties Advisory Committee. Under the Ottawa Agreement (q.v.) substantial concessions were made in favour of Commonwealth goods. *See* IMPORT DUTIES ACT 1958.

Import Duties Act 1958 An Act consolidating a series of duties imposed by Britain at various dates since 1915, using a standard form of classification (the "Brussels Nomenclature") adopted by many other countries. *See* IMPORT DUTIES ACT 1932; MCKENNA DUTIES; OTTAWA AGREEMENT.

Import Duty *See* CUSTOMS DUTY.

Import Licence   A Board of Trade licence required for all goods imported into Britain.   A licence may be an "open general licence" permitting the unrestricted importation of certain goods in accordance with schedules which are published from time to time.   Sometimes an "individual open licence" may be issued, granting to a particular importer the unrestricted right to import a certain commodity as long as the licence is valid.   Frequently a "specific import licence" is issued to cover shipments up to a certain value only.

Import Quota   The maximum amount of a commodity, fixed by the Government, that can be imported into a country during a specified period.   The usual procedure is for import licences to be issued to the countries supplying the commodity in question, the licences stating the maximum amount of the commodity each country is permitted to supply.

Import Surcharge   An extra charge.   On 27th October, 1964, Britain's Labour Government imposed a surcharge of 15 per cent on the value of imported goods (excluding foodstuffs and raw materials) in an effort to discourage imports and overcome an adverse balance of payments problem.   This was reduced to 10 per cent on 27th April, 1965.   The legislation imposing the charge expired in November, 1966, and the charge lapsed accordingly.

Importing Houses   Business houses which import goods from overseas in order to sell them in their own country.

Imports   Goods and services bought from abroad.

"In the Bank"   A situation existing when the commercial banks are restricting credit and the discount-houses are able to raise cash only by taking bills to the Bank of England for re-discount; the money-market is then described as being "in the Bank".   *See* LENDER OF LAST RESORT.

Income   The wealth, measured in money, which is at the disposal of an individual or a community, per year or other unit of time; it may be regarded as a flow of purchasing power which may be expended at once on goods or services or retained for the purposes of capital accumulation.

Income Tax, Progressive   A system of graded tax payments, individuals with small incomes paying a smaller proportion of their incomes than individuals with large incomes.   The system is based on the theory of diminishing marginal utility.   *See* MARGINAL UTILITY, LAW OF DIMINISHING.

Income Tax, Proportional   A system of tax payments so designed that people pay in direct proportion to their incomes.

Income Velocity of Money   *See* VELOCITY OF CIRCULATION.

Incomes Policy   *See* NATIONAL INCOMES POLICY.

Increasing Returns, Law of   *See* VARIABLE PROPORTIONS, LAW OF.

Index, Actuaries Investment A share index published until December, 1962, when it was superseded by the Financial Times—Actuaries share indices. *See* INDICES, FINANCIAL TIMES—ACTUARIES SHARE.

Index, Financial Times Industrial Ordinary Share A geometric index, calculated and published by the *Financial Times* twice daily, at noon and at the close of Stock Exchange (q.v.) for the day. Constituents of the index are thirty market leaders, representing a cross-section of British industry.

Index Numbers Figures or indices which disclose the relative change, if any, in prices, costs, etc., of goods and services between one period of time and some other period of time selected as the "base period". *See* INDEX, ACTUARIES INVESTMENT; INDEX, FINANCIAL TIMES INDUSTRIAL ORDINARY SHARE; INDEX NUMBERS OF INDUSTRIAL PRODUCTION; INDEX OF RETAIL PRICES; INDEX OF RETAIL SALES; INDEX OF WEEKLY EARNINGS; INDEX OF WEEKLY WAGE-RATES; INDICES, FINANCIAL TIMES-ACTUARIES SHARE; INDICES OF TRAMP SHIPPING FREIGHTS; INDICES OF WHOLESALE PRICES; SHARE INDICES, THE TIMES; STATIST INDEX, THE.

Index Numbers of Industrial Production Index numbers designed to measure, at regular intervals, changes in the volume of production in particular industries, groups of industries and industry as a whole. Wherever possible, index numbers of production are based on physical units of output, e.g. tons of steel, as this procedure eliminates the influence of price changes. In some industries, physical output would be a misleading measure of output; in such cases output is measured by the value of output (deflated to constant prices), or the quantity of materials used. When grouping the products and industries together to give an overall index of industrial production the following method is used. Product by product the percentage change in production is compared with some base period; in order to combine these percentages a system of weighting is adopted which expresses the significance of the products in the economy (that is, the net output of the industry in the base period). The index of industrial production is therefore a weighted average of the percentage movements of the indicators. Over time the relative values of the net outputs will alter, and it is necessary to revise the index occasionally and to use revised weights. When this is done, the series becomes discontinuous and movements through time are lost.

The index which is used today and which is published in the *Monthly Digest of Statistics* provides a general measure of monthly changes in the volume of industrial production in the United Kingdom. The index uses weights applicable to 1963. About 800 production series, individually weighted, are incorporated in the index. *See* GROSS AND NET OUTPUT.

Index of Retail Prices An index which measures monthly changes in the level of retail prices. The prices taken into account by the index are "weighted"; the basis of the weighting is provided by regular inquiries into household expenditure. The index is published in the Ministry of Labour Gazette and the Monthly Digest of Statistics.

The former "cost of living index" was replaced in 1947 by the Interim Index of Retail Prices; this interim index was replaced in 1956 by the Index of Retail Prices. From January, 1963, onwards the index has been calculated with prices at 16 January 1962 taken as 100. From 1963 onwards the weights have been revised in February each year on the basis of information derived from the Family Expenditure Survey for the three years ended the previous June, adjusted to correspond with the levels of prices ruling in January of each year. Expenditure is divided into ten main groups—food, alcoholic drink, tobacco, housing, fuel and light, durable household goods, clothing and footwear, transport and vehicles, miscellaneous goods and services. Expenditure covered by the index does not include income tax payments, insurance contributions and premiums, or mortgage payments for house purchase.

Index of Retail Sales An index published in the Board of Trade Journal; separate index numbers are given for different kinds of shops and different types of retailer.

Index of Weekly Earnings An index covering earnings in the manufacturing industries and some of the principal non-manufacturing industries.

Computed at six monthly intervals from information collected from inquiries into earnings and hours of work of wage earners in the last pay week of April and October each year.

The index reflects changes in the amount of overtime and short time or absenteeism and changes in the earnings of piece workers and other payment-by-result workers due to changes in the efficiency of operatives and machines.

Index of Weekly Wage Rates An index providing a measure of the average movement in the wage rates for men, women and juveniles, separately and in combination.

The number of industries and services selected for inclusion in the index is 80, including agriculture, mining, manufacturing, transport, national and government service, cinema, theatres, etc.

The rates of wages are the minimum or standard rates of wage as fixed by voluntary collective agreement between organisations of employers and work people, or arbitration awards, or statutory minimum rates.

The rates are those of manual wage-earners, including shop assistants, but excluding clerical, technical and administrative workers.

The base date of the Index of Rates of Wages is 31 January 1956; the base date of the old index was 30 June 1947.

Indices, Financial Times–Actuaries Share Indices of share prices published daily in the *Financial Times*. Details of the constituents and computation of the indices are given in the booklet *Guide to the F.T.–Actuaries Share Indices* (St. Clements Press Ltd.).

Indices of Tramp Shipping Freights Two indices prepared by the Chamber of Shipping of the United Kingdom of tramp shipping freights, one for voyage-charter and one for time-charter. They are published in the *Annual Digest of Statistics*.

Indices of Wholesale Prices   Board of Trade price indices arranged in groups
as follows:
  (a) Price indices of materials used in broad industrial groups, e.g. textile
       industries, house-building;
  (b) Price indices of the output of broad industrial groups, e.g. chemical
       and allied products, clothing and footwear;
  (c) Price indices of materials (mostly imports) used in industry, e.g. raw
       cotton, imported soft-wood;
  (d) Price indices of the output of particular industries, e.g. coal, carpets
       and rugs.
All these indices are published in the Board of Trade Journal.

Indifference Analysis   A technique developed in recent years by economists
to help construct a more satisfactory theory of consumers' demand.   It
involves the use of the indifference curve (q.v.).

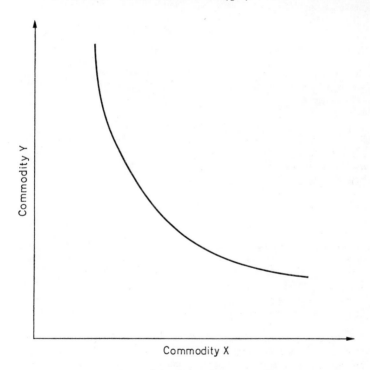

FIGURE 5   INDIFFERENCE CURVE

Indifference Curve   The locus of all exchanges (or substitutions) of one commodity for another which gives the consumer the same amount of satisfaction.
Between all possible combinations the consumer will be indifferent, i.e. he
will feel himself no better off, and no worse off, whichever combination he has.

See Figure 5. The slope of an indifference curve is negative; as the quantity of X increases, that of Y must decrease.

Indifference Map   A family of indifference curves. *See* INDIFFERENCE CURVE.

Indirect Taxes   *See* TAXES.

Individualism   The name given to a political and economic system that favours the development of the individual rather than that of the state or other association; it is the antithesis of collectivism and socialism. Individualism has found strong advocacy among the English speaking peoples. As a philosophy it rested on the teachings of Adam Smith (1723–1790) and Jeremy Bentham (1748–1832) and was accepted with some modification by John Stuart Mill (1806–1873). Its most extreme exponent was Herbert Spencer (1820–1903). The creed of the individualist is that the best results for mankind can be attained by giving free play to individual energy and initiative, applying this principle both in the sphere of industry and in that of morals, with as little interference by government as possible. Since about 1880, there has been a strong reaction against individualism. *See* LAISSEZ-FAIRE.

Indivisible Plant   Plant which must be used on a large-scale, or not at all, if it is to fulfil its functions. The minimum size is determined by technical considerations.

Induction   The act or process of reasoning from particular cases to general conclusions. It is a method by which truths of scientific value are obtained which are not directly deducible from principles already known. The inductive method may be employed to test the findings of economic theory developed by the deductive method. Alfred Marshall expressed the opinion that "induction and deduction are both needed for scientific thought as the right and left foot are both needed for walking". There is no one method, therefore, which can be properly called the method of economics. *See* DEDUCTION.

Industrial and Commercial Finance Corporation Ltd.   A financial services institution, established in 1945 by the English and Scottish banks with the approval of the Bank of England and the Government, with the purpose of assisting the business man who requires finance for expansion or development which it is not practicable or convenient to raise by way of banking facilities or a public issue of shares. It assists, therefore, small and medium-sized companies.

Finance is provided in several forms, including long-term loans and/or share capital; amounts range from £5,000 to £200,000 and over on a first application. In January 1966 the total amount advanced by the Corporation exceeded £78 m. Loans are from 10 to 20 years with a fixed rate of interest charged on the outstanding amount only.

A Plant Purchase Scheme enables customers to buy industrial plant, machinery and commercial vehicles over periods of up to five years. The leasing of plant and equipment is also arranged. *See* FINANCE CORPORATION FOR INDUSTRY LTD.; FINANCE CORPORATIONS.

Industrial Courts Act 1919 An Act introduced for the purpose of providing improved machinery for the settlement of disputes. It gave the Minister of Labour power to set up an Industrial Court, consisting of an independent chairman and representatives of employers and work people, to which industrial disputes might be referred with the consent of the parties concerned. The Minister was also empowered to appoint a Court of Inquiry, to ascertain the facts relating to any industrial dispute. In 1951, the Industrial Disputes Tribunal was established as an alternative to the Industrial Court; it ceased to operate in 1959.

Industrial Development Certificate A certificate required from the Ministry of Technology, under The Distribution of Industry Act 1945 (q.v.) in respect of any initial construction or extension of a factory with over 5,000 sq. ft. of floor area. Through the granting or refusal of Industrial Development Certificates the Board of Trade controls the siting of industry; the purpose is to direct suitable new industries away from the congested regions and into the Development Districts (q.v.). Even with a Certificate, an industrialist must still obtain local planning permission (q.v.).

Industrial Estates Corporations Financed and controlled by the Ministry of Technology public corporations which build factories for rent or sale either in advance, or to meet the known requirements of a particular firm. Between 1960 and 1965 an average of 70 factories were built each year.

Industrial Reorganisation Corporation A Corporation set up in 1966 by the British Government as a further aid to its industrial policies. With an initial capital of £150 million, the Corporation provides loans or purchases shareholdings in companies in order to promote rationalisation schemes. While the capital involved is relatively small, the Corporation is able to finance a larger volume of transactions by disposing of its investments as projects become financially viable. *See* RATIONALISATION.

Industrial Revolution Name given to the economic changes which took place in Britain during the latter half of the 18th century and the first half of the 19th century. Until about 1700, the spinning wheel, the hand loom and the plough had altered little but they were now proving unequal to the new demands made upon them. The opening up of the world's markets was giving an unprecedented opportunity to exchange home produce for foreign raw materials. The first of a series of new inventions came when John Kay (1704–1764) of Bury, Lancashire, invented the flying shuttle which greatly quickened the weaving of cloth. Hitherto the weft was passed through the warp by the weaver; now it was thrown across a much wider space by a mechanical device. The result of this invention was the need for a greater supply of yarn. In 1764, James Hargreaves (1720–1778) invented the spinning jenny. In 1768, a mob of spinners, fearful that the new machine would put them out of work wrecked his home and machines. In 1769, Richard Arkwright (1732–1792) invented an improved spinning machine; it spun a finer and stronger thread by using a system of rollers driven by water power. But both this invention and the spinning jenny gave place to Crompton's "mule", which combined the principles of both inventions. Samuel Crompton (1753–1827) developed his hybrid machine in 1779; it produced a still stronger and finer cotton yarn. Although many frames were broken by hand-spinners who feared unemployment, a new industry was founded in which large fortunes were made. In 1785, Edmund Cartwright (1743–1823) invented the first mechanical loom and began a revolution in weaving. In 1789, he developed a machine for wool-combing. It was not until the early years of the 19th century, however, that the loom was perfected and came into general use. Gradually both the hand spinner and the hand weaver disappeared, unable to compete with the new machines.

The year 1766 marked the beginning of another phase in the Industrial Revolution in the application of steam power to the textile and other industries, although it was many years before steam power became of universal application in industry. James Watt (1736–1819), the Scottish engineer, successfully adapted the ponderous steam pump which had long been used in mines into a practical engine to drive the machines of spinners and weavers. Watt's steam engine was first used in the cotton mills and soon in all the textile industry. In the iron industry too great changes were taking place. Abraham Darby (1677–1717) had already discovered that iron could be smelted with coke; in 1709 he set up a foundry at Coalbrookdale in Shropshire for this purpose. By 1760 this technique had become well-established, setting up a demand for more coal. The iron-industry was further revolutionised by Henry Cort (1740–1800) who made possible the utilisation of coal and mechanical appliances in the final stages of the manufacture of iron-goods. Simultaneously a steel industry was being developed in Sheffield. To carry the growing quantities of coal required for smelting and household purposes, a whole network of inland waterways developed; the main roads were also improved and reconstructed. The year 1820 marked the next distinctive phase with the development of the railways and the introduction of machine tools. Transport developments opened up the markets of England, allowing raw materials and fuel, and manufactured articles, to be transported cheaply to all parts of the country.

At the same time the steady drift of population from the country to the towns was proceeding at an unprecedented rate. Soon the majority of people were leading an urban, rather than a rural, life. In addition, the population had grown considerably. In 1750, there were perhaps some six million people in England and Wales; by 1850 this figure had grown to 20 million. Of these a growing proportion had to be fed with imports from the new food-producing countries of the world. Agriculture at home also underwent great changes in organisation and methods, much improving productivity. In this period, the economic structure of England was completely altered. Steam and machines had driven out most of the hand work in the principal industries of the country. The majority of people, now divorced from the soil, depended upon wages earned in the various industries. All this contributed to higher wages and greater efficiency in production. One of the finest tributes to capitalism was paid by Karl Marx himself. In the *Communist Manifesto*, in a reference to the bourgeoisie, he wrote, "It has been the first to show what man's activity can bring about. It has accomplished wonders far surpassing Egyptian pyramids, Roman aqueducts, and Gothic cathedrals;

it has conducted expeditions that put in the shade all former Exoduses of Nations and Crusades." But Marxist Socialism (q.v.) was based upon the apparent failings, not successes, of the capitalist free-enterprise economy; and he was not alone in recognising these failings. Benjamin Disraeli (1804–1881) in his book *Sybil*, or "a tale of two nations", included the following passage: "Since the passing of the Reform Act the altar of Mammon has blazed with triple worship. To acquire, to accumulate, to plunder each other by virtue of philosophic phrases, to propose a Utopia to consist only of wealth and toil, this has been the breathless business of an enfranchised England, until we are startled from our voracious strife by the wail of intolerable serfage."

Industrial Training Act 1964   An Act to promote the better training of apprentices. The Act requires the Minister of Labour to appoint a Central Training Council to advise him on the exercise of his functions under the Act and on matters concerned with industrial training which he refers to it. It consists of a chairman, employer and trade union members, educationalists, the chairmen of a number of industrial boards and those with a special interest in training. The Act also empowers the Minister to set up Training Boards in industries, after consultation with the employers and trade unions concerned. These Boards comprise equal numbers of trade union and employers' representatives and a smaller number of educational members. The Training Boards undertake a wide range of functions covering all aspects of training. They have the power to impose a levy on firms in the industry concerned and also to give grants to those providing approved training. Each Board is expected to assess its industry's training requirements and to make recommendations on the nature, content and length of training, and on the further education course which it considers necessary. Boards are able to provide their own training courses for apprenticeships and other forms of training.

Industrial Training Board   *See* INDUSTRIAL TRAINING ACT 1964.

Industrial Union   *See* TRADE UNIONS.

Industry   In its widest sense, all the manifold activities of a country which provide employment, but more narrowly those activities concerned with the production of goods rather than services. Specifically, an industry comprises all those activities which are directed to the production of a given class of goods, e.g. aircraft, ships, machine tools, foodstuffs, etc. An industry may be composed of many business units as in agriculture, or perhaps only one business unit as in the case of coal. An individual firm may make a wide range of dissimilar goods, and thus be participating in the activities of several industries.

Infant Industry   A young and growing industry, often considered not quite able to stand on its own feet in the face of foreign competition. Such industries may be afforded the protection of a tariff (q.v.), or granted a subsidy, until strong enough to stand alone. Experience suggests, however, that tariffs and subsidies, once introduced, are not so easily removed. *See* PROTECTION.

In-Feeding   The supply of goods and services from within an organisation.

Inferior Goods   *See* GIFFEN GOODS.

Inflation   A condition in which the volume of purchasing power is constantly running ahead of the output of goods and services, with the result that as incomes and prices rise the value of money falls.   Since the Second World War all countries have experienced varying degrees of persistent inflation; some countries such as Hungary and Greece experienced hyper- or runaway-inflations which were quite disastrous.   Geoffrey Crowther has expressed the view that the term "inflation" should not be used where rising prices are merely indicating a revival from a depression, the word "reflation" being more appropriate.   Conversely a retreat from inflation may be described as "disinflation" whenever it falls short of a genuine deflation (q.v.).   Both "disinflation" and "reflation" signify a movement of credit, prices and wages downwards or upwards to an "equilibrium" at which consumers' expenditure is no more, and no less, than is sufficient to buy the goods available.   John Maynard Keynes thought that only when a "further increase in the quantity of money produces no further increase in output and entirely spends itself on an increase in the cost unit fully proportionate to the increase in effective demand" could the condition be appropriately designated as one of true inflation.   An increase in the volume of purchasing power may be both a cause and an effect of inflation; a cause in so far as it leads to higher prices through increased demand and costs of production, and an effect in that rising prices lead to demands for higher money incomes. Whether an inflation is a "demand-pull" inflation or a "cost-push" inflation the total effect is a spiralling of prices and incomes.   While any marked inflationary trend may be quite harmful to an economy such as Britain's in which the prices of her exports must be kept competitive, many economists tend to regard a gentle upward trend in prices and incomes as stimulating to the economy.   It certainly reduces the burden of fixed interest payments on past debts, although less fair to new lenders who tend to look for higher rates of interest to compensate for the falling value of money.   *See* INFLATION, COST-PUSH; INFLATION, DEMAND-PULL; "UNEASY TRIANGLE", THE.

Inflationary Spiral   An upward trend of prices, which is partly the result and partly the cause of increases in wages and salaries and other incomes such as profits, dividends, interest and rent.

Inflation, Bottleneck   *See* INFLATION, DEMAND-SHIFT.

Inflation, Cost-Push   Inflationary trends initiated by pressure for higher incomes, greater spending not being accompanied by a corresponding increase in goods and services.   Cost-push inflation may also arise from increases in the prices of imported raw materials.

Inflation, Creeping   Inflation (q.v.) characterised by a slowly rising price level.

Inflation, Demand-Pull   Excessive demand for goods and services, the symptoms of which are rising prices and scarcities of labour and materials; bidding raises the prices of these resources which leads to further increases in the prices of goods and services.

Inflation, Demand-Shift Or bottle-neck inflation, inflation (q.v.) which arises without an increase in aggregate demand for goods and services should the structure of demand (q.v.) change more rapidly than resources can be shifted. This may occur in its most acute form during a change from a war to a peace economy in which government expenditure falls and consumer spending increases fairly rapidly, the physical changeover in factory production from war goods to consumer goods lagging behind. Thus demand outstrips supply in the consumer sector and prices temporarily rise. Demand-shift inflation is a short-term phenomenon, offering no explanation of long-term or secular inflation.

Inflation, Suppressed Inflation (q.v.) suppressed by price controls and regulations; it implies the existence of "redundant money" or potential demand for goods which, if unleashed, would create active inflation. Redundant money accumulated in Britain during the Second World War, partly as a result of heavy Government spending and Budget deficits. Redundant money also accumulated in the form of post-war credits (q.v.); sterling balances owned abroad were another form of redundant money, adding to the potential demand for British goods.

Information Agreement Also known as an open price agreement, or price reporting agreement, an agreement whereby a number of firms undertake to inform each other regularly about past, current and sometimes future prices, and other relevant data such as costs, discounts, rebates, conditions of sale, turnover and often the names of buyers. The information is generally collated and distributed by a central agency, often a trade association. Agreements of this nature fall into two main types; those in which notification is given prior to a change in price ("pre-notification agreement") and those in which notification is only given after a change in price has taken place ("post-notification agreement"). An information agreement serves as a means for co-ordinating the behaviour of suppliers participating in a given market; it may result in consciously parallel policies with regard to prices, particularly in an oligopoly (q.v.), thus largely paralysing price competition. Information agreements appear to be introduced whenever price-fixing agreements become illegal. In the United Kingdom certain information agreements have been found contrary to the public interest by the Restrictive Practices Court (q.v.).

Information Theory Mathematical theory describing the coding and transmission of information; it is used in tele-communications and may eventually have a place in studying communication problems in organisations.

Infrastructure Services regarded as essential for the creation of a modern economy, e.g. power, transport, housing, education and health services.

Inheritance Tax A tax levied on what is received by the individual heirs to an estate.

Inland Bill of Exchange A bill which is both drawn and payable within the British Isles, or drawn within the British Isles upon a person resident therein. Any other bill is known as a "foreign bill". *See* BILL OF EXCHANGE.

Innovation In a general sense, the technical, industrial and commercial steps which lead to the marketing of new manufactured products and to the commercial use of new technical processes and equipment. *See* INVENTION.

Input–Output Analysis The quantitative analysis of inter-industry relations. All transactions that involve the sale of products or services within an economy during a given period are arranged in a square indicating simultaneously the sectors making, and the sectors receiving, delivery. The preparation of input-output tables has significantly added to our knowledge of the industrial economy in past periods.

Inputs Materials and factor services fed in at one end of the production process and used in the process of production.

Installed Load Tariff A tariff for the supply of electricity consisting in its simplest form of a unit charge plus a standing charge related to the number of kilowatts of installed electrical load on a premises. *See* TARIFF (b).

Instalment Credit Credit (q.v.) to finance the purchase of consumer goods, repayable by a series of payments over a period of time.

Institutional Investors A group of investors who have funds to invest as a consequence of the conduct of their businesses. The group includes insurance companies, banks and investment trusts, and industrial companies who administer their own pension schemes or have other funds available.

Instrumental Industries Industries engaged in making or repairing instruments of production, in particular machinery of all kinds, ships and vehicles.

Insurance The elimination of risk of loss by the payment of premiums to an insurance company which undertakes to pay for specified losses; the losses of the few are thus met from the premiums of the many. Insurance services fall into the following classes: (a) fire, and other hazards such as riots, explosion, earthquake and hurricane; (b) accident, including motor, third party liability and personal; (c) marine, both hull and cargo; (d) aviation, both hull and cargo; and (e) life and endowment. *See* LLOYD'S; UNDERWRITING.

Interest The price paid by a borrower to a lender, usually on the basis of X per cent of the capital per annum. The elements of interest are:

    (a) a payment for the risk of loss of capital by the lender;
    (b) a payment for making the arrangement;
    (c) a payment varying with the state of the market in respect of the demand for, and supply of, capital, known as "net" or "pure" interest.

Thus the rate of interest tends to equate the supply of money available for borrowing and the demand for loans.

Long-term interest rates are usually higher than short-term rates, due to a greater risk of a change in the rate of yield of securities over a long period. The two rates tend to rise and fall together.

Generally, a low rate of interest and a plentiful supply of capital encourages expansion; a high rate with scarce capital checks it.

In the "agio" theory, usually associated with Professor von Böhm-Bawerk, it is argued that the fundamental reason for interest lies in the fact that a man prefers present to future satisfactions. Interest may be said to represent the loss in satisfaction experienced by postponing the consumption of goods. It is this surplus of present over future satisfactions that is said to explain the payment of interest. Hence the expression "interest is the price of time". John Maynard Keynes (1886–1946) defined interest as "the price which equilibrates the desire to hold wealth in the form of cash with the available quantity of cash". *See* LIQUIDITY PREFERENCE.

Interest, Classical Theory of Rate of A theory that the rate of interest, under the play of market forces, comes to rest at the point where the amount of investment at that rate of interest is equal to the amount of saving at that rate. John Maynard Keynes (1886–1946) argued that the total amount of saving was influenced by many factors, and that the rate of interest merely influenced individual decisions as to what proportion of savings would be invested in industry and how much held as cash. *See* INTEREST; KEYNESIAN REVOLUTION; LIQUIDITY PREFERENCE.

Interest, Natural Rate of The rate of interest which preserves the status quo of an economy.

Interest, Neutral Rate of The rate of interest consistent with full employment; from this aspect it may be described as the "optimum rate of interest". *See* INTEREST, NATURAL RATE OF.

Interim Dividend A dividend (q.v.) paid out of profits not yet audited.

Interlocking Directorships An arrangement under which individual directors have seats on the boards of various companies within the same group.

Intermediate Areas Areas of Britain, not being development areas (q.v.), in which the rate of economic growth gives cause, or may give cause, for concern.

Internal Economy *See* ECONOMIES OF SCALE.

International Atomic Energy Agency United Nations organisation formed in 1957 to promote the utilisation of atomic energy for electricity generation and radioactive isotopes in medicine, agriculture and industry.

International Bank for Reconstruction and Development (I.B.R.D.) Bank set up under the Bretton Woods Agreement (q.v.) in December 1945 for two purposes: to help finance the rebuilding of war-devastated areas and to aid in the advancement of less-developed countries. Nearly one-third of all funds have gone for power projects. Besides lending funds, the Bank provides technical advice to governments or other borrowers on a wide range of development problems. It undertakes general economic surveys for governments wishing to study resources and to plan long-range programmes of development. The Bank has also lent its "good offices" to help governments solve economic or financial disputes. The Bank's loan funds come in part from members' subscriptions to capital shares. The powers of the Bank are vested in a Board of Governors. It is often referred to as the World Bank.

International Centre for the Settlement of Investment Disputes (I.C.S.I.D.) An international organisation the purpose of which is to provide the parties to certain international investment arrangements with a forum to which they may turn for the settlement of any disputes. It came into being on 14th October, 1966. The Centre was created by the Convention on the Settlement of Investment Disputes between States and Nationals of Other States, a Convention intended to encourage the growth of private foreign investment for economic development. The Convention was the result of the initiative of the International Bank for Reconstruction and Development (q.v.).

International Co-Operation Administration A U.S. government agency which replaced the Foreign Operation Administration (q.v.) on 30th June, 1955, assuming responsibility for supervising all U.S. foreign-aid programmes, including economic and technical aid.

International Credit Clubs Set up to meet demands for medium-term credit, each "club" consists of a number of European finance houses or banks which introduce instalment credit business to their foreign partners on a reciprocal basis. Credit is extended to the foreign customer, not to the exporter; such schemes have advantages for small firms which are unable or unwilling to grant credit. The main "clubs" are the European Credit Union, Amstel Club and Eurocredit. Each club is represented in Britain by one of the major finance houses already providing instalment credit in Britain.

International Currency A currency internationally acceptable as a means of settling debts. Gold has almost universal acceptability for the settlement of major debts, but is otherwise inconvenient. United States dollars and British sterling have wide acceptability; probably some 25–30 per cent of international trade is conducted in sterling. *See* KEYNES PLAN; SPECIAL DRAWING RIGHTS; TRIFFIN PLAN.

International Development Association (I.D.A.) An affiliate of the International Bank for Reconstruction and Development (q.v.). It was formed in 1960 to help developing nations by extending financial aid on easy terms. I.D.A. finances carefully studied and well prepared projects. It will help countries whose credit standing has not enabled them to borrow from the Bank, and it is prepared to finance a wide variety of projects, e.g. by extending credits for municipal water supply, industrial estates and special training programmes.

International Economics A branch of economic science concerned with economic transactions across national frontiers, e.g. exchange of goods, movements of capital, emigration, etc.

International Finance Corporation (I.F.C.) A United Nations agency, established in 1956 as an affiliate of the International Bank for Reconstruction and Development (q.v.), to help finance productive private undertakings by investing in them, without government intervention or guarantee. It invests only in the less-developed areas, and in enterprises which are primarily industrial. I.F.C. will not, however, finance more than half of the total cost of an enterprise.

International Gold Pool An organisation established in 1961 by a number of central banks to operate in the London market for the purpose of stabilising the price of gold. The participating countries were the United States of America, Belgium, Italy, Netherlands, Switzerland, Western Germany and the United Kingdom. France was also a member but ceased to take an active part in the pool from July, 1967, onwards. Early in March, 1968, the demand for gold reached a record level, the price pressing against the effective ceiling price of $35 per fine ounce maintained by the gold pool. At the request of the United States authorities the London gold market was closed on Friday, 15th March, 1968, and did not re-open until 1st April, 1968. During this period an emergency meeting was held in Washington of the governors of the seven central banks still participating in the gold pool arrangement. The outcome was a decision to abandon the gold pool. Gold would continue, however, to be transferred between monetary authorities on the basis of $35 per fine ounce but the authorities undertook no longer to sell, nor necessarily to buy, in the market. In effect a two-tier system for gold was created, as in the market the price of gold would be free to find its own level.

International Labour Organisation (I.L.O.) International organisation set up in 1919 by the Treaty of Versailles to help under-developed countries make most efficient use of their manpower by improving factory processes and training supervisors and workers in new techniques, and generally improve working conditions. The I.L.O. has developed a "world labour code" comprising some 230 conventions and recommendations relating to working conditions and employees' welfare. In 1946 the I.L.O. became affiliated to the United Nations.

International Liquidity The ability of countries to meet their international debts and settle their international transactions. Countries keep reserves of gold and foreign currencies and settle their indebtedness to other countries by means of either a transfer of gold or payments in their own or foreign currencies. A country in temporary balance-of-payments difficulties may seek the assistance of the International Monetary Fund (q.v.).

International Monetary Fund An international financial institution set up on 27th December, 1945, as a result of the Bretton Woods Agreement (q.v.) of the previous year. It is an association of governments designed to: (a) promote international monetary co-operation through a permanent institution; (b) facilitate the expansion and balanced growth of international trade; (c) promote exchange stability, maintain orderly exchange arrangements among members, and avoid competitive exchange depreciation; (d) assist in the establishment of a multi-lateral system of payments in respect of current transactions between members; and (e) provide members with an opportunity to correct maladjustments in their balance of payments (q.v.) without resorting to measures destructive of national and international prosperity. The Fund has over 100 members. Each member government has been set a quota to be paid into the Fund, payable partly in gold and partly in the member's own currency; the quota determines the member's voting power and the amount of foreign exchange that it may draw from the Fund. A member may purchase foreign exchange, paying its own currency, but the member must "repurchase" its own currency within three or, at the outside, five years to maintain the balance in the Fund pool. Currencies drawn from the Fund may be used to relieve a member's balance of payments difficulties; the funds may not be used for military purposes or for programmes of economic development. The aim is to assure the maintenance of fixed exchange rates in the face of short-term fluctuations; many countries have been helped in this way. Each member undertakes to establish and maintain an agreed par value (q.v.) for its currency, and to consult the Fund on any change in the initial parity.

In addition, the Fund consults with members on their international financial situation and on specific problems as they arise. On request, the Fund furnishes expert missions to advise and assist governments in working out monetary problems on the spot. In any event, members are kept informed of the latest developments. Policies are laid down by a Board of Governors, representing all members, which normally meets annually. Many of its powers are delegated to a Board of Executive Directors. In recent years, the resources of the Fund have been supplemented by the Group of Ten (q.v.) agreements. *See* SPECIAL DRAWING RIGHTS.

International System of Units (SI) An international metric system of weights and measures. It is a collection of units and multiples derived from six basic units:

> Metre (for length)
> Kilogramme (for weight)
> Second (for time)
> Ampere (for electric current)
> Kelvin (for absolute temperature)
> Candela (for luminous intensity)

The degree Celsius is used for the customary temperature interval. *See* METRIC SYSTEM.

International Trade Or foreign trade, the exchange of goods and services between independent countries or states.

International Trade Organisation (I.T.O.) An organisation which was to have been set up when the Havana Charter was ratified in 1947–8 to encourage international co-operation in commercial policies and activities, draw up rules of fair trade and reduce barriers to world business activity. An Interim Commission for I.T.O. was set up, with headquarters at Geneva, and a secretariat was appointed. The Organisation has not, however, come into existence because of the U.S. refusal to ratify the Havana Charter, but some of its objectives have been embodied in the General Agreement on Tariffs and Trade (q.v.) which came into force on 1st January, 1948. The staff originally appointed to work for the I.T.O. Interim Commission has become the G.A.T.T. secretariat. *See* ORGANISATION FOR TRADE CO-OPERATION.

International Transactions In this context, economic transactions including financial transactions and capital movements, among independent countries or states.

Interstate Commerce Commission (U.S.) A body responsible for federal, as distinct from state, transport in the U.S.A. It has comprehensive powers over railroad rates and services and highway common carriers, and over certain classes of coastal and inter-coastal shipping. It has limited powers also to regulate petroleum pipelines.

Intra-European Payments Agreement (I.E.P.A.) A payments system which operated between member countries of the Organisation for European Economic Co-operation (q.v.) between July 1948 and July 1950, for the purpose of stimulating intra-European trade and commerce. The scheme was administered in detail by the Bank for International Settlements (q.v.). It was superseded by the European Payments Union (q.v.).

Intra-Firm and Inter-Firm Comparisons Comparisons of business efficiency made between the units of the same firm, or between firms within the same industry, in order to stimulate improved performance. The members of an industry often collaborate in the regular publication of statistics and organisations are set up to define, collect and compare financial and operating ratios on a confidential basis. The more common ratios used in inter-firm comparisons are:

$$\frac{\text{Net Profit}}{\text{Capital employed}} \qquad \frac{\text{Fixed Assets}}{\text{Stocks}}$$

$$\frac{\text{Total capital employed}}{\text{Liquid Assets}} \qquad \frac{\text{Fixed Assets}}{\text{Depreciation Provision}}$$

$$\frac{\text{Current Assets}}{\text{Current Liabilities}} \qquad \frac{\text{Fixed Interest Capital}}{\text{Equity Capital}}$$

Introduction, Stock Exchange *See* STOCK EXCHANGE INTRODUCTION.

Invention A new technique or piece of equipment for the performance of tasks. A labour-saving or capital-saving invention will reduce the cost of labour and of capital respectively per unit of output, but the total demand for these factors of production may not be reduced if wider markets are obtained through a fall in selling price consequent upon a fall in the costs of production. *See* INNOVATION.

Inventories Part of a manufacturer's working assets consisting of raw materials to be used in a product, goods in process of manufacture, and finished goods ready for distribution to customers.

Inventory Turnover The value of sales over say a year divided by the value of the inventory at the end of that year.

Investment In economic science, capital expenditure on physical productive assets, e.g. machinery, factory buildings, roads, bridges, houses, and so on, and stocks. Investment plus consumption equals the gross national product at factor cost (q.v.). As a financial term, investment embraces purchases of stock exchange securities, or deposits of money in banks, building societies, or other financial institution, with a view to income and, in appropriate cases, capital gains (q.v.).

Investment Appraisal An assessment of whether investment in a proposed project will show a satisfactory rate of return; various alternative projects may be examined to ascertain which should give the greatest return on capital invested over any given period of time. *See* PROFITABILITY OF ALTERNATIVE PROJECTS, METHODS OF COMPARING

Investment, Deepening Investment which increases the total output of a given labour force by increasing the productivity (q.v.) of that force, within a given framework of technical knowledge. *See* INVESTMENT; INVESTMENT, WIDENING.

Investment Demand Schedule A list of quantities of investment likely to be demanded in respect of a corresponding list of rates of interest. In a given state of expectation in respect of profit from investment, a larger quantity of investment is demanded the lower the rate of interest, i.e. the quantity of investment demanded is a decreasing function of the rate of interest.

Investment Dollars Dollars of a special type which an investor in the United Kingdom is allowed to purchase to pay for non-sterling securities. Sometimes known as "security", "premium" or "switch" dollars. They are bought and sold freely in the London money market, mainly by banks and stockbrokers. Purchases and sales of investment dollars must be reported to the Bank of England. Investment dollars are for investment purposes only.

Investment Grants Introduced by the British Government in January, 1966, to replace tax allowances on investment in industry. They are flat-rate payments towards expenditure by industry on machinery and plant for use in manufacturing, construction and privately owned mining and quarrying work. The standard rate of grant is normally £20 per £100; in development areas (q.v.) the rate is normally £40 per £100.

Investment Intentions The plans of business organisations to add to stocks or to fixed capital equipment.

Investment, Negative The process of absorbing stocks.

Investment Opportunity Line Description given by Professor Irving Fisher to a transformation curve representing a function relating the income a firm may obtain in successive years from the employment of a given set of resources in different ways.

Investment Ratio The proportion of a country's resources devoted to investment.

Investment, Socialisation of The control of the investment of capital in industry by a public authority using state funds. Lord Keynes in his *General Theory of Employment, Interest and Money* (1936) thought that a somewhat comprehensive socialisation of investment would prove the only means of securing an approximation to full employment, although he felt that this need not exclude all manner of compromises and devices by which public authority could co-operate with private initiative.

Investment Trust A public corporate body, registered under the Companies Acts, which invests funds in a wide range of stocks and shares thus "spreading the risk" more effectively than could be achieved by an individual investor with much smaller funds. The capital of the investment trust is derived mainly from public issues of debentures (q.v.), preference shares and ordinary shares, which are quoted on the stock exchanges. The small investor may thus buy shares in a trust which in turn is using the capital of many investors to acquire a wide range of securities which will provide a reasonably high and secure income over a long period of time. Dividends are distributed annually. *See* UNIT TRUST.

Investment, Widening Investment to increase production utilising existing techniques, conventional labour/capital ratios, and the already established time-pattern of production; in other words, investment which increases production, but not productivity (q.v.). *See* INVESTMENT; INVESTMENT, DEEPENING.

Invisible Earnings An element in the balance of payments (q.v.) which includes: (a) services in the field of commerce and finance; and (b) earnings of British holdings of property and enterprises abroad. As invisible exports tend to exceed in value the services rendered by overseas countries to Britain and the earnings of foreign capital invested in Britain, the net earnings contribute to offsetting deficits in visible trade. Government military and non-military spending overseas and contributions to international organisations represent invisible imports. The net receipts of U.K. shipping companies while a large item in the overseas accounts make only a small contribution to net earnings. Civil aviation also yields little or no net earnings. Travel represents a deficit as more Britons travel abroad than overseas residents visit Britain. However, financial and allied services; underwriting and other insurance; interest, profits and dividends from overseas investments, all yield a substantial net surplus. Over the past 5 years net earnings have averaged almost £170m. per year.

Invisible Trade *See* BALANCE OF PAYMENTS.

Iron and Steel Board A Board set up to supervise the development and expansion of the steel industry following de-nationalisation in 1953. All capital expenditure by a steel company over £100,000 had to be sanctioned by the Board, which was also given power to fix maximum prices. The Board's guiding aim was to set prices at the lowest level compatible with expanding and efficient production. The heavy steelmakers' associations recommended their members to treat the Board's maximum prices as fixed prices, and not to charge less for their products. This recommendation had to be defended before the Restrictive Practices Court (q.v.). The argument submitted was that competition must lead to a "price war". This argument was not accepted and the Restrictive Practices Court held that the price-fixing agreement between Britain's heavy steelmakers was contrary to the public interest.

Iron and Steel Corporation of Great Britain A public corporation to which the securities of the steel companies were transferred upon nationalisation in 1949. In 1953 the steel industry was denationalised, but a measure of public supervision was retained through the setting up of an Iron and Steel Board (q.v.). *See* BRITISH STEEL CORPORATION.

Iron-Law of Wages *See* WAGES, THEORIES OF.

Irredeemable Debenture A debenture (q.v.) containing no provision for the repayment of the principal in normal circumstances. If the company goes into liquidation however, the debenture has a prior claim to repayment. *See* PRIOR CHARGE.

Irredeemable Security A security issued with no date of redemption laid down. *See* SECURITIES.

Iso-Cost Map A graph or diagram in which the variations of the cost of supply with distance from any centre of supply can be shown by means of isopleths.

Iso-Outlay Curves Curves or contours graphically connecting all those combinations of input quantities which can be bought for the same outlay.

Isoquant A curve, every point on which represents the same quantity of output but a different combination of the factors of production. *See* Figure 6. If the relative price of one unit of capital and one unit of labour is represented by AB, then the point of tangency X gives the combination of those factors which produce the output Q at minimum cost. It is at this point that the marginal rate of substitution of the factors of production is exactly equal to their relative price. The isoquant in relation to the producer may be compared with the indifference curve (q.v.) in relation to the consumer.

Issue *See* PUBLIC ISSUE.

Issue Price In respect of public issues and offers for sale of equities (q.v.), the prospectus price of the shares. In placings it is the price of the shares to clients; in offers for sale by tender it is the price determined by the tendering. *See* PLACING; OFFER FOR SALE; OFFER FOR SALE BY TENDER; PUBLIC ISSUE.

Issued Capital That part of the authorised capital of a company which has been subscribed. Such capital may be fully-paid-up, or partly paid up.

Issuing House Financial firm specialising in the issuing or floating of new securities for governments, municipalities and companies. The issuing house undertakes that the whole of a new issue of securities will be sold and makes all necessary arrangements such as advertising the prospectus, etc.; arrangements are made with underwriters to take such part of the issue as is not subscribed to by the public, paying the underwriter a fee of so much per cent. *See* ISSUING HOUSES ASSOCIATION.

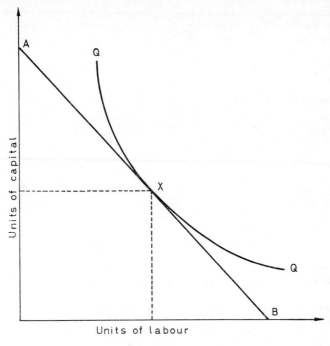

FIGURE 6 ISOQUANT

Issuing Houses Association An Association, formed in 1945, to promote the common interests of Issuing Houses. *See* ISSUING HOUSE.

143

J

Jarrow In the "thirties", a town of some 36,000 population whose livelihood depended almost entirely on a single shipyard—Palmer's Yard. In 1934 the yard was closed and 57 per cent (some 6,000 persons) of the insured population were unemployed. In 1937 the Special Areas Commissioners acquired the yard for industrial development. The fate of Jarrow was described by Ellen Wilkinson (1891–1947) in her book, *The Town that was Murdered*.

Jawbone (U.S.) Descriptive of verbal appeals as an aspect of the voluntary approach to the implementation of monetary policy. During periods when restraint in bank lending is desirable, the Federal Reserve Board and Reserve Banks may appeal to the commercial banks to scrutinise loan applications particularly carefully giving priority to loans which will add to productive capacity. *See* MORAL SUASION.

Jenkins Committee A Committee charged with the task of reviewing the Companies Act 1948. The most immediate of the Committee's proposals was that companies should give full and up-to-date information on the real value of assets, turnover, profits, reserves, etc. Such information was already supplied by the more progressive companies to their shareholders. *See* COMPANIES ACTS 1948 AND 1967.

Job Production The manufacture of an article to a customer's specification. *See* BATCH PRODUCTION; MASS PRODUCTION.

Jobbers *See* STOCKJOBBER.

Joint Demand A situation which exists when the satisfaction of a want involves two or more separate commodities being used in conjunction with each other, e.g. knives and forks, petrol and motor-cars, pens and ink, records and record players.

Joint Industrial Councils Or Whitley Councils, permanent joint bodies of employers and employees whose function is to consider matters affecting the progress and well-being of the trade concerned from the point of view of all those engaged in it, so far as is consistent with the general interests of the community.

Joint Products A situation in which a single productive process results in the production of two or more products, e.g. the rearing of cattle produces both meat and hides.

Joint-Stock Banks Deposit banks whose business is mainly or exclusively in the United Kingdom, e.g. the clearing banks, the Scottish banks (q.v.), the Northern Irish banks and other domestic banks which are members of the British Bankers' Association.

Joint Supply A situation in which the supply of one commodity inevitably involves the supply of another, e.g. beef and hides. An increase in the supply of beef involves an increase in the supply of hides; an increased demand for one may be accompanied by reduced prices for the other.

Junking (U.S.) The replacement of obsolete machines by better machines.

K

Kaffirs South African mining shares.

Kennedy Round A description used for negotiations which led to an extensive and substantial reduction of tariffs. The U.S. Trade Expansion Act, 1962, empowered the U.S. President (then President John F. Kennedy) to cut tariffs by up to 50 per cent on a wide range of goods, subject to reciprocity. Ministers of G.A.T.T. member countries met in 1963 to decide the broad lines that the negotiations should take and agreed that negotiations should begin on 4th May, 1964, in Geneva. After three years of Kennedy Round negotiations it was decided on the 15th May, 1967, that tariff reductions of up to 50 per cent on industrial commodities would become effective by 1972 between the participating countries. These extensive tariff reductions mean that tariffs are no longer a formidable barrier to trade and the result should be an accelerated expansion of world trade. Other non-tariff barriers, such as quotas, remain however, while primary producing countries did not fare well in the Kennedy Round negotiations. *See* GENERAL AGREEMENT ON TARIFFS AND TRADE (G.A.T.T.); TARIFF (a).

Key Industry An industry (q.v.) which by reason of its size, location, product, or other characteristic, possesses a dominating influence within a sector of the economy or in the economy as a whole.

Keynesian Revolution Appellation for the profound changes in fundamental economic thinking brought about by the challenging contributions of John Maynard Keynes (1884–1946). Keynes (pronounced Canes) was educated at Eton and King's College, Cambridge. In 1913, after a short period at the India Office, he published his first book "Indian Currency and Finance". In 1919, he was principal Treasury representative at the Versailles peace conference, but resigned following profound disagreement with some of the aims of the conference. His views subsequently found expression in a treatise *The Economic Consequences of the Peace.* In 1925, he opposed the return to a gold standard embodying his arguments in another treatise *The Economic Consequences of Mr. Churchill* (later incorporated in his book *Essays in Persuasion*). He was outspoken in his criticisms of the failure to deal with the chronic unemployment problems of the inter-war years, advocating large-scale public works on loan account as one of the remedies. This was a view strongly opposed by the Treasury of that day, as exemplified in the

White Paper *Memorandum on Certain Proposals Relating to Unemployment* published in 1929.

In 1930, Keynes published the first of his two main works *A Treatise on Money* in which he sought to establish certain fundamental equations relating changes in the purchasing power of money to relative changes in savings and investment. In 1936 appeared Keynes' most famous work *The General Theory of Employment, Interest and Money*. The *General Theory* is basically an analysis in terms of fundamental economic principles of the causes of unemployment, that is, unemployment over and above "frictional" unemployment arising from people changing jobs. In it he argued that there were fundamental errors in the premises underlying classical and neo-classical economic theory and that the automatic self-righting qualities that had been attributed to the economic system were fictitious. For example, traditional theory held that in the case of the labour market, as in that of other markets, the price of labour tended to be adjusted to a level at which all labour would find employment. According to this theory, therefore, labour had only to lower its price for full employment to be restored. The *General Theory* analyses the possibility of stable equilibrium with high unemployment with no natural forces tending to redress it, irrespective of the price of labour. Employment, Keynes argued, was determined by total effective demand which depended upon the propensity to consume and the propensity to invest. Traditional theory maintained that if there was a tendency for voluntary saving to exceed voluntary investment, the rate of interest would fall thus stimulating investment and reducing savings until the two balanced. Keynes maintained that the rate of interest did not do this; he argued that the rate of interest was not directly affected by the balance between savers and those who wanted to invest in capital equipment, but was affected by the balance of advantage in holding money as compared with other assets, i.e. by the degree of "liquidity-preference". If under the influence of liquidity-preference the rate of interest is such that, when there is full employment, the amount which people wish to save exceeds the amount required for capital outlay, effective demand for goods and services will be less than adequate. Redundant stocks will appear accompanied by a fall in profit margins; the consequent reduction in orders for goods will drive down the level of employment. A point will be reached at which the total which individuals wish to save no longer exceeds the amount required by business undertakings. Thus the "equilibrating mechanism" was not the rate of interest but the level of employment. The idea that supply creates its own demand (*See* SAY'S LAW OF MARKETS) disappeared, together with the idea that unemployment is due primarily to the unwillingness of people to work for sufficiently low wages. The practical policy which flowed from Keynes' theory was that the banks should influence the rates of interest towards a level that would stimulate as much new capital outlay as was required to absorb the savings that would occur when the economy was fully employed. This policy should be coupled with one of public works, e.g. the construction of public utilities and houses. Investment would have a "multiplying" effect in raising effective demand. Keynes' "General Theory" evoked a storm of controversy, although in the following ten years many became converted to his way of thinking. Indeed, the White Paper on *Employment Policy* (Cmd. 6527) published in 1944 marked official recognition of the victory of the Keynesian Revolution—the Government now accepts responsibility for the maintenance of a "high and stable level of employment".

Keynes was very much concerned both during and after the Second World War with "lend-lease" and loan negotiations. He led the British delegation at the Bretton Woods Conference in 1944. It was at this Conference that a scheme for international currency, mainly devised by Keynes, was put forward by the British Treasury. Known as the "Keynes Plan" it aimed at increasing multi-lateral trade through stable exchange rates and freely convertible currencies. It envisaged the setting up of an international institution (as indeed happened in the form of the International Monetary Fund) and the introduction of an international unit of account, which Keynes called "Bancor". The Americans put forward the White Plan and the decisions taken at Bretton Woods represented a compromise between the two schemes. Keynes, who had received a peerage in 1942, died in 1946. In 1951 appeared Sir Roy Harrod's *Life of John Maynard Keynes*. See BRETTON WOODS AGREEMENT; LIQUIDITY PREFERENCE; PROPENSITIES TO CONSUME AND SAVE; MULTIPLIER; SAVINGS EQUAL INVESTMENT; WASHINGTON AGREEMENT.

Keynes Plan A scheme for an international currency, devised by Lord Keynes (1884–1946), put forward by the British Treasury prior to the Bretton Woods Conference in 1944. Its aim was to increase multilateral trade (q.v.) through stable exchange rates and freely convertible currencies; it envisaged the setting up of an international monetary fund and the introduction of an international unit of account which was to be known as "Bancor". The Bretton Woods Agreement (q.v.) was the product of a compromise between the Keynes Plan and the White Plan put forward by the United States. *See* KEYNESIAN REVOLUTION.

Kite A bill, often called an "accommodation bill" (q.v.), drawn on a person who has received nothing in return. It is an expedient for obtaining credit for a short period.

"Knock Out" Agreement An agreement by a dealer to give a person a consideration for abstaining from bidding at an auction sale. Such an agreement is illegal under the Auctions (Bidding Agreements) Act 1927.

L

Labour One of the "factors of production" (q.v.); the combination of all exertions by individuals, whether they be manual, physical or mental, directed towards the production of wealth (q.v.). Labour is quantitative, involving both effort and time; it is also qualitative, both intelligence and skill determining its efficiency.

Labour-Costs Per Unit of Output The cost of the labour in real terms involved in making each unit of output from a factory. High wages associated with high productivity may mean a lower labour cost per unit than low wages associated with low productivity.

Labour, Division of *See* DIVISION OF LABOUR.

Labour-Intensive Description of industries in which there is a considerable use of labour in relation to the amount of capital equipment, per unit of output. In a labour-intensive industry, capital charges may amount to only 20 per cent or less of the costs of production, excluding raw materials and fuel. *See* CAPITAL-INTENSIVE; RESEARCH-INTENSIVE.

Labour-Mix In a business enterprise, the proportion of salary-earners to wage-earners.

Labour, Mobility of The ease of movement of labour between areas and occupations. Movement from one area to another is known as geographic or lateral mobility. Occupational movement is described as vertical mobility.

Labour, Productive and Non-Productive Productive labour is all effort, by hand and brain, which contributes to the supply of goods and services which command a price. The definition thus embraces the work of bricklayers, machinists, labourers, engineers, solicitors, teachers, civil servants and nurses. Adam Smith (1723–1790) adopted a more narrow view, regarding labour as productive or non-productive according as the efforts in question did or did not result in the production of tangible material objects. Today even labour involved in the production of material objects is not considered productive if the objects produced have no exchange value.

Labour, Specialisation of *See* DIVISION OF LABOUR.

Labour Turnover The number of workers who leave, or are replaced, in a given period expressed as a percentage of the average number of workers employed during the period.

Labour Unit A term used by John Maynard Keynes (1883–1946) in the sense of a unit of ordinary labour; labour that was paid, for example, twice as high as ordinary labour being counted as two labour units. Labour could be made homogeneous by this device.

Lag, Decision-Making Time-lag between the receipt of information by a decision-maker and the taking of action on it; this is partly because there is a minimum time in which a thoughtful and wise decision can be made, and partly because there is often institutional inflexibility about decision-making, e.g. the need for decisions to be embodied in an annual Budget.

Lag, Informational Time-lag between the occurrence of an event and the appearance of the statistics relating to it. Thus the policy-maker tends to see only "yesterday", not "today".

Lag, Policy-Effect Time-lag between the implementation of a policy and its full direct and indirect effects on the economy, or a particular industry or business.

Lagged Relationship Between x and y, a relationship in which the value of y at any point in time depends on the value of x at a previous point in time, e.g. what is produced now (y) is not determined so much by present prices but, as production takes time, by prices (x) prevailing at some previous time when production plans were made.

Laggers *See* ECONOMIC INDICATORS.

Laissez-Faire A policy of non-interference by the State in economic affairs. The underlying philosophy is that man is moved predominantly by self-interest and that there exist certain immutable laws which produce a natural harmony. It is argued that if everyone is left alone to pursue his own interests (to produce, buy and sell, borrow and lend) without outside interference, then the result will be to the mutual benefit of all. The laws of supply and demand will ensure the best deployment of capital and labour; the function of government is, therefore, to act as umpire and not to take part in the game.
Historically, laissez-faire was the expression of the new individualism as applied to industry; it constituted a revolt against all ecclesiastical and government interference in the affairs of commerce and industry. Its evolution can be traced back to the 15th century. By the early 19th century most economists and the governing classes in Britain had come to believe in laissez-faire. The policy found its advocates in Adam Smith (1723–1790), David Ricardo (1772–1823), Thomas Robert Malthus (1766–1834), John Stuart Mill (1806–1873) and John Locke (1632–1704). The practical expression of the philosophy did much to ensure the development of commerce and industry. The system did not produce all the good results that were expected, and the reaction to its failings found expression in factory and health legislation, trade unionism and socialism. In western countries today state intervention in the economic sphere is widespread and increasing; in communist countries it is all embracing. As Sir Hubert Henderson has remarked—"A considerable departure from

laissez-faire is necessary in order to realise the theoretical results of laissez-faire".

Land One of the factors of production (q.v.) It is virtually fixed in quantity, although the supply of useful land may be increased by the use of fertilisers, irrigation and machinery. Land, in the economic sense, includes natural resources such as coal, oil and water. It has no cost of production, and in this respect differs fundamentally from the other two factors, labour and capital.

Land Commission A commission which came into being in Britain on 6th April, 1967. It has two main functions:

(a) to collect for the Treasury (q.v.) a special tax on property development values known as the "betterment levy". Any normal increase in the market value of property, without any development element, is not subject to this levy and is taxed as a capital gain. Local authorities and other public bodies, housing associations, and some charities are exempt from the levy; and,

(b) to acquire, manage and dispose of land which, in its opinion, is "suitable for material development". The commission can acquire land by agreement or by compulsory purchase (the latter only when the land has planning approval). It can sell its land to any developer, public or private. It may sell land for housing at less than the market price. Land may be disposed of under a special tenure known as Crownhold, in which the commission retains to itself all future development value.

Laspeyres' Index A type of index often used for measuring changes, e.g. in prices. It is relatively easy to construct and uses base-period weights. The index utilises the following method:

$$\frac{\Sigma P_n\, q_o}{\Sigma P_o\, q_o}$$

where, P_o = price in the base-year; q_o = quantity in the base-year; and P_n = price in the year being considered. In times of rising prices, the index tends to over-estimate price increases. The reason for this is that no account is taken of the possible fall in the consumption of those goods whose prices have grown fastest, or of the possible increase in consumption of those goods whose prices have fallen, relatively speaking. *See* PAASCHE INDEX.

Lay Days Number of days allowed for the loading and unloading of a ship. For any days taken in excess of the agreed number "demurrage" (q.v.) becomes payable.

Lead Time The elapsed time between the placing of an order and receipt of the goods.

Leaders *See* ECONOMIC INDICATORS.

Lease An arrangement whereby the use of land or buildings is granted by a landlord, or lessor, to a tenant, or lessee, for a specified term of years at an agreed annual rental.

Least Squares Method A mathematical procedure for computing the average relationship between two variables. The two variables may be shown as a series of points on a "scatter" diagram; a straight line may indicate the general or average relationship between the two variables. The "best straight line" is that which minimises the sum of the squares of deviations of the observed values from the line. The equations for obtaining this minimum sum are:

$$\Sigma(y) = Na + b\Sigma(x)$$
$$\text{and } \Sigma(xy) = a\Sigma(x) + b\Sigma(x^2)$$

when x and y = the variables; N = the number of pairs of variables; and a and b = constants. The two equations are secured by substituting the original values of x and y; these equations are then solved simultaneously for a and b, the generalised equation for the average relationship being:

$$y = a + bx$$

The least squares method is used extensively in economic computation for estimating secular trends. *See* REGRESSION ANALYSIS.

Legacy Duty A tax levied on what is received by the individual heirs to an estate.

Legal Tender Money which a person is obliged by law to accept in payment of a debt. Under the Decimal Currency Act 1969 token money is declared to be legal tender up to certain amounts, e.g.
- (a) for bronze coins, up to twenty new pence or four shillings;
- (b) for coins of not more than ten new pence or two shillings, up to five pounds;
- (c) for cupro-nickel or silver coins of more than ten new pence or two shillings, up to ten pounds.

In terms of coins issued, this means the 2p, 1p and ½p can be used to pay amounts up to 20p or 4s; the 10p and 5p for payments up to £5; and the 50p can be used for payments up to £10. Bank of England (q.v.) notes, under the Currency and Bank Notes Act 1928, are legal tender to any amount.

Lender of Last Resort A traditional role of the Bank of England (q.v.); it is the one bank which will never refuse assistance to discount houses, if it is asked for. The Bank will rediscount at Bank Rate (q.v.) acceptable bills of exchange or Treasury bills tendered by the discount houses; or more commonly the discount houses will be lent money, also at Bank Rate, against "eligible paper" such as bills of exchange, Treasury bills or short-term government securities, for a minimum period of seven days. The discount houses may become short of money by the calling in of loans by the commercial banks (q.v.). As they borrow for very short periods and lend for somewhat longer periods, this right to borrow from the Bank of England is essential for their operations. *See* DISCOUNT HOUSE.

Letter of Credit (a) An order in writing from a banker to his agent abroad, or to a banker abroad, to authorise the payment of a sum of money to the person named in the letter; (b) An arrangement facilitating early payment for goods despatched overseas. An overseas seller will stipulate in his contract with the buyer concerned that the buyer shall establish a letter of credit in the seller's favour. This provides that, as soon as the seller has the documents, such as Bills of Lading (q.v.), showing that the goods are in course of shipment, he can present them to a bank for payment.

Letter of Hypothecation A letter from an exporter to his bank authorising it, in the event of the importer failing to accept or pay a bill of exchange (q.v.), to sell the goods exported and remit the proceeds less expenses. If the bank makes an advance to the exporter such a letter enables it to recover the loan by selling the goods, if the importer does not pay.

Letter of Regret A letter conveying regret sent to an applicant who has applied for new shares in response to an offer for sale but has been unsuccessful. *See* ALLOTMENT LETTER.

Letter of Renunciation Method by which a shareholder may assign part or all of his rights to subscribe to a "rights issue" (q.v.) to someone else.

Leverage (U.S.) The ratio between bonds and preferred stock in relation to common stock. A stock has a "high leverage" if the company has a large proportion of bonds and preferred stock in relation to the amount of common stock. *See* CAPITAL GEARING.

Lien The right to retain the property of another person until debts due from that person have been paid.

Life The assumed length of "life" of a capital asset, expressed in years, adopted for the purpose of economic appraisals or in making provision for depreciation (q.v.). A "life" is the estimated average life for the class of asset considered having regard to physical life and to obsolescence. Examples are:

	Years
Power stations	30
Chemical plant	11
Motor vehicles	10
Houses	60
Warehouses	60
Factory buildings	45
Office buildings	45

Lighterage Charges made for the conveyance of goods by lighter or barge.

Limited Liability An arrangement, authorised by statute since 1855, under which a shareholder in a business cannot lose more than the amount he has paid for his shares (i.e. the fully paid amount). The introduction of the principle of limited liability has been one of the most important developments in modern industrial organisation. With limited liability investors are more willing to lend money and it provides a means of financing large-scale production or projects. To the investor, it opens up an opportunity for spreading risks by holding shares in a large number of different companies. Without limited liability, every person sharing in the ownership of a business is jointly responsible for the debts of his firm to the full extent of his private resources. British bankruptcy law is extremely exacting; a bankrupt may be left with only the clothes he wears, his bedding and the tools of his trade. Limited liability companies are of two types, private limited companies (q.v.) and public limited companies (q.v.).

Limited Order   Instruction to a stockbroker (q.v.) to buy or sell shares at specified prices only. *See* MARKET ORDER.

Limiting Factor   A factor in the activities of an undertaking which at a particular point in time or over a period will tend to limit the volume of output.

"Line and Staff" Administration   A system of administration. The "Line" consists of a chain of administrators responsible for deciding on policy and its execution. The "Staff" comprises the technical advisers to each level in the line; they advise on the best technical means of carrying out the policy decided by the "Line".

Linear Programming   A mathematical technique for allocating limited resources to a number of activities in the most effective manner. For example, it can be applied to the problem of how best to use a fleet of vehicles taking varying quantities of material from production points to a changing number of consumer points.

Liquid Assets   Assets either in the form of money, or which can be quickly converted into money. The liquid assets of a commercial bank are coin, notes, and balances at the Bank of England; money at call or short notice; and discounted bills.

Liquid, To be   To hold cash.

Liquidation   The conversion of assets (q.v.) into cash, when they are not already in that form. In terminating or winding-up a business, "going into liquidation" means not only converting assets into cash but also the paying of all business debts and the distribution of the balance of cash, if any, among the owners of the business. *See* BANKRUPTCY; OFFICIAL RECEIVER.

Liquidity   The ability to meet current financial liabilities in cash.

Liquidity Preference   The degree of preference for holding money instead of securities (q.v.). If the "liquidity-preference" of the community increases, this means that the demand for money increases, while the demand for securities falls. Lord Keynes defined three motives for the holding of money:
  (a) the transactions motive, i.e. the need for cash to meet current requirements;
  (b) the precautionary motive, i.e. to have something in hand to meet unforeseen contingencies;
  (c) the speculative motive, arising from uncertainty regarding the future rate of interest.
  Expressed mathematically, the quantity of money which the public will hold when the rate of interest is given is $M = L(r)$, where M is the quantity of money, L the function of liquidity-preference and r the rate of interest.

Liquidity Preference Theory of Interest A Keynesian theory which attributes the rate of interest to the demand for and supply of money and money substitutes, with demand being determined by liquidity preference (q.v.) and the supply by banking policy. Liquidity preference is held to vary inversely with the rate of interest, and vice versa. Thus when interest rates are high little cash is demanded by the economy because liquidity preference is weak. Conversely, when interest rates are low, more cash is demanded as liquidity preference is strong. *See* INTEREST; LOANABLE FUNDS THEORY OF INTEREST.

Liquidity Ratio The ratio of 28 per cent which British banks conventionally maintain between their liquid, or relatively liquid, assets including cash, money at call and short notice (q.v.), Treasury bills and commercial bills, and their total deposits. Until September, 1963, it was a convention that this ratio should be 30 per cent; at the request of the banks it was agreed by the Bank of England (q.v.) that the ratio should be lowered to 28 per cent. *See* CASH RATIO (a).

Listed Security A security recognised by a stock exchange (q.v.) for trading on that exchange. *See* SECURITIES.

Liverpool Cotton Exchange A highly organised market for cotton. Cotton is graded by the Liverpool Cotton Association, which consists of merchants, brokers and spinners. The prices quoted on the market are for immediate delivery i.e. "spot" (q.v.) and for future delivery, i.e. "futures" (q.v.). Thus cotton may be sold before it arrives at port, and indeed even before the crop has been harvested.

Lloyd's The Corporation of Lloyd's, a City institution which pioneered marine insurance, brought a greater measure of safety to shipping, and built up a complicated information service with signal stations and agents throughout the world. Insurance has not been confined to marine risks, however, and it is now possible to insure at Lloyd's against almost any kind of risk. Anyone wishing to accept insurance business at Lloyd's must satisfy the governing committee that he is a man of wealth and reliability. Those admitted as members of the society carry on insurance business through appointed representatives known as underwriters. The society has about 4,500 members. Lloyd's has grown enormously in size since it began in the coffee house of Edward Lloyd, near the Tower of London, about 1734.

Lloyd's List A daily paper which sets out the movements of ships the world over and is thus indispensable not only to those engaged in marine insurance, but also to shippers, wharfingers, exporters, importers and many others. *Lloyd's List*—London's oldest daily newspaper—and *Lloyd's Shipping Index* which is separate from *Lloyd's List*, are both published daily by Lloyd's and keep track of the latest movements of over 13,000 ocean-going vessels. *See* LLOYD'S REGISTER OF SHIPPING.

Lloyd's Register of Shipping A society of underwriters, shippers and merchants. The society not only compiles a complete list of all ships in the world over 100 tons: it has laid down definite ship-building standards, and through over one thousand surveyors, stationed at the principal ports at home and abroad, sees that these standards are put into effect. When these surveyors are satisfied they will class a ship A1. *See* A1 AT LLOYD'S.

Load Factor The total number of units actually sent out from a plant during a period (usually a year) expressed as a percentage of what would have been sent out if the plant had been worked at maximum capacity throughout the period.

Load/Rate Tariff A tariff for the supply of electricity in which the consumer pays a standing charge related to the demand he subscribes for, and when his demand is less than the subscribed demand the units consumed are charged at a low price; when his demand is above the subscribed demand the units of electricity in excess are charged for at a relatively high price. This form of tariff is used extensively in Norway. *See* TARIFF (b).

Loanable Funds Theory of Interest A theory that interest rates are determined by the supply of, and the demand for, funds available for lending. The supply of such funds is determined mainly by: (a) the extent of savings, and (b) the net increase in deposit currency. The demand for such funds is determined mainly by: (a) the opportunities for new capital formation, and (b) the desire to increase cash balances. The theory has much in common with the liquidity preference theory of interest. *See* INTEREST; LIQUIDITY PREFERENCE THEORY OF INTEREST.

Local Employment Acts 1960 to 1966 Government measures applied to areas with unemployment in excess of a certain proportion of the working population. They provide for three estate management corporations, one each for England, Wales and Scotland, and give the Government and local authorities special powers to attract industry to development districts (q.v.). By 1963, about £75 m. worth of aid had been provided under the Acts to start 340 projects. These were expected to provide 80,000 new jobs.

Local Taxes *See* RATES.

Location of Industry, Factors Influencing The factors influencing the location of industry may be defined as:
  (a) Availability and cost of raw materials of satisfactory quality and security of future supplies;
  (b) Delivery costs of sending the final product to markets of sufficient size and certainty, and competitiveness of the product in those markets;
  (c) Availability of labour having regard both to number and degree of competence required;
  (d) Transport and communications;

(e) Level of local costs generally (rents, rates, wages, etc.);
(f) Adequacy of local resources such as water supply and facilities for waste disposal;
(g) Availability, reliability and cost of fuel;
(h) Availability of local specialised industries and services;
(i) Load bearing requirements for site;
(j) Cost of site development (land cost, levelling, filling, drainage, roads, etc.);
(k) Possibility of development of site for additional plant in due course;
(l) Availability of housing, local transportation, schools, churches, hospitals and recreation facilities;
(m) Planning and development restrictions and inducements.

Clearly the "weighting" given to each of these items will vary according to the type of business activities involved. The primary reason for a plant location study by a company is to find a site at which a plant of suitable size can produce the highest return on invested capital; the aim is to establish the optimum size of plant at the optimum location. The problem of location involves highly complex studies concerned not only with present but also future conditions and changing patterns, and often involves difficult decisions. *See* DISTRIBUTION OF INDUSTRY ACT 1945; LOCAL EMPLOYMENT ACTS 1960 TO 1966.

Lock-Out The refusal by an employer to admit his employees to their place of work. Opposite of strike (q.v.).

Loco Buyer to pay all transport costs.

Lombard Street An expression used to denote the London Money Market. *See* MONEY MARKET.

"London and Cambridge Economic Bulletin" A supplement prepared for *The Times* (Business News) by the London and Cambridge Economic Service. The editorial committee comprises members of the London School of Economics and the University of Cambridge.

London Commodity Exchange A market for almost every commodity which does not have an exchange of its own, e.g. cocoa, jute, rubber and sugar.

London Discount Market Or money market, a market the principal function of which is to match the needs of the borrowers of money for short periods of time with the funds available from the lenders of such money. The money market comprises the twelve discount houses of the City of London, the commercial banks (q.v.), the accepting houses, and the Bank of England (q.v.). *See* ACCEPTING HOUSE; DISCOUNT HOUSE; LONDON DISCOUNT MARKET ASSOCIATION; MONEY MARKET.

London Discount Market Association An Association of the twelve discount houses of the City of London. Each of the twelve houses enjoys the privilege of a Loan Account at the Discount office of the Bank of England. The Bank of England never refuses to lend to members of the Association. *See* LENDER OF LAST RESORT.

London Gold Market A major free market for gold bullion. The market was closed between September, 1939, and March, 1954. It was closed again briefly between 15th March and 1st April, 1968, as a result of a crisis in gold. Since 29th December, 1958, all currently earned sterling in the hands of non-residents has been freely convertible into gold. The gold market is served by five firms dealing in gold bullion; representatives of the firms meet each working day to fix the official London gold price, but prices may vary considerably during the course of a day. *See* INTERNATIONAL GOLD POOL.

London Metal Exchange Founded in 1881, an Exchange for the sale of copper, tin, lead and zinc. All business is conducted by or through the members of the "Ring". Dealings, mainly in futures, are settled verbally across the Ring, the members making "bids" or "offers". Closed during the Second World War, the Exchange was fully restored by the early 1950s.

Long A description of a buyer or holder of securities (q.v.) who has more of a particular security than he has contracted to deliver; the "longs" are usually those who have bought expecting a rise in prices. *See* SHORT.

Long- and Short-Period As defined by Alfred Marshall (1842–1924), the long-period is one in which there is time for the supply of those things which are used in producing a commodity to adapt themselves to demand whereas the short-period does not allow such a movement. Depending on the case in mind, therefore, the short-period could vary from an hour to several months or even years.

Loose Times Times prescribed by management for the completion of certain tasks, which are over-generous.

Loss and Gain Account (U.S.) *See* PROFIT AND LOSS ACCOUNT.

Loss Leader A good sold by a retailer below normal retail price, not for the purpose of making a profit on the sale of the good, but for the purpose of attracting customers likely to purchase other goods at his shop. Under the Resale Prices Act 1964, it is lawful for a supplier to withhold goods from a retailer who has been using goods of the same description as loss leaders.

Lump Sum Contract A type of contract under which the contractor agrees to undertake and complete constructional works for a given price; if costs exceed price the loss is borne by the contractor.

Luxury A commodity or service which satisfies a secondary need in respect of food, clothing, shelter or entertainment. While the nature of a luxury may suggest an elastic demand, much depends in a particular case on the availability of close substitutes; thus a particular luxury may have a quite inelastic demand. *See* NECESSITY.

M

"Macmillan Gap" A "gap" in the pre-war capital market which consisted of a lack of provision for the supply to smaller and medium-sized firms of long-dated capital in amounts too small for a public issue. The Macmillan Committee's Report made proposals for dealing with this need. New institutions such as the Industrial and Commercial Finance Corporation Ltd. and the Charterhouse Industrial Development Co. Ltd. have come into existence to meet the situation. *See* FINANCE CORPORATIONS; MACMILLAN REPORT.

Macmillan Report The Report of the Committee on Finance and Industry, 1931.

Macro-Economics A branch of economics (q.v.) concerned with the analysis of the economy in the large, i.e. with such large aggregates as the volume of employment, saving and investment, the national income, and so on. *See* MICRO-ECONOMICS.

Malthusian Theory of Population A theory of population developed by Thomas R. Malthus (1766-1834) and published in *An Essay on the Principle of Population* in 1798. The essence of the theory may be summarised as follows:
  (1) That population would soon outstrip the means of feeding it, if it were not kept down by vice, misery or self-restraint;
  (2) That in a state of society where self-restraint does not act at all, or only acts so little that we need not think of it, population will augment until the poorest class of the community have only just enough to support life;
  (3) That in a community where self-restraint acts effectually, each class of the community will augment until it reaches the point at which it begins to exercise that restraint.

Population, Malthus declared, tended to increase in a geometrical progression, whereas the means of subsistence increased in only arithmetical progression. The *Essay* was recast in a second edition in 1803; in this the author somewhat modifies his gloomy forbodings, hoping that personal restraint might prove an effective factor in the check to an increasing population.

Managed Currency A currency system which is not based on a metallic standard such as the "gold standard" (q.v.) which was regarded, in its pure form, as a more or less automatic system, but is one in which the quantity of money in the country is regulated by the monetary authorities.

Management Accounting The services which an accountant can offer to management to assist in the formulation of policy, the control of its execution and the assessment of its effectiveness.

Management Ratios A method of providing management with information in which the levels of various activities in a business are measured one against another. For example:

(1) $\dfrac{\text{Production costs}}{\text{production}}$

(2) $\dfrac{\text{Production overheads}}{\text{production}}$

(3) $\dfrac{\text{General and Administration Costs}}{\text{production}}$

(4) $\dfrac{\text{Production}}{\text{assets employed}}$

Manchester School A group of men, active during the period 1820–1850, who advocated free trade and opposed most encroachments into laisser-faire (q.v.) in economic and social matters. Bright and Cobden were prominent leaders of the group.

"Manchester School, The" A quarterly publication of the University of Manchester, England, devoted to economic and social subjects.

Manufacturing Industry Or secondary industry, the processing of raw materials into finished products. *See* EXTRACTIVE INDUSTRY.

Marginal To the economist, a term meaning "extra". *See* MARGINAL ANALYSIS, ETC.

Marginal Analysis A tool of analysis found in all branches of economic theory, marginal analysis is concerned with the utility of successive units of a commodity or service and with the costs of successive units of a factor of production. *See* "MARGINAL" REVOLUTION.

Marginal Consumer A consumer who would increase or reduce the consumption of something by one unit if the price of that something fell or rose very slightly.

Marginal Cost The additional cost of producing each successive increment of output; the cost of producing M + 1 units, minus the cost of producing M units.

Marginal Costing The ascertainment of the cost of producing an additional unit. This is achieved by differentiating between fixed costs (q.v.) and variable costs (q.v.). The effect on profit of changes in volume and type of output may then be considered.

Marginal Costs, Long-Run The costs of supplying on a continuous basis those services and products which can be costed separately; they include provision for the replacement of fixed assets needed for the continued provision of services, together with a satisfactory rate of return on capital employed.

Marginal Costs, Short-Run The additional costs of increasing output in the short-run.

Marginal Demand Price, Law of Diminishing A proposition that an increase in the amount of a commodity that a person has will, other things being equal, diminish his marginal demand price for it. A corollary of the Law of Diminishing Marginal Utility.

Marginal Efficiency of Capital The earning power of the last increment of capital invested; or, as defined by Keynes in his *General Theory of Employment, Interest and Money* (1936), "the relation between the prospective yield of one more unit of a type of capital and the cost of producing that unit."

Marginal Firm A firm which is the last to enter, or the first to leave, a particular line of production. It is not necessarily the least efficient firm and may, indeed, be the most efficient.

Marginal Land Land which is the last to be brought into, or the first to be taken out of, a particular line of production. This will not necessarily be land which is just worth cultivating.

Marginal Producer A producer who would be just induced to produce a certain commodity at the prevailing level of profits being obtained from it, but if profits fell slightly would withdraw from production.

Marginal Product The amount added to the total product by the addition of one more unit of capital-and-labour. George J. Stigler in his "Theory of Price" makes five propositions regarding the marginal product: (a) The sum of the first n marginal units is equal to the total product of n units of capital-and-labour; (b) When the average product is increasing, the marginal product is greater than the average product, but it does not follow that the marginal product increases when the average product increases; (c) When the average product is decreasing, the marginal product is less than the average product; (d) When the average product is at a maximum, the marginal product equals the average product; and (e) the addition or subtraction of a fixed sum from all of the total products will have no effect on the marginal product.

Marginal Productivity The productivity of the last unit of a factor of production.

Marginal Productivity Theory of Wages *See* WAGES, THEORIES OF.

Marginal Profit The difference between the selling price and the marginal cost (q.v.) of an article.

Marginal Propensities to Consume and Save Concepts developed by John Maynard Keynes (1884–1946), in his *General Theory of Employment, Interest and Money*, which represent the fractions of each extra unit of income which are, respectively, consumed and saved. Their sum is unity, i.e. MPC + MPS = 1. Keynes argued that, as a "normal psychological law", when the real income of the community increases or decreases, its consumption will increase or decrease but not so fast. Expressed mathematically:

$$\triangle Y_w > \triangle C_w$$

where Y_w = income in terms of wage units, and C_w = consumption in terms of wage-units, both terms being positive.

Hence $\dfrac{\triangle C_w}{\triangle Y_w}$ = marginal propensity to consume

and $\dfrac{\triangle I_w}{\triangle Y_w}$ = marginal propensity to save

These concepts are important because they indicate how the next increment of output will be divided between consumption and investment.

Thus $\triangle Y_w = \triangle C_w + \triangle I_w$

where $\triangle C_w$ = increment of consumption, and $\triangle I_w$ = increment of investment.

See MULTIPLIER; PROPENSITIES TO CONSUME AND SAVE.

Marginal Propensity to Import Analogous to the marginal propensity to consume, the marginal propensity to import can be defined as:

$$m = \frac{\triangle M}{\triangle Y} \text{ or } \frac{\triangle M}{\triangle V}$$

where, $\quad$ M = value of all imports (including services);
$\qquad\qquad$ Y = national income;
$\qquad\qquad$ V = total expenditure on consumption and investment goods.

This term was first used by F. W. Paish.

Marginal Purchaser A person who is on the margin of doubt as to whether to buy an article or spend the money on something else, and who just buys.

Marginal Rate of Substitution The amount of commodity Y necessary to offset the loss of one unit of commodity X. The marginal rate of substitution of Y for X increases as the quantity of Y increases relative to that of X. Equality of marginal rates of substitution means that a person could not increase the sum total of his satisfaction by the substitution of one good or service, at the margin, for another.

Marginal Revenue The revenue derived from the sale of an additional unit. It equals the total revenue from N units minus the total revenue from N − 1 units. Under conditions of perfect competition the marginal revenue is constant and is equal to average revenue or price. This is not the case in respect of imperfect or monopolistic competition in which the output of each supplier influences price. To sell an additional unit in these conditions requires a lowering of the price of the marginal and all other units of the supply. The marginal revenue is thus less than the price of the product.

"Marginal" Revolution A description accorded to the contributions of William Stanley Jevons (1835–1882), Carl Menger (1840–1921) and Leon Walras (1834–1910), who solved the apparent conflict between value and utility by recognising that it was the specific utility depending on the last available or marginal unit of a commodity, and not the generic utility, which determined its value. Jevons did not employ the adjective "marginal", using the term "final utility" instead. He published his "Theory of Political Economy", embodying this new theory, in 1871. In the same year Menger produced a similar work in Vienna which is considered the best non-mathematical statement of the principle of marginal utility. Walras' work appeared three years later in Switzerland. The "marginal" approach to the theory of value opened a new period in the history of economic thought.

Marginal Significance *See* MARGINAL UTILITY.

Marginal Social and Private Net Products Concepts associated with the name of A. C. Pigou, the marginal social net product is the total net product of physical things, or objective services, due to the marginal increment of resources in any given use or place, no matter to whom any part of this product may accrue; the marginal private net product is that part of the total net product of physical things, or objective services, due to the marginal increment of resources in any given use or place which accrues in the first instance, i.e. prior to sale, to the person responsible for investing resources there. Pigou's thesis was that, in general, industrialists are interested not in the social, but only in the private, net product of their operations. Self-interest will tend to bring about equality in the values of the marginal private net products of resources invested in different ways; but it will not tend to bring about equality in the values of the marginal social net products, except when marginal private net product and marginal social net product are identical. When there is a divergence between these two sorts of marginal net product, self-interest will not, therefore, tend to make the national dividend (q.v.) a maximum. Such divergences between the social and private net product are likely to occur even under conditions of simple competition. Pigou's view stands in sharp relief to the opinions of the Classical School (q.v.). For example, David Ricardo said, "Where there is free competition the interests of the individual and that of the community are never at variance."

Marginal Unit The marginal unit is the last to be added, or the first to leave a supply.

Marginal Utility The extent to which a consumer's satisfaction would be increased or decreased if he had one more or one less unit of a commodity.

Marginal Utility, Law of Diminishing A proposition that the marginal utility (q.v.) of a commodity to anyone, other things being equal, diminishes with every increase in his supply of it. Alfred Marshall stressed an implicit condition in this law—that we do not suppose time to be allowed for any alteration in the character or tastes of the person concerned. The law explains why most demand curves (q.v.) slope downward to the right, indicating that more goods will be bought at any price than at a higher price. Purchasers tend to equate marginal, not total, utilities.

Marginal Utility of Money The increase or decrease in total utility (q.v.) resulting from the addition or subtraction of one unit of currency to or from the total supply of money of a consumer.

Marginal Value The price at which consumers will just be induced to buy the last increment of the supply of a commodity.

Market An area, however large or small, where buyers and sellers are in sufficiently close contact with each other to ensure that the price of a commodity tends to be the same in all parts of the market, allowance being made for transportation costs, tariff barriers, and other obstacles.

There are markets for all kinds of goods, services, raw materials, foodstuffs, manufactured goods, labour, currency, and so on. A market may be confined to a village or town, or be international in scope. *See* IMPERFECT MARKET; PERFECT MARKET; SPOT MARKET.

Market Conduct The behaviour of firms in changing prices, outputs, product characteristics, selling expenses and research expenditure. Market conduct is influenced by market structure (q.v.).

Market, Imperfect *See* IMPERFECT MARKET.

Market Order Instruction to a stockbroker (q.v.) to buy or sell shares at the best offer price or the best bid price prevailing at the time the instruction is given. *See* LIMITED ORDER.

Market Overt Generally a market held on such days and in such a place as may be prescribed by charter, custom or statute. In the City of London, a market overt means every shop in which goods are exposed for sale, for such things only as are usually sold in the shop.

Market, Perfect *See* PERFECT MARKET.

Market Performance The performance of a firm or industry in a market measured against specified criteria. These criteria or goals may include: (a) the efficient employment of scarce factors of production to yield the greatest possible real income; (b) the full employment of the factors of production; (c) growth and progressiveness in enlarging and improving the flow of goods and services; and (d) equity in the distribution of income.

Market Research A management aid which involves the systematic collecting, recording and analysing of data about problems relating to the marketing of goods and services. Industrial marketing research is confined to industrial markets, marketing activities and inter-industry relationships, whereas consumer marketing research is concerned with the needs and demands of ordinary people. A sub-division of marketing research is "sales analysis" which involves an analysis of data obtained from the internal sales records of a firm.

Market, Sensitive *See* SENSITIVE MARKET.

Market Structure The economically significant features of a market (q.v.) which affect the behaviour of firms in the industry supplying that market. The main elements of market structure are: (a) concentration (q.v.) and concentration ratio (q.v.); (b) product differentiation (q.v.); (c) barriers to the entry of new firms; (d) growth rate of market demand; (e) price elasticity of market demand; (f) ratio of fixed to variable costs in the short run. *See* MARKET CONDUCT.

Market Supply Curve A curve on a graph showing the relationship between the prices of a commodity and the quantities which traders are willing to sell at each of those prices.

Marketing Board An organisation set up to assist producers in the marketing of their product. A number of marketing boards have been established in Britain, e.g. to market eggs, milk and wool. *See* AGRICULTURAL MARKETING ACT 1931.

Markings The daily recording and publication of the prices at which bargains (q.v.) are done on the Stock Exchange (q.v.). It is the task of the unauthorised clerks to fill in, or "mark", special recording slips provided for this purpose.

Mark-up The percentage of profit added to the cost price of goods by traders in order to determine their selling prices.

Marshall Aid *See* EUROPEAN RECOVERY PROGRAMME.

Marshall Plan *See* EUROPEAN RECOVERY PROGRAMME.

Marshall's Theory of Markets A proposition by Alfred Marshall that the larger the market for a commodity the smaller generally are the fluctuations in its price, and the lower the percentage on the turnover which dealers charge for doing business in it.

Marxist Socialism A creed developed by Karl Marx (1818–1883) which had its origin in the conditions created by the Industrial Revolution (q.v.). Of middle class origin, Marx was born on the 5th May 1818 in the city of Trier. He graduated in his home town and then went on to University, first at Bonn and later at Berlin, where he studied jurisprudence, history and philosophy.

He concluded his course in 1841, submitting a doctora ·dissertation on the philosophy of Epicurus. In his views Marx was still a follower of the German philosopher, Hegel. From University, Marx became editor of a Cologne newspaper. Under his editorship the revolutionary trend of the paper became more and more pronounced until in 1843 the Government decided to suppress it altogether. In the same year Marx married Jenny von Westphalen, whose family belonged to the Prussian nobility. In the autumn they moved to Paris, Marx attempting to launch a new radical newspaper. In 1844, Frederich Engels visited Marx and from that time became his closest friend. They both took an active part in the life of the revolutionary groups in Paris and it was during this period that they worked out the theory and practice of revolutionary socialism. In 1845, Marx was banished from Paris, moving to Brussels. There Marx and Engels joined the Communist League; at the request of this League they drew up the famous *Communist Manifesto*. When the revolution broke out in 1848, Marx was banished from Belgium; a year later he moved to London where he lived in dire poverty until his death thirty-four years later. In London, Marx spent a large part of his time in the British Museum, preparing and writing his great work *Das Kapital*. In 1883, two years after the death of his wife, Marx also died. They were buried in Highgate cemetery. Not more than eight people attended Marx's funeral. Engels delivered an address and by way of conclusion said, "The greatest living thinker will think no more. Soon the world will feel the void left by the passing of this Titan . . . his name and his work will live for centuries to come".

Marx attempted to show that the capitalist system could not by its very nature survive, that it would in the course of time be replaced by socialism, and that the class which would effect the revolution would be the new industrial working-class or "proletariat". He formulated the "materialist interpretation of history", viewing society as something undergoing constant change with one event linked to another by a cause and effect relationship. He argued that social classes take shape in response to their share in, and control of, wealth production; thus at any time the class which has the greatest economic power has the greatest political power. He saw the history of all hitherto existing society as the history of class struggles—to quote the *Communist Manifesto*, "Freeman and slave, patrician and plebeian, lord and serf, guild-master and journeyman, in a word, oppressor and oppressed stood in constant opposition to one another, carried on an uninterrupted, now hidden, now open fight, a fight that each time ended, either in a revolutionary reconstitution of society at large, or in the common ruin of the contending classes". In a capitalist system the "bourgeoisie" and the government are one. Marx drew attention to what he called a "contradiction" in the capitalist system, that although production was increasing by leaps and bounds, the workers had not the power to demand a greater share in the new wealth. Marx's argument ran that, in the light of the spectacle of great wealth on the one hand and poverty on the other, the working people would eventually rise and seize power from the ruling classes. Having won, the workers "by hand and brain" could then go forward to the building of socialism—a state of society in which all the means of production, distribution and exchange, are owned in common. Yet even at the time Marx wrote, the facts were not quite as he stated them. The poor were growing rather better off, and the falling mortality rate for children pointed to a real rise in living standards. He did not foresee the growing influence of trade unions, the impact of democracy, or the possibility of progress through evolution.

Mass Production The large scale manufacture of a standardised product by the use of specialised labour and capital equipment.

"Mate's Receipt" A receipt, signed by the mate of a ship, which may be given instead of a bill of lading (q.v.). Later this can be exchanged with the shipowners for a bill of lading.

Mathematical Analysis, Use of Calculus in Calculus, a method of calculation founded simultaneously and independently by Isaac Newton (1642–1727) and Gottfried Willhelm Leibnitz (1646–1716), used as a central technique in mathematical analysis related to economics. The differential calculus deals with the rate of change of a function, and the integral calculus with the inverse of differentiation.

Mathematical Analysis, Use of Greek Letters in A technique for extending the range and flexibility of the notation of mathematical analysis by the use of letters from the Greek alphabet. Table 1 gives the Greek alphabet together with the corresponding English letter in mathematical usage and the purposes for which the letters are used.

TABLE 1

GREEK ALPHABET

	Greek	English	General Usage
α	alpha	a	
β	bēta	b	constants
γ	gamma	c	
κ	kappa	k	
λ	lambda	l	
μ	mu	m	constants, parameters
ν	nu	n	
ξ	xi	x	
η	ēta	y	variables
ζ	zēta	z	
π	pi	p	
ρ	rho	r	special constants or variables
σ	sigma	s	
τ	tau	t	
ϕ	phi	f	
Φ	cap. phi	F	functional operators
ψ	psi	g	
Ψ	cap. psi	G	
δ	delta	d	
Δ	cap. delta	D	operators indicating increments in variables
Σ	cap. sigma	S	summation sign
ϵ	epsilon	—	a small positive constant
θ	thēta	—	a positive fraction

167

Mathematical Analysis, Use of Symbols in The use of symbols common to the whole field of mathematics and relevant in the mathematical analysis of economic problems. These symbols are given, with their meanings, in Table 2.

TABLE 2

MATHEMATICAL SYMBOLS

Symbol	Meaning
$\simeq$, or $\doteqdot$, or $\triangleq$	Approximately equal to
$\equiv$	Identical with
$>$	Greater than
$<$	Less than
$\not>$	Not greater than
$\not<$	Not less than
$\geqslant$	Equal to or greater than
$\leqslant$	Equal to or less than
$+$	Plus
$-$	Minus
$\pm$	Plus or minus
$\times$, or .	Multiplied by
$\div$, or $/$	Divided by
$=$	Equal to
$\neq$	Not equal to
$\propto$	Proportional to
$\gg$	Much greater than
$\ll$	Much less than
$\parallel$	Parallel to
$\perp$	Perpendicular to
$\sqrt{}$	Square root of
$\sim$	Of the order of
∞	Infinity
$\to \infty$	Tend to or approach infinity
Σ	Sum of
Π	Product of
$\lfloor \nu$, or n!	Factorial
$\exists$	There exists
ϵ, δ	Small positive numbers
δx, or Δx	Increment
D	Operator (d/dx)
$\dfrac{dy}{dx}$	Differential coefficient of the function y in respect of x
$\partial/\partial x$	Partial Differential
	Integrals:
$\int y\,dx$	(a) Indefinite
$\int_a^b y\,dx$	(b) Definite
$\oint y\,dx$	(c) Around a closed contour
exp x	e^x (exponential function)
log x	$\log_e x$
Limit f(x) x$\to$a	Limit of f(x) as x tends to a
e	2.71828 . . .(base of natural logarithms)
π	3.14159 . . .
	Efficiency

Mathematical Economics The application of the techniques of mathematical analysis to economic variables, with the object of discovering relationships between those variables. The relationship between variable numbers is symbolised by the term "function". Thus demand is a function of price, price being taken as the independent variable. Instances of variable numbers or quantities in economics are prices, incomes, costs of production, amounts of goods bought or sold on a market, and the amount of factors of production employed by a firm or industry. These can all be converted into numbers of units; some into physical units, others into money or "value" units. Economic relationships are expressible, therefore, by means of mathematical functions. There is a curve corresponding to each function to interpret a relationship between two economic variables, e.g. demand and supply curve. Diagrams of this sort may be used to throw into prominence arguments which are being advanced. The application of mathematical techniques in economics is discussed in Professor R. G. D. Allen's well-known book *Mathematical Analysis for Economists*. Much valuable work is being carried on today at Cambridge and London in the development of mathematical models to take account of all the variables of the nation's economy. *See* ECONOMETRIC MODELS; MATHEMATICAL SCHOOL.

Mathematical Model *See* ECONOMETRIC MODEL.

Mathematical School A school of economists who have adopted a mathematical approach to economic problems. The English economist William Stanley Jevons (1835–1882) belonged to both the Mathematical and Final Utility Schools. In 1862, he presented a paper to the British Association entitled "The General Mathematical Theory of Political Economy". A full exposition of mathematical economics was contained in a work by Léon Walras (1834–1910) of the University of Lausanne entitled *Éléments d'Économie politique pure*, which appeared in 1874. He applied mathematical analysis to a régime of perfectly free competition. Some economists today consider mathematics of limited use in economics; others regard it as an indispensable tool in the study of the workings of the economic system and perhaps the principal way in which applied economics can hope to effectively contribute to national economic forecasting. *See* ECONOMETRIC MODELS for a reference to the work of Professor Richard Stone at Cambridge; *and* MATHEMATICAL ECONOMICS.

Mature Economy *See* ECONOMIC GROWTH, STAGES OF.

Maturity The date upon which a bond (q.v.) or debenture (q.v.) is due to be repaid.

Maximum Demand The largest demand for a good or service by consumers measured over a given period. The period may be of any length such as a half-hour, a day, or a year. *See* SIMULTANEOUS MAXIMUM DEMAND.

Maximum Demand Tariff A tariff for the supply of electricity which, in its simplest form, consists of two parts, a unit charge and a charge levied on the number of kilowatts of electricity of maximum demand registered over, say, half-an-hour. *See* TARIFF (b).

May Report (1931) The Report of the Committee on National Expenditure, headed by Sir George Ernest May, which forecast a large deficit in the budget. It recommended that Government expenditure, including unemployment pay, should be reduced and taxation increased.

McKenna Duties Tariffs introduced by Britain in 1915 with the primary object of cutting down bulky and inessential imports, such as motor-cars from the U.S.A., to save dollars and cargo space. Although intended as a war measure, the tariffs remained after the war, serving as a protection to the home car producer. They were merged into the general tariff in 1938. The McKenna Duties represented a break from Britain's traditional free trade policy since 1860.

Median That value in a distribution which exceeds in magnitude half the values and is exceeded by half the values. When the number of terms is odd, the median is located on the middle term; when the number is even the median is located as halfway between the two middle terms. In the case of a frequency distribution it is the value which will divide the total number of frequencies into halves.

Memorandum of Association A document to be submitted to the Registrar of Companies when seeking registration of a company. The memorandum sets out the name of the company (which in the case of a limited liability company must include "Limited" as its last word), the objects of the company and the amount and sub-division of its authorised (or nominal) share capital. It must be signed by two persons if the company is to be a private one, or by seven if it is to be a public company. *See* ARTICLES OF ASSOCIATION; COMPANY, LEGAL FORMATION OF A.

"Memorandum on Certain Proposals Relating to Unemployment" A White Paper (Cmd. 3331) prepared by the Treasury and published in 1929 to show why a programme of public works designed to relieve unemployment (which had long been above 10 per cent and was shortly to rise to 20 per cent of the labour force) could bring no lasting benefit. The Paper argued that the total fund of saving is given, and if more is used for home investment, foreign lending, and consequently the export surplus, would be reduced correspondingly; there would be no advantage to the economy as a whole. Keynes and other economists regarded the White Paper as "neo-classical theory in action" and the argument a complete fallacy. The White Paper stands in sharp contrast to the White Paper on *Employment Policy* (q.v.) of 1944 in which the Government, accepting responsibility for the maintenance of a "high and stable level of employment" for the first time, recognises the role of public investment and public works in maintaining this level of employment.

Mercantilism A political and economic policy, well-established in England during the 17th and early 18th centuries, aimed at increasing national wealth and power; by means of regulations and endeavour it was hoped to make England supreme among other commercial nations. Mercantilism rested upon five principles:

(1) The state had the duty to foster national welfare by adopting the appropriate economic and power policies, though this involved the exploitation of neighbours and colonies;

(2) The health of the national economy depended partly upon an increase of population; and partly upon,

(3) An increase in the mass of precious metals in the country;

(4) That foreign trade must be stimulated, for only through a favourable balance of trade could the quantity of precious metals be increased— "the most important of the means which make a kingdom without mines abound in gold and silver";

(5) Commerce and industry were of greater importance as branches of the national economy than agriculture.

These ideas no doubt served their purpose; indeed Mercantilism was perhaps the only practicable policy at the time. The phase passed and the views of the Classical School (q.v.) began to take the stage.

Merchant Banks Banks whose business consists mainly of the accepting of commercial bills and the financing of trade.

Merchanting A type of trade which consists of buying goods in one overseas country and selling them in another. Many of these transactions are negotiated in the London Produce Exchanges and other centres.

Merger A union of two or more firms in a transaction by which one absorbs the other(s), or a new firm is created utilising the assets of the absorbed firms.

Metric System A system of weights and measures in which the kilogramme and the metre are the basic units. The system is decimal throughout. The metric system forms the basis of the more recent International System of Units (SI) (q.v.). In May, 1965, the British Government announced that a gradual change to the metric system of weights and measures was favoured. The Government considered it desirable that the greater part of industry should have made the change by 1975. The training of engineering and other students in the new system has already commenced. There can be little doubt that SI units will become, in time, the accepted international metric system.

Micro-Economics A branch of economics (q.v.) concerned with the analysis of the behaviour of individual consumers and producers. *See* MACRO-ECONOMICS.

Middleman An intermediary between producer and consumer, undertaking for profit the task of distribution.

Milk Act 1934 Legislation under which the British Government subsidised the Milk Marketing Board so that milk was made available to schoolchildren at a price of a halfpenny for one-third of a pint, needy cases receiving milk free. *See* MARKETING BOARD.

Minimum Wage Legislation Protective legislation to establish minimum wages for workers in certain industries. The need for such legislation has usually arisen because the trade unions in the industries concerned have been either non-existent or too weak to negotiate wage rates for their members. The Trade Boards Acts of 1909, 1913 and 1918 set up Trade Boards for this purpose. The Wages Councils Act of 1945 repealed earlier legislation and set up Wages Councils with powers to propose regulations fixing remuneration and holiday conditions. The former Trade Boards became Wages Councils. These Councils fix the remuneration of over one million employees. Legislation was consolidated in the Wages Councils Act of 1959. Other legislation has been introduced to deal with particular cases, e.g. the Agricultural Wages Act and the Catering Wages Act.

In Canada minimum wages for all or some forms of factory employment have been established by statute in all provinces, applicable in most cases to both men and women. These minimum statutory wages are set on an hourly basis in some provinces and on a weekly basis in others.

Mint   A place where money is coined. *See* ROYAL MINT, THE.

Mint Par of Exchange   Under a Gold Standard, the relative value of the coins of different countries. The rate of exchange between two countries on the Gold Standard will only vary from this by the cost of the transport of gold between the two centres.

Mixed Economy   An economy in which resources are allocated partly through the decisions of private individuals and privately-owned business enterprises and partly through the decisions of the Government and state-owned enterprises. The two sectors are known as the private and public sectors, respectively.

Mobility   The ease with which the factors of production (q.v.) can be transferred from one avenue of employment to another.

Mode   The value around which the items in a distribution tend to be most heavily concentrated.

Monetary Movements   An element in the balance of payments (q.v.) account which shows how the balance on current account (q.v.) and long-term capital account (q.v.) is settled, by increasing or decreasing sterling liabilities to non-residents. Payment may be in sterling, gold or convertible currencies.

Monetary Policy, Objectives of   The Report of the Committee on the Working of the Monetary System (Cmnd. 827, para. 69) summarises the objectives in pursuit of which monetary measures may be used:

    (a)   a high and stable level of employment;
    (b)   reasonable stability of the internal purchasing power of money;
    (c)   steady economic growth and improvement of the standard of living;
    (d)   some contribution, implying a margin in the balance of payments, to the economic development of the outside world;
    (e)   a strengthening of London's international reserves, implying a further margin in the balance of payments.

Money Any generally accepted medium of exchange; something that will be accepted by most people in exchange for goods and services and for the payment of debts, e.g. bank notes, coin and bank deposits. In some societies stones, shells, tobacco and feathers have been generally accepted. Gold, silver and copper have been popular as they do not deteriorate with time or wear out quickly; they have a high value per unit of weight and are divisible into fairly small units. Money confers complete liquidity (q.v.) on its holder. *See* MONEY, FUNCTIONS OF; MONEY SUPPLY.

Money at Call and Short Notice Day-to-day loans to the money market (q.v.) which earn relatively low rates of interest and may be called in at short notice.

Money, Functions of The ways in which money serves as: (a) a medium of exchange, permitting the separation of exchange into the two distinct acts of buying and selling; (b) a measure of value, in serving as a unit in terms of which the relative values of different commodities and services can be expressed; (c) a standard for deferred payments, permitting the calculation of payments due at some future date; and (d) as a store of value, permitting saving.

Money Market A market for short-term loans, the main business of which is conducted by bill brokers, discount and accepting houses, and the commercial banks. The principal commodities dealt in are bills of exchange (q.v.), trade bills (q.v.), and Treasury Bills (q.v.). *See* LONDON DISCOUNT MARKET.

Money Supply A supply comprising three streams: (a) metallic currency (coins); (b) paper money (notes); and (c) current account deposits. In the United States of America the supply consists of: (a) Treasury currency and coin; (b) Federal Reserve notes; and (c) demand deposits (checking accounts).

Monometallism The basing of a monetary system on the use of one metal, usually gold. *See* BIMETALLISM.

Monopolies Commission A Commission first set up in 1949 as the Monopolies and Restrictive Practices Commission under an Act of the previous year. It was re-constituted in 1956 as the Monopolies Commission under the Restrictive Trade Practices Act of that year. The Commission consisted initially of not less than 4 nor more than 10 persons appointed by the President of the Board of Trade. It is an independent statutory body, with its own officers and staff, whose function is to inquire into the existence and effect on the public interest of monopolies in the supply, processing and export of goods, and of certain restrictive practices not dealt with by the Restrictive Practices Court (q.v.) which is a separate body. For the purposes of the Commission, the term monopoly is defined as a condition where one supplier or a group of inter-connected bodies corporate, or a number of concerns which act together in such a way as to restrict competition, control at least one-third of the supply of specific goods, either in the United Kingdom as a whole, or in some specified area of the United Kingdom. The Commission only inquires into matters referred to it by the Board of Trade. It is not an executive body and can only investigate, report and recommend; its Reports are made to the Board of Trade who are responsible for laying them before Parliament. The Government decides what action should be taken. The recommendations of the Commission, if accepted by the Government, could be enforced by an Order laid before Parliament. Up to 1963, the Commission submitted 25 Reports. The Commission's recommendations led to the abandonment of various types of restrictive practices in the industries surveyed usually after agreement between the Board of Trade and the industry concerned without resort to powers of compulsion.

The Monopolies and Mergers Act 1965 gave the Board of Trade powers to refer to the Monopolies Commission mergers and take-overs which would establish or intensify a monopoly situation, or where the assets to be taken over exceed £5 m. The Monopolies Commission was also expanded to cover service industries.

Monopolistic Competition Competition which exists when each of two or more sellers supplies a considerable part of the market with which they are connected. *See* PRODUCT DIFFERENTIATION.

Monopoly A firm which produces a sufficiently large proportion of the total output of a commodity to enable it to influence the price of the commodity by variations in output. This implies that there are no close substitutes for the commodity and that the firm faces no imminent threat from competitors, existing or potential.

The Monopolies commission (q.v.) has the task of enquiring into single firm monopolies or oligopolies, defined as firms that supply one-third or more of the output of a product. *See* ABSOLUTE MONOPOLY; OLIGOPOLY.

Monopoly Agreements Agreements between individual firms which have effect as if a single monopoly existed. These agreements are of three kinds:
  (a) to control prices, e.g. price rings;
  (b) to control output, e.g. cartels, commodity restriction schemes;
  (c) to divide the market, e.g. before the Second World War, Imperial Chemical Industries Ltd., made an agreement that the European markets should be left to I. G. Farben Industrie and the American markets to du Pont, while both concerns agreed to leave the Commonwealth to I.C.I. *See* CARTEL; COMMODITY RESTRICTION SCHEME; PRICE RING.

Monopoly, Discriminating A monopoly which charges different prices to different customers for the same commodity. By breaking up the market into various parts in this way, and by charging in each part of the market that price which will maximise profits, the monopolist may hope to increase his total profit. Much depends, of course, on the extent to which a market may be effectively broken up.

Monopoly Profit Profit greater than normal profit (q.v.).

Monopsony A buyer's monopoly.

"Monthly Digest of Statistics" A Digest prepared monthly by the Central Statistical Office which contains the principal official statistics for such matters as expenditure on the gross domestic product; revenue and expenditure of central and local government; population; births, marriages and deaths; distribution of man-power in Great Britain; unemployment; industrial production; fuel and power; building and civil engineering; food and agriculture; external trade; transport and communication; finance; wages and prices; and distribution. An Annual Digest is also published.

Moon-Lighting The practice of having a second full or part-time job.

Moral Suasion One of the instruments used by the Bank of England in controlling the activities of the commercial banks (q.v.); it comprises the making of recommendations to the commercial banks who may prefer to act on these rather than wait for action to be forced on them through the use of the Bank-rate (q.v.) and open-market operations (q.v.), or the issue of a directive. *See* JAWBONE (U.S.); TREASURY DIRECTIVE.

Mortgage The conveyance of property by a debtor (mortgagor) to a creditor (mortgagee) as security for a debt, with a condition that the property shall be reconveyed on payment of the debt.

Mortgage Debenture *See* DEBENTURES.

Most favoured Nation Clause A clause which may be included in a commercial treaty between two nations that they will mutually grant to each other any favourable treatment which either may accord to a third nation in respect of customs duties.

Motivation Research A group of techniques developed by behavioural scientists which are used by marketing researchers to discover factors influencing marketing behaviour. *See* MARKET RESEARCH.

Multilateral System of Settlements *See* EUROPEAN MONETARY AGREEMENT (E.M.A.).

Multilateral Trade The sale of goods in one country and the use of the proceeds in the purchase of goods from another; trade between several countries.

Multiplier A ratio indicating the effect on total employment or on total income of a specified amount of a real capital investment. This important economic concept shows how fluctuations in the amount of investment (q.v.), although small in relation to the national income, are capable of generating fluctuations of much greater magnitude in total employment and income; in other words, putting one man out of employment due to a cutting back of investment leads to more than one man's loss of employment and earnings. The multiplier applies equally to the expansion of employment as well as to contraction. In

Britain in 1938, it is thought that the multiplier was about two, i.e. the setting to work of one of those who were then unemployed would have led to an average employment and wages for one other man.

The reasons for this amplification are as follows. Let us visualise a situation in which the country's resources are not fully utilised. The Government, eager to provide useful work and to tackle social problems, launches a large-scale slum clearance and re-housing programme. To carry out this task it is necessary to employ more workers in the building industry and in all the ancillary industries, e.g. brickmaking, cement manufacture, pre-fabrication, etc. All this activity is covered by the amount of initial investment which covers the cost of labour and all the materials required. Incomes of all kinds will increase by the amount of the additional investment. As earnings increase so will expenditure (although not by as much). The spending of those who have benefited directly will create secondary employment in other industries —food, clothing, entertainment, etc. The recipients in these industries will, in turn, have more to spend, creating tertiary employment. The increase in income to which the original investment gave rise will be multiplied as prosperity spreads.

If we assume that the people concerned save a fixed proportion of their incomes, say 10 per cent, the expansion in income will be ten times the expansion in savings and therefore ten times the expansion in investment. Thus an increase in investment by £1 m. will generate an extra £10 m. in income. The multiplier in this case is ten. The greater the marginal propensity to consume, the greater the multiplier.

The concept of the "multiplier" was first introduced into economic theory by Richard F. Kahn in an article "The Relation of Home Investment to Unemployment" (*Economic Journal*, June, 1931). He laid down general principles by which to estimate the actual quantitative relationship between an increment of net investment and the increment of aggregate employment which will be associated with it. The concept was incorporated into John Maynard Keynes' *General Theory of Employment, Interest and Money*. As the multiplier is the ratio between employment or income and investment, it is thus the reciprocal of the ratio of savings to income, i.e. the reciprocal of the marginal propensity to save. Let the marginal propensity to consume (MPC) = q (assuming $O \leqslant q \leqslant 1$) and the initial sum invested = x, then the total increase in national income =

$$x(1 + q + q^2 + \ldots + \infty) = \frac{x}{1-q}$$

If the series is not infinite, i.e. for any limited period, t, the increase in the national income =

$$x(1 + q + q^2 + \ldots q^t) = \frac{x(1-q^t)}{1-q}$$

It is however clear that as a point of full employment of all resources is approached, the multiplying effect of new investment must become more limited. If new investment is made at a time of full employment (labour and materials being obtainable only by attracting them from other uses) then there can be no multiplying effect in terms of employment, but only in money incomes. If the gross national product has been unaffected by the new investment, the total effect on the economy will have been solely inflationary. The maximum beneficial effect of the multiplier will only be experienced when increasing investment in times of heavy unemployment, or when cutting back investment at the time of a boom. *See* MARGINAL PROPENSITIES TO CONSUME AND SAVE.

Mutual Economic Assistance, Council For (Comecon) *See* COUNCIL FOR MUTUAL ECONOMIC ASSISTANCE (COMECON).

Mutual Security Agency (U.S.) A U.S. government agency which replaced the Economic Co-operation Administration (q.v.) in December 1951, having the declared object of providing for the general welfare of the U.S.A. by furnishing military, economic and technical assistance to friendly nations in the interest of international peace. The Mutual Security Agency was replaced in August, 1953, by the Foreign Operations Administration (q.v.).

N

Name Day *See* TICKET OR NAME DAY.

National Accounts Classification A part of the Financial Statement (q.v.) presented to the British Parliament on Budget Day each year setting out the transactions of the public sector in accordance with the principles and definitions used in the statistics of national income and expenditure compiled by the Central Statistical Office; the effect of these transactions on the rest of the economy are shown.

National Association of British Manufacturers A national organisation (formerly the National Union of Manufacturers) founded in 1915 representing manufacturing industry, particularly medium-sized and smaller firms. Its membership totalled over 5,000 individual firms and 60 affiliated trade associations. In August, 1965, its functions were taken over by the new Confederation of British Industry (q.v.).

National Bank (U.S.) An incorporated commercial bank chartered by the government of the United States of America. *See* STATE BANK.

National Board for Prices and Incomes A Board set up by the Government in 1965 to keep prices and incomes under review. Its terms of reference are outlined in the White Paper "Prices and Incomes Policy" (Cmnd. 2639). The Board comprises an independent chairman, a number of independent members, a businessman and a trade unionist. Some of the members are part-time. The work is conducted in two separate divisions, the Prices Review Division and the Incomes Review Division. The Prices Review Division investigates any price or group of prices, manufacturing, wholesale or retail of goods and services in private and nationalised industry. The Government retains direct responsibility for all references to the Prices Review Division. Some of these result from complaints made to the Government by individuals, interested parties or independent bodies; others are directly selected by the Government as meriting detailed investigation. The Incomes Review Division investigates claims and settlements relating to wage and salary increases, reductions in hours and other improvements in conditions of service, whether in the private sector or the public services; cases in which a revaluation of pay levels or an overhaul of the pay structure seems to be indicated for economic and social reasons; the level of earnings in an industry or sector; and where appropriate cases of increases of money incomes, other than wages and salaries. As in the case of prices, the Government retains responsibility for references to the Division. In addition to the permanent appointments to the Board, panels of businessmen and trade unionists are appointed to assist the two divisions with the investigation of particular cases. The Board is not a statutory body. Persuasion and pressure of public opinion are relied upon to ensure that the findings and recommendations of the new body are accepted by the parties concerned. The Prices and Incomes Act 1967 may be invoked to delay increases in prices and incomes for up to seven months.

National Bus Company An authority set up under the Transport Act, 1968, which assumed responsibility for the bus interests of the Transport Holding Company in England and Wales, taking over most of the main network of local bus services outside the municipalities. The Company operates through subsidiary companies.

National Coal Board A body created by the Coal Mines Nationalisation Act of 1946 to take control of most of the coal mines in England, Wales, and Scotland. The Board's statutory duty is to develop the industry efficiently and provide coal in such quantities and at such prices as to further the public interest. Today production has been confined to the 400 or so most efficient mines, but this number is likely to be progressively reduced as the demand for coal diminishes in the coming years.

National Debt The debts of the British Government, accumulated largely through borrowing from the British people over many years. In 1968/69 the National Debt amounted to some £33,000 m. The Debt comprises:
  (a) Funded Debt—consols, War loans, etc., which have no contractual repayment date;
  (b) Unfunded Debt—floating debt (mainly short-term borrowing against Treasury bills); other internal debts such as "dated" securities, National Savings Certificates, Defence Bonds, Premium Bonds, National Development Bonds, etc.; and external debt such as the United States and Canadian Loans raised after the Second World War.

National Debt Commissioners Appointed in 1786, Commissioners whose primary function is to create sinking funds for the reduction of the national debt (q.v.); other duties are undertaken such as the investment and financial management of large government funds, e.g. Post Office Savings Bank (q.v.) funds, Trustee Savings Banks (q.v.) funds, and the National Insurance Fund.

National Development Bonds A Government security issued in 1964 to replace Defence Bonds (q.v.), various issues of which had been running since 1939. The new bonds carry a fixed rate of interest of 7 per cent per annum.

National Dividend That part of the objective income of the community, including income from abroad, which can be measured in money terms. An alternative description of the National Income (q.v.).

National Economic Development Council ("NEDDY") A Council set up by the Government in 1961 with the following objects:

(a) To examine the economic performance of the nation with particular concern for plans for the future in both the private and the public sectors of industry.

(b) To consider together what are the obstacles to quicker growth, what can be done to improve efficiency and whether the best use is being made of our resources.

(c) To seek agreement upon ways of improving economic performance, competitive power and efficiency; in other words, to increase the rate of sound growth.

The Council is responsible for indicative planning only, responsibility for final decisions on matters of national policy remaining with the Government. The proposal for a National Economic Council was first put forward by the then Chancellor of the Exchequer, Mr. Selwyn Lloyd, on 25th July 1961, as part of a group of measures for dealing with a balance of payments crisis. Meetings were subsequently held between the Chancellor and employers' organisations and with the T.U.C. Late in 1961 the Council was set up with Sir Robert Shone as the first Director-General. The Council has twenty members. The first meeting of the Council was held on 7th March 1962. At a subsequent meeting on 9th May, the Council decided that the first main task should be the preparation of a report studying the implications of an average annual rate of growth of 4 per cent for the period 1961–66. A Report on the growth of the United Kingdom Economy, 1961–66, was submitted to the National Economic Development Council by the Director-General on 24th January 1963. The Council approved the 4 per cent growth objective for the whole of the economy. It was estimated that productivity would have to contribute 3.2 per cent of the growth. From 1951 to 1961, the average annual increase in productivity was about 2 per cent. The additional increase in the growth of the national product would come from an increasing labour force. It was also recognised that exports would have to grow by 5 per cent a year to meet import requirements and to provide a surplus on current account of £300 m. for increased aid to developing countries, overseas investment, and provide an additional small overall surplus to function as a reserve. The Council has subsequently produced and published several general and special reports on various aspects of the economy.

In 1964, the Government transferred the Council's responsibilities for drawing up a long-term economic plan to the Department of Economic Affairs. However, the Council remains the parent body for the "little Neds" whose task is to study the problems of particular industries. *See* ECONOMIC DEVELOPMENT COMMITTEES.

National Freight Corporation A publicly-owned authority, established under the Transport Act 1968, responsible for all freight services provided by the public sector of the transport industry which originate by road. Operating from 1st January, 1969, the Corporation has the duty of providing integrated road and rail freight services in Great Britain, using road and rail transport to the best advantage. The Corporation has taken over from British Rail commercial responsibility for the freightliner services, and all the road haulage and shipping activities formerly undertaken by the Transport Holding Company.

National Giro *See* GIRO.

National Income A measure of the money value of the goods and services becoming available to a nation from economic activity during a prescribed period. It can be calculated by three different methods:

(1) By adding all the incomes generated in the country by economic activity—wages and salaries, earnings of professional people, incomes of farmers, business profits, pay of the armed forces, rent and "net income from abroad" (but excluding transfer payments (q.v.) such as interest on the national debt, retirement pensions, family allowances or grants to students). The money value or price of a commodity or service (without indirect tax) is exactly equal to the sum of the various incomes generated in its production.

(2) By adding together the values of all the goods and services produced in a country, i.e. prices minus indirect taxes, while avoiding double counting (the value of raw materials must not be counted again in the value of finished products).

(3) By adding the values of what has been consumed (deducting indirect taxes) and what has been invested in the country to give a total expenditure.

Whichever method is adopted, the final gross amount should be the same. Allowance may be made for the depreciation of assets to give a "net" figure. As the National Income includes only those incomes, whether individual or corporate, which are derived from the current production of goods and services, it can be described as the sum of the incomes of the factors of production (q.v.), or factor incomes. The sum of domestic factor incomes measures the total output of goods and services available within the nation and is described as the Gross Domestic Product at Factor Cost. It should be noted, however, that the National Income comprises not only domestic incomes, but also net income received from abroad. For this reason, the National Income is described as either the Gross or Net National Product at Factor Cost, depending on whether or not depreciation is allowed for. The national accounts of the United Kingdom are published annually in a Blue Book on National Income and Expenditure. Quarterly estimates of the national income appear in the Monthly Digest of Statistics (q.v.).

A growth in National Income in money terms may be due to genuine economic progress, or it may be due to:

(a) inflation and a fall in the value of money;

(b) growth in population, the average income per head remaining the same; or

(c) simply a growth in services for which people pay, which were previously provided "free". For example, the preparation of meals at home is a service not included in the national income; but if the family decide to eat at a restaurant the cost of the service (but not the raw materials which are counted anyway) is added to the national income. Thus, anything given and not hired or sold is not recorded. Neither is produce consumed directly by producers.

Thus, a country's computed National Income may rise while the standard of living remains stationary or actually falls; if more women go out to work the National Income is increased, but there is no deduction for the loss of "free services" at home; finally, if we all paint our own houses the National Income shows a decline. However, it is relatively easy to adjust the National Income figures for changes in the value of money, and the other odd features do not make much material difference. The National Income is a good guide to what is happening to the total volume of goods and services.

The greatest weakness of the National Income accounts is that they are no sure guide to the material standard of living of a particular section of a community. In other words, it is a guide to the size of the cake, but no guide to the size of the slices which are going to different categories of person in a community. On the other hand, if the total volume of production of goods and services is small, then the average standard of living will be low, however equitable the distribution. It is generally accepted in Britain that the initial distribution of the National Income is inequitable; the Government seeks to reduce the great inequality of incomes through the use of the techniques of progressive income tax and death duties. In addition, a substantial portion of the money raised is used for the provision of social benefits which tend to raise the standard of living of the middle and lower income groups. In both Britain and the United States there are still extremes of wealth and poverty; but not as great as in Africa or India.

Table 3 shows the national income and expenditure accounts for 1968. *See* GROSS DOMESTIC PRODUCT AT FACTOR COST; GROSS DOMESTIC PRODUCT AT MARKET PRICES; GROSS NATIONAL PRODUCT AT FACTOR COST; GROSS NATIONAL PRODUCT AT MARKET PRICES.

TABLE 3

THE NATIONAL INCOME

£ million
1968

Expenditure

Consumers' expenditure	27,045
Public authorities' consumption	7,565
Gross fixed investment	7,734
Value of physical increase in stocks and work in progress ..	241
Total domestic expenditure at market prices	42,585
Exports and property income from abroad	10,380
less Imports and property income paid abroad	−10,541
less Taxes on expenditure	−6,951
Subsidies	885
Gross National Product at Factor Cost	**36,358**

£ million
1968

Factor Incomes

Income from employment	25,046
Gross trading profits of companies[1,2,3]	5,194
Gross trading surplus of public corporations[1,3]	1,338
Gross trading surplus of other public enterprises[1]	111
Income from self-employment[1]	2,785
Rent[4]	2,324

Total domestic income before providing for depreciation and stock appreciation	36,798
less Stock appreciation	−650
Residual error	−226

Gross Domestic Product at Factor Cost	**35,922**
Net property income from abroad	436

Gross National Product	**36,358**
less Capital consumption	−3,380
National Income	**32,978**

[1] Before providing for depreciation and stock appreciation.

[2] Selective employment tax is included on a cash basis and refunds or premiums are allowed for when they are received.

[3] From the end of July 1967 the British Steel Corporation is included in public corporations and the companies then nationalised are no longer included in the company sector.

[4] Before providing for depreciation.

"National Income and Balance of Payments White Paper" A publication of the Central Statistical Office presented to Parliament just before the Budget each year. It contains preliminary estimates of the main national accounts tables for the latest year, together with comparable figures for earlier years. The White Paper also includes the balance of payments accounts.

"National Income and Expenditure" A publication of the Central Statistical Office issued annually at the beginning of September. This Blue Book contains detailed tables and covers all aspects of the national accounts.

National Incomes Commission ("Nicky") A Commission set up by the Government in July 1962, for the purpose of giving consideration to the repercussions on the national economy of individual pay settlements. The Commission was asked to take into account in its deliberations:

    (a) the need to keep a sound relationship between the aggregate of money incomes and the rate of increase of national productivity;

    (b) the need to pay a fair reward for the work concerned;

(c) the manpower requirements of the occupation or industry under review;

(d) the repercussions which a given settlement might have on other employments.

The Commission was asked to publish its views. The Final Report of the Commission (Cmnd. 2583) condemned agreements in the ship-building and engineering industries as inflationary and against the public interest. With the setting up of the National Incomes and Prices Board in 1965, the Commission was terminated. *See* NATIONAL BOARD FOR PRICES AND INCOMES.

National Incomes Policy A policy of restraint in relation to increases in personal incomes with the object of slowing down inflationary trends. The object is to keep increases in personal incomes broadly in line with increases in productivity in industry. Restraint in wage claims has been called for by the British Government several times since the Second World War. In 1948, the Government issued a White Paper on Personal Incomes, Costs and Prices which had a limited effect in checking wage increases, partly due to some support elicited from the Trades Union Congress and partly due to increased resistance by some employers to wage demands. The effect was, however, short-lived. A later appeal by Mr. Macmillan in 1956 elicited little response. In the 1960s Mr. Selwyn Lloyd introduced a "guiding light" for permissible movements in incomes of about $2\frac{1}{2}$ per cent per annum, being broadly in accord with increases in productivity at that time. His appeal was pushed with energy, but soon crumbled in the face of economic forces.

One difficulty has been the natural wariness of the Trades Union Congress in approaching the appeal for "wage restraint". Indeed, the T.U.C. leaders have refused to commit themselves on wages without a similar commitment from the employers in respect of prices and profits. In 1961, the T.U.C. joined the National Economic Development Council (q.v.), but only on condition that incomes policy should not be put on the agenda. Against the wishes of the T.U.C. Mr. Selwyn Lloyd established a National Incomes Commission (q.v.), but this body achieved little. In the meanwhile the Federation of British Industry has examined proposals for "disciplining" prices and profits. These proposals were:

(a) a variable profits tax;

(b) a scheme for registration of price changes:

(c) prices complaints procedure.

The first proposal was designed to ensure that profits did not rise faster than wages, by seeing that any excess went to revenue. The second and third proposals were designed to make it difficult for firms to make unjustifiable price increases. The F.B.I. Working Party reported in March, 1964, that none of the three schemes were administratively workable.

It is very difficult to hold down wages when the demand for labour exceeds supply at the nationally negotiated wage-levels. The phenomenon of "wage drift" (q.v.) has crept in with wages being raised above the nationally agreed rates by individual employers trying to attract or retain workers. This is a process which goes on, particularly at low levels of unemployment, without pressure from the unions. The most an Incomes Policy could hope to achieve would be restraint in the pressure for higher wages by unions. It could not hope to constrain "demand-pull" inflation. In any event if a national agreement between the Government, employers and trade unions is implemented it could not be applied uniformly over the whole field of industry; some sections would get more, others less, than the overall permissible increase each year. The problem of constraining incomes is one facing every Western country; it is perhaps of most critical importance to Britain so dependent as she is on selling competitively abroad. It should be noted that the negative phrases "pay pause" or "incomes restraint" have been replaced by the more positive sounding description "a planned growth of incomes". The meaning is the same.

In 1965, a new "norm" for increases in all money incomes was established, this being an annual average increase of 3 to 3½ per cent; the implication being that if some got more, others would get less. Subsequently a ceiling of 3½ per cent per annum was adopted, not as a "norm" but as an "absolute maximum". However, an acceptable productivity agreement might permit a pay increase above the maximum. *See* PRODUCTIVITY AGREEMENTS; "UNEASY TRIANGLE", THE.

National Institute of Economic and Social Research (N.I.E.S.R.) A research body established in 1938 to increase knowledge of the social and economic conditions of contemporary society. It is financed by grants from foundations, governmental agencies and companies. In conducting research the staff of the Institute co-operate with the universities and other academic and industrial bodies. The Institute publishes the quarterly "National Institute Economic Review".

National Plan A plan for economic growth in the United Kingdom published by the British Government in 1965; a basic objective was to achieve a 25 per cent growth in the national product by 1970 accompanied by a favourable balance of payments (q.v.). The gross targets of the plan were abandoned following the introduction of deflationary measures in July, 1966, to correct an adverse balance of payments situation.

National Research Development Corporation A body set up by the Government in 1948 to make financial assistance available for suitable research projects undertaken by private industry or private individuals.

National Savings Certificates Introduced during the First World War and normally obtained through the British post office, a form of investment specially designed for the small saver; interest, which is free from income tax, surtax and capital gains tax, takes the form of accruals to the capital value and is paid out only on the encashment of certificates. *See* DEFENCE BONDS; NATIONAL DEVELOPMENT BONDS; PREMIUM SAVINGS BONDS; "SAVE AS YOU EARN".

Nationalisation State ownership and control of any of the means of production, distribution or exchange. Nationalisation was for many years an important item in the policies of the British Labour Party and the objective of the common ownership of the means of production, distribution and exchange remains enshrined in Clause Four of the Party's Constitution. In practice, the Party has limited its aims to the nationalisation of certain basic industries— coal, gas, electricity, transport, iron and steel, and water. The Conservative Party has also engaged in limited schemes of national ownership. Those concerns falling within state ownership in Britain include the:

(a) Post Office (1657);
(b) Central Electricity Board (1926);
(c) British Broadcasting Corporation (1927);
(d) London Passenger Transport Board (1933);
(e) British Sugar Beet Corporation (1937);
(f) British Overseas Airways Corporation and British European Airways (1939 and 1946 respectively);
(g) Bank of England (1946);
(h) Coal Mining Industry (1947);
(i) Cable and Wireless (1947);
(j) Inland Transport (1948);
(k) Electricity Supply Industry (1948);
(l) Gas Industry (1949);
(m) Iron and Steel Industry (1951 and 1967).

See BRITISH STEEL CORPORATION; PUBLIC CORPORATION.

Near Money   Assets readily convertible into money (q.v.), e.g. deposit accounts, deposits with savings banks and building societies, and certain short-term government securities. In the United States of America "near money" comprises time and savings deposits in commercial banks, deposits at mutual savings banks, savings and loan shares, U.S. Savings Bonds and U.S. Securities due in less than one year.

Necessity   A commodity or service which satisfies a primary need in respect of food, clothing or shelter. While the nature of a necessity may suggest an inelastic demand, much depends in a particular case on the availability of close substitutes; thus a particular necessity may have a quite elastic demand. *See* LUXURY.

Negotiable Instrument   A claim, the title to which passes by delivery. Examples of such claims are bills of exchange, cheques, promissory notes, share warrants, dividend warrants, and debentures payable to bearer. Transfer is by delivery only. A bill of exchange (q.v.) payable to a certain person "only" is not a negotiable instrument. Neither is a cheque with "not negotiable" written on it. Bills of lading, dock warrants, share certificates and postal orders are not negotiable. A creditor is not bound to take a negotiable instrument in payment of a debt; he may insist on payment in legal tender (q.v.).

Net Investment   The value of investment (q.v.) after allowing for the wearing-out or depreciation (q.v.) of existing assets.

Net National Product at Factor Cost   The Gross National Product at Factor Cost (q.v.), minus depreciation (q.v.). *See* NATIONAL INCOME; GROSS NATIONAL PRODUCT AT MARKET PRICES.

Net United Kingdom Rate Tax payable by a company after allowing for double taxation relief (q.v.).

Network Analysis A generic term for the whole range of "network techniques" including Critical Path Analysis (q.v.) and Programme Evaluation and Review Technique (q.v.). All are methods of planning a complex project in a logical way by analysing it into its component parts and recording them as a network, model or diagram. These techniques assist in controlling the inter-related activities of a project from initiation to completion.

Net Worth The financial value of a business to the proprietor(s). It represents assets minus current liabilities.

New Deal The policy inaugurated by President Roosevelt in the U.S.A. in 1933 in order to overcome the great economic crisis which had broken out at the end of 1929.

The New Deal consisted of a series of far-reaching economic and social measures which were not only in sharp contrast with the previous attempts to end the depression by orthodox "deflationary" means, but also contrary to many American traditions. The Administration started on a programme of industrial recovery through public works, and an ample supply of cheap credit. The dollar was devalued by 40 per cent. Housing legislation provided for large scale construction of houses with public guarantees and subsidies. The Reconstruction Finance Corporation granted loans to finance the Government's schemes. A number of other authorities (such as the Works Progress Administration and the Civilian Conservation Corps) were created to employ the workless and to stimulate economic activities. Unemployment relief was regulated and enlarged. The Social Security Act introduced general social insurance in the U.S.A. The Agricultural Adjustment Act provided for large scale assistance to farmers.

The New Deal met with considerable resistance in the beginning and certain parts were repealed by the U.S. Supreme Court; its basic portions were, however, upheld. The New Deal helped to reduce the number of workless in the U.S.A.

Newgo See NEW TIME.

New Time Transactions effected on the London Stock Exchange two clear days before the contango day (q.v.), for settlement on the second ensuing account day, i.e. "new account", "next time", "new time" or "newgo".

New Towns Completely new towns which have been built under the New Towns Acts 1946 and 1965 to house the surplus populations of large cities or to form new communities around existing industries. A Development Corporation is in charge of each new town. About twenty new towns have been developed in Britain since the Second World War.

"No Par Value" Shares (U.S.) Shares which have no nominal value (q.v.) This type of share is illegal in Britain.

Nominal Value   The nominal value of a share is the value given to shares when they are created, e.g. £1, 5s., 1s., etc. For example, the £1 nominal shares of a company may now stand in the region of £3 or £4, which is known as the market price.

Nominee Shareholder   A bank, firm of stockbrokers or other institution, which holds shares on behalf of clients.

Non-Cumulative Preferred Stock (U.S.)   Preferred stock (q.v.) the dividend on which, if unpaid, does not have to be paid later. *See* CUMULATIVE PREFERRED STOCK.

Non-Recourse Finance   Finance (q.v.) provided by a specialist finance company which, for a commission, assumes financial responsibilities on behalf of an exporter. The company passes on to the exporter any down-payments credited from the overseas buyer and most of the amount remaining due within fifteen days of shipment, this being without recourse once the goods have been accepted by the buyer.

Non-Voting Shares   Shares which do not entitle the holder to vote at the General Meetings of the company. The purpose of issuing these shares is to raise additional capital from the public while control is retained by the holders of the voting shares. It has often been argued that the issue of non-voting shares should be prohibited by law.

Normal Price   The long-run price of a commodity, defined by Alfred Marshall as the "value which economic forces would bring about if the general conditions of life were stationary for a run of time long enough to enable them all to work out their full effect".

Normal Profit   The average rate of reward per unit of output in an industry or sector of the economy over a period of time. Normal profit is the minimum rate of profit necessary to ensure that a sufficient number of people will be prepared to invest, undertake risks and organise production. The rate differs from industry to industry, according to the degree of risk and difficulty involved. Industries in which the rate of reward is above normal will tend to expand; those in which rewards are below normal will tend to contract. This may in some instances be a slow and erratic process; in others fairly rapid. Costs of production, in an economic sense, include an allowance for normal profit.

O

Obsolescence The loss in value of physical assets due to technological changes which have led to more efficient assets, rather than due to physical deterioration.

Odd-Lot Anything less than a round-lot (q.v.) of one hundred shares.

Odd-Lot Broker (U.S.) A broker who caters for odd-lot customers, i.e. customers who wish to sell or buy shares or stock in lots of less than one hundred, the minimum number for trading on the stock exchange. In making-up round lots of one hundred the odd-lot broker is able to engage in selling and buying. His purchases of round lots may be split between customers.

Offer The price at which a person is ready to sell; purchase price. Hence to "buy at best offer". *See* BID.

Offer for Sale The offer of new securities to the public, not on behalf of the company itself, but by one or more holders to whom they have already been issued. Normally the holder is an issuing house (q.v.) which has bought the new issue from the company concerned and is now offering them to the public at a slightly higher price, the difference covering the expenses of the offer. *See* OFFER FOR SALE BY TENDER; PLACING; PUBLIC ISSUE; RIGHTS ISSUE.

Offer for Sale by Tender An exceptional method of making a new issue of equities (q.v.). As in the case of an offer for sale (q.v.) an issuing house (q.v.) purchases the shares from the company prior to issue. On the basis of a prospectus, tenders are invited from the public for the shares; however the prospectus only states a minimum price and tenders are to be made above this price. After the tenders have been received, the issuing house then fixes a price at which the shares are to be sold. The company receives the full price of the shares, less the remuneration of the issuing house. Between 1959–1963, there were only eighteen issues by this method, fifteen of these occurring in the last quarter of 1963. *See* PLACING; OFFER FOR SALE; RIGHTS ISSUE; STOCK EXCHANGE INTRODUCTION.

Offices, Shops and Railway Premises Act 1963 The first comprehensive legislation in Britain regulating working conditions in offices, shops and railway premises. In broad general terms, the Act provides for the health, safety and welfare of office workers, etc. The Factories Acts make similar provision for workers in factories.

Official Receiver An official appointed under the Bankruptcy Acts by the Board of Trade to take control of a bankrupt's properties until a trustee is appointed. An official receiver has also to take charge of the winding-up of a company that has failed. *See* BANKRUPTCY; LIQUIDATION.

Official Support Buying (e.g. of sterling, gilt-edged securities) by the Bank of England (q.v.) or a Government agency to support the market price. *See* GOVERNMENT BROKER.

Oligopoly A situation in which a market, or a large part of a market, is supplied by a small number of firms each of which possesses a significant degree of economic influence. Each firm is strong enough to influence the market but not strong enough to disregard the reactions of competitors. There is a tendency in such markets for competition to shift from price to non-price matters such as quality, service and advertising.

Oligopsony The equivalent of oligopoly (q.v.) on the buyers' side of the market.

Oncost A charge made on the direct cost of production of a commodity as a contribution to the recovery of indirect expenses. *See* FULL COST PRICING.

"One Off" Production The production of an article to suit the particular requirements of a customer. Opposite of mass production (q.v.).

One-Way Callable Stock Stock which cannot be redeemed by the holder, but which can be redeemed at the sole discretion of the issuing authority.

Open Market Operations The buying or selling of Government stocks on the open market by the Bank of England, for the purpose of making the Bank Rate (q.v.) more effective in regulating the volume of credit. Payments in respect of such stocks which are made by, or to, customers of the commercial banks affect the size of the cash reserves held by those banks at the Bank of England. Through the necessity of maintaining a minimum ratio of 8 per cent between the cash reserve and the total volume of deposits, any change in the cash reserve will influence directly the total volume of deposits and loans. The system works as follows. If the Bank of England buys £x m. of Government stock on the Stock Exchange, it pays the sellers by cheques drawn on itself. Most of these sellers then pay their cheques into their accounts at the various commercial banks. Settlement of these cheques results in the total balances of the commercial banks at the Bank of England being increased up to £x m. Since these balances are regarded as cash (and may be drawn in cash) an increase in cash held by a commercial bank will raise its cash reserve ratio above 8 per cent. It will then be in a position to increase its lending until the ratio falls again to 8 per cent. Open market operations of this kind increase the volume of purchasing power available to the community; the effect may be to stimulate industrial and commercial activity of all kinds. Conversely, a sale of Government securities by the Bank of England leads to a reduction in the cash reserves of the commercial banks and hence to a shrinking of the volume of deposits and loans; the effect is deflationary. Many economists consider the Bank Rate (q.v.) ineffective unless accompanied by open market operations. There is much in this view, although the Bank Rate does determine directly the rate of interest for loans to the nationalised industries from the Exchequer, and loans to local authorities through the Public Works Loan Board (q.v.). It also determines by custom the rates of interest which are charged for overdrafts. Since 1951, the British monetary authorities have used two other methods for influencing the credit policies of banks in addition to Bank Rate and open market operations. One method has been the Treasury Directive (q.v.), and the other the device of Special Deposits (q.v.).

"Open Price" Agreement Agreement under which firms notify their trade association about their prices, costs, orders and output and the figures are disseminated throughout the trade. The expectation is that the diffusion of this information will lead to a uniformity of prices among the several producers.

Opening Prices The prices at which business first commences on the floor of the Stock Exchange (q.v.) at the official opening time.

Operating Cost Ratio (U.S.) Operating costs expressed as a proportion of the value of net sales.

Operating Profit (U.S.) The value of net sales minus total operating costs.

Operating Ratios Ratios indicating the operating efficiency of a business. Examples of operating ratios are:

$$\frac{\text{Cost of Sales}}{\text{Stock (including stores and work in progress)}}$$

$$\frac{\text{Stock of Finished Goods}}{\text{Production costs for period}}$$

$$\frac{\text{Trade Creditors}}{\text{Purchasers}}$$

Operating Revenues (U.S.) Money received by a railroad or a utility from its customers for goods or services supplied.

Operational Research The application of scientific and mathematical techniques to complex problems arising in the direction and control of systems of men, machines, materials and money, to improve the speed, quality and cost of performance. The approach normally involves the development of a symbolic model of the system, incorporating measurements of factors such as chance and risk, in an attempt to predict and compare the outcomes of alternative decisions, strategies or controls.

Opportunity-Cost The real cost of satisfying a want, expressed in terms of the cost of the sacrifice of alternative activities. For example, if capital funds could earn 7 per cent elsewhere, then that is their cost in present use.

Optimum Allocation of Resources The direction of resources towards their most productive uses, ensuring that the maximum satisfaction or gain is being obtained by the individual, firm or community allocating those resources.

Optimum Firm A firm in which the costs of production per unit of output are at a minimum, having regard to the existing state of technical knowledge and managerial ability. Expansion up to this size is accompanied by falling average costs as a result of economies of scale (q.v.); beyond this point costs begin to rise due to the diseconomies arising from the increasing scarcity of the factors of production (q.v.), increasing selling costs (q.v.) or managerial difficulties. The optimum is not a fixed point, but changes with every development in techniques and machinery, movements in the rate of interest, or improvements in facilities for buying, selling or research. Furthermore, the optimum firm is not a simple concept; there is an optimum size for technical production, for finance, for marketing, for management and for risk. All these optima have to be reconciled as far as possible to the best advantage. For the multi-product firm, there is an optimum output for each of the firm's product lines; hence the view is sometimes taken that there is no real limit to the size of the firm as a co-ordinating organisation, providing that the managerial organisation can be suitably adapted.

It is only under conditions of perfect competition, however, that the optimum output will coincide with the earning of maximum profits. Maximum profits are made when output has expanded to a point where marginal revenue equals marginal cost. In the circumstances of imperfect competition (q.v.) or monopoly (q.v.) the optimum size may not necessarily be reached, or it may be exceeded. However, in a competitive world the firm with the lowest average costs per unit of output in the long, as well as in the short, term is most likely to survive and to retain the support of investors. Firms therefore *tend* to optimise output.

Optimum Output Output at which factors of production are combined in the most efficient way, i.e. the output at which the average cost of production is at its lowest point. Only under conditions of perfect competition (q.v.), however, will this be the point of maximum profit. In conditions of imperfect competition (q.v.), or real life conditions, the point of maximum profit may well be away from the optimum output.

Optimum Population The ideal size of population, which will yield the highest possible material return per head of population. As Cannan has expressed it: "The optimum for population is the right movement which will give the largest return to industry in the long run, the interests of the people of all generations being taken into account." The optimum for population is closely related to the available supplies of other factors of production; the optimum will therefore change with changes in the supply of other factors. *See* OVER-POPULATION: UNDER-POPULATION.

Option   The right to buy or sell shares or property within a stated period at a predetermined price. *See* SHARE OPTIONS.

Optional Capital   The difference in capital cost between two projects or schemes, which are true alternatives, e.g. the difference in capital cost between two suitable machines one of which is more expensive that the other but offers higher efficiency. A higher rate of return may be required from optional capital than from basic investment.

Ordinary Shares   The equities of a limited company. They carry the right to the residue of a company's assets after it has paid all its creditors and preference shareholders, and share in the distribution of profits, if any, after the prior claims of the preference-share holders and debenture holders have been met. Whatever the amount of profit, it is rare for all of it to be handed out in dividends to shareholders. Prudent directors of companies put part of the profits into the reserve fund. This fund may then be used to expand the business, instead of relying solely on additional borrowed capital.   *See* EQUITIES; NON-VOTING SHARES.

Organisation for Economic Co-Operation and Development (O.E.C.D.)   An organisation which came into being on 30th September, 1961, succeeding the Organisation for European Economic Co-operation (O.E.E.C.) (q.v.). The O.E.C.D. was set up under a Convention signed in Paris on the 14th December, 1960, by the Member countries of the O.E.E.C. and by Canada and the United States. This Convention provides that the O.E.C.D. shall promote policies designed: (a) to achieve the highest sustainable economic growth and employment and a rising standard of living in Member countries, while maintaining financial stability, and thus to contribute to the development of the world economy; (b) to contribute to sound economic expansion in Member as well as non-member countries in the process of economic development; (c) to contribute to the expansion of world trade on a multi-lateral, non-discriminatory basis in accordance with international obligations. The Members of O.E.C.D. are Austria, Belgium, Canada, Denmark, France, the Federal Republic of Germany, Greece, Iceland, Ireland, Italy, Japan, Luxembourg, the Netherlands, Norway, Portugal, Spain, Sweden, Switzerland, Turkey, the United Kingdom and the United States.

Organisation for European Economic Co-Operation (O.E.E.C.)   An organisation established in 1948 to allocate aid received under the European Recovery Programme (q.v.) among the participating countries, subject to the approval of the Economic Co-operation Administration (q.v.) in Washington, and to generally stimulate intra-European trade. It was superseded in 1961 by the Organisation for Economic Co-operation and Development (q.v.).

Organisation for Trade Co-operation (O.T.C.)   An international organisation set up by the parties to the General Agreement on Tariffs and Trade (q.v.) to administer the General Agreement.

"Other Things Being Equal" An essential qualification to many statements in economic theory in order to eliminate, for the time being, consideration of other disturbing influences.

Ottawa Agreement An Agreement negotiated at Ottawa in 1932, between the United Kingdom and the Dominions, together with India, under which the principle of "Imperial Preference" was established. By this Agreement, the United Kingdom substantially reduced in favour of Commonwealth goods the import duties imposed by the Import Duties Act of 1932 on foreign goods. In return, the Dominions agreed to grant preferential duties in respect of United Kingdom manufactured goods and colonial produce. The Agreement brought about a remarkable change in the direction of Britain's external trade, greatly increasing the proportion of trade undertaken with the Commonwealth countries. *See* IMPORT DUTIES ACT 1932.

Outage Cost The costs of non-availability of plant due to breakdown, overhaul, or simply failure to complete the construction of a project by a scheduled date, arising from the use of less efficient methods or the absence of any alternative service.

"Outer Seven" A term often used to describe the members of the European Free Trade Association (q.v.).

Output Quantity of goods manufactured by a factory, or the quantity of material extracted from a mine, quarry, etc., or services produced, during a given time.

Output Response Function A hypothesis that if the aggregate effective demand for goods and services within an economic system steadily increases output will increase, but ultimately at a diminishing rate of response. This relationship will be the net result of several factors: (a) reduced unemployment associated with increasing scarcity of suitable labour; (b) longer hours of work, but not longer than acceptable to the labour force; (c) attraction of married women and other "marginal" workers into the labour force, but with a subsequent "drying-up" of this source of additional labour; (d) increased productivity with more effective utilisation of capacity, associated with increasing difficulty in securing further improvement; and (e) increasing scarcity of raw materials in relation to increasing requirements. See Figure 7, which assumes that both demand and output are measured from a fairly high base level, that is a level at which the economy is beginning to experience difficulty in making a fully proportionate response in output to further increments of effective demand.

Out-Turn Actual attainment, as opposed to an estimate.

Outwork Minor productive operations carried out in private homes for factories. Outwork is paid for on the basis of output.

Overcapacity Excess productive capacity likely to arise in an industry subject to constant fluctuations in the demand for its products. Overcapacity or surplus capacity may also arise from long term changes in demand.

Overdraft *See* BANK OVERDRAFT.

Over-Full Employment A situation in which the demand for labour is too high, the number of vacancies greatly exceeding the number of people seeking work. The effect may be to produce a "cost-push" inflation, unless productivity (q.v.) rises faster than monetary incomes. *See* INFLATION, COST-PUSH; FULL EMPLOYMENT.

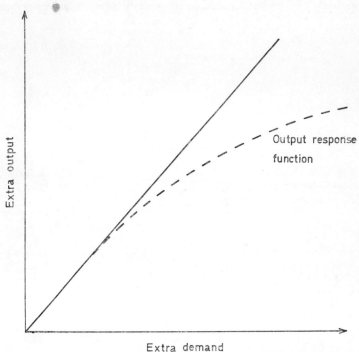

Output response function

Extra output

Extra demand

FIGURE 7   OUTPUT RESPONSE FUNCTION

Overheads Costs not directly chargeable to any unit produced. They include rent of premises, salaries of salesmen and research, salaries of directors, etc. and all other general expenses, as opposed to costs of raw materials, wages, etc., the proportion of which that goes into each unit can be determined.

Over-Population A condition when the marginal product of labour is less than the existing average output per head for the country as a whole. Thus, if the population were slightly reduced, the average output per head would be raised. *See* OPTIMUM POPULATION; UNDER-POPULATION.

Over-Subscription A situation in which the value of the applications for a new issue of securities (q.v.) exceeds the value of the securities offered. *See* ALLOTMENT LETTER; LETTER OF REGRET.

Over-the-Counter Market A market operated by security dealers for stocks not listed on stock exchanges.

Overtrading A situation in which a firm has little working capital.

Oxford Economic Papers Founded in 1938 as a medium for the publication of important material in the field of theoretical and applied economics; currently published in three numbers per year by the Oxford University Press.

P

Paasche Index A type of index for measuring changes, e.g. in prices. It utilises current period weights, but since current-year weights are seldom known, the index is difficult to construct. The index utilises the following method:

$$\frac{\Sigma\, P_n\, q_n}{\Sigma\, P_0\, q_n}$$

where P_0 = price in the base-year; P_n = price in the year under consideration; and q_n = quantity in the year under consideration. The index has the disadvantage that in times of generally rising prices it tends to under-estimate price increases. *See* LASPEYRES' INDEX.

Paid-Up Capital That part of the issued capital (q.v.) which is paid up by the shareholders.

Paper Gold *See* SPECIAL DRAWING RIGHTS (S.D.RS.).

Par *See* AT PAR.

Par Exchange Rate *See* PAR VALUE.

Par Value Or par exchange rate, the price of one country's currency in terms of another. The value of each currency is expressed in terms of gold; from these valuations the rates are obtained. The initial par value of the pound sterling, established with the International Monetary Fund (q.v.) in December, 1946, was 3.58134 grammes of fine gold per pound sterling, or 403.000 U.S. cents per pound sterling. In September, 1949, the par value of the pound was changed to 2.48828 grammes of fine gold, or 280.000 U.S. cents per pound. In November, 1967, the par value of the pound sterling was changed to 2.13281 grammes of fine gold, or 240.000 U.S. cents per pound. *See* DEVALUATION CRISES, 1949 AND 1967.

Paradox of Value A paradox in which an essential to life, such as water, is normally little valued, but a luxury, such as diamonds, carries a high price. The explanation lies in the fact that the amount of water available is normally so great that its marginal utility (q.v.) is zero. In respect of diamonds, the stock is small and the demand great; the marginal utility is high. It was William Stanley Jevons (1835–1882), Carl Menger (1840–1921) and Léon Walras (1834–1910) who resolved the apparent conflict between value and utility by recognising that it was the specific utility depending on the last

197

available, or marginal unit of a commodity, and not generic utility, which determined its value.

Parent Company   A firm that controls one or more other firms through stock ownership.

Paris Bourse   The French equivalent of the London Stock Exchange.   *See* BOURSE; STOCK EXCHANGE.

Paris Club   *See* GROUP OF TEN.

Partial Equilibrium Analysis   *See* EQUILIBRIUM THEORY.

Participating Preference Share   Preference share (q.v.) which also entitles the holder to a limited share in residual profits.

Participating Preferred Stock (U.S.)   Preferred stock (q.v.) which, under certain conditions, shares in earnings beyond the normal stated dividend.

Partnership, Limited   A partnership which includes limited partners whose financial obligations to the firm are limited to the amount of capital they have invested. This arrangement is permissible under the Limited Partnership Act 1907. A limited partner is debarred, however, from taking an active share in the management of the firm. There are not many partnerships of this type in Britain. Canadian law also permits this form of business unit.   *See* PARTNERSHIP, THE.

Partnership, The   An association of persons carrying on a business in common with a view to profit. It may comprise any number of people from 2 to 20 (10 in the case of a bank). The liability undertaken by partners is unlimited— each partner is personally liable for debts incurred by the firm to the full extent of his private fortune. Sole proprietors (q.v.) often turn their businesses into partnerships. It is a way of obtaining additional capital and sharing both risks and management functions. It is easy to form and dissolve a partnership. *See* PARTNERSHIP, LIMITED.

Passenger Transport Authorities   Authorities set up under the Transport Act, 1968, in the four main English conurbations outside London—Tyneside, Merseyside, South-East Lancashire-North-East Cheshire and the West Midlands. The task of these authorities is to integrate and develop the public passenger transport services over large coherent areas.

Patent   A grant from a government to a person or persons conferring for a specified time the exclusive privilege of making, using or selling a new invention. Thus an inventor gains the right to exclude all others from duplicating his invention for use or sale. Patents seek to encourage more inventive activity but restrict competition, furthering monopoly in various ways.

Pay-Back Method A method of comparing the profitability of alternative projects; the object is to determine over what period the net cash generated by an investment will repay the cost of the project:

$$\text{Pay-back period} = \frac{\text{Cost of Project}}{\text{Annual Increase in Income}}$$
(after tax)

The most serious drawback of the pay-back method is that it takes no account of the life of the investment, and ignores the timing of proceeds.

Pay Day *See* ACCOUNT DAY.

P.A.Y.E. "Pay as you earn" system of collecting Income Tax, i.e. the deduction each week or month of the tax on that week's or month's earnings. System introduced in 1944.

"Paying-in-Slip" Form used for paying into an account at a bank, notes, coins and cheques.

Payment by Results A technique for increasing productivity (q.v.); it includes piece-work methods of payment, incentive bonuses, and other schemes relating earnings to output.

Payroll Tax A tax imposed by a Government on the wages-bill of a business. In the United States a payroll tax was authorised by the Social Security Act, 1935, to provide for unemployment insurance and, in certain cases, for workmen's compensation. In Australia, a payroll tax is levied on employers at the rate of 2½ per cent on all wages and salaries paid, subject to an exemption of $20,800 per year. Rebates have been allowed for employers achieving certain specified increases in export sales. In Britain, a payroll tax was introduced in 1966 under the description of "selective employment tax" (q.v.). In addition, national insurance contributions and graduated pension contributions are levied on the number of persons employed in a business. Some economists hold the view that such a tax discourages firms from "hoarding" labour which they may not really need at a particular time, but are afraid to lose.

"Penal" Terms Severe terms or conditions imposed by the Bank of England (q.v.) in respect of loans to discount houses, made in the Bank's capacity as "lender of last resort" (q.v.). Although the Bank of England will never refuse to lend at last resort to the twelve discount houses which form the London Discount Market Association, the Bank dictates the terms on which it will lend particularly in respect of the rate of interest payable on money so borrowed and the period for which cash may be borrowed; as a matter of policy it always makes these terms "penal" and thus borrowing is kept to a minimum. Loans are usually for a minimum period of seven days and at Bank Rate; these terms are severe as money can normally be borrowed from day-to-day in the money market and at a rate of interest anything from 1 to 1¾ per cent below Bank Rate (q.v.). *See* DISCOUNT HOUSE.

Perfect Competition A concept used in economic analysis, for the purpose of exposing the basic forces common to all markets. On the supply side it implies (a) *Many Firms*, competing with each other, but each supplying so small a proportion of the total output as to be unable to exert a perceptible influence on the market price by changes in output; each firm is a "price-taker", and not a "price-maker"; (b) *A perfectly elastic supply of the factors of production*, each firm being able to increase output without driving up the level of wages, interest or rent; (c) *Mobility*, firms being completely free to enter or leave the industry without artificial hindrances; (d) *Complete knowledge*, each firm being fully informed about the activities of other firms in the industry and, in particular, their profitability. On the demand side, the concept implies (a) *Many purchasers*, no single buyer being able to perceptibly influence the market price by varying the size of his purchases; (b) *Complete knowledge*, each buyer knowing what price is being asked for a particular commodity in every part of the market; (c) *Absence of transport difficulties or costs*, which might prevent or impede a purchaser from taking full advantage of slight differences in prices for the same commodity in various parts of the market; (d) *Homogeneity of product*, the product of any firm being accepted by the purchaser as an exact substitute for the product of any other firm. The concept of perfect competition is as much removed from reality as the concept of absolute monopoly, imperfect competition being a better general description for a modern economy based on free enterprise. *See* IMPERFECT COMPETITION.

Perfect Market A concept sometimes used in economic theory for the purpose of studying certain effects, in which it is assumed that there are no transfer costs of goods from place to place so that uniform prices would be established everywhere, and that every seller is in contact with every buyer and every buyer in contact with every seller. *See* IMPERFECT MARKET.

Perfect Market Transparency The objective of price information agreements; a market is perfectly transparent for the sellers if all sellers know exactly the prices asked and obtained by their competitors, the terms of sale, the quality of their competitors' products and the names of their customers. The result may be conscious parallelism (q.v.) with regard to prices, particularly in an oligopoly (q.v.), paralysing price competition. *See* INFORMATION AGREEMENT.

Personal Cheque Service A simple chequing service provided by banks instead of a full banking service to meet the needs of people requiring a standard, limited banking service, provided at the lowest possible cost.

Personal Loans from Banks A method of borrowing available in Britain to credit-worthy customers who wish to spread the cost of certain items of expenditure over a period of time. They are granted for fixed periods normally ranging from six to twenty-four months and are repayable by equal monthly instalments. The loans are intended to assist the purchase of consumer durables such as motor cars, sewing machines, refrigerators, washing machines and furniture.

Phantom Competition The quotation by customers of other suppliers' prices at lower levels than the true ones. *See* COMPETITION.

Phillips Curve Developed by Professor A. W. Phillips of the London School of Economics, a graphical curve which plots annual price changes (%) against unemployment rate (%). The curve suggests that as unemployment declines, wages and prices must rise; conversely as unemployment rises, wage and price increases tend to diminish. It is recognised that education, training of the unskilled, employment for hard-core unemployed, and facilitating the movement of people in search of jobs to where jobs are available, has the effect of "shifting" the Phillips curve in the direction of more employment with less inflation. Figure 8 illustrates a Phillips curve for the United States for the years 1960–1968.

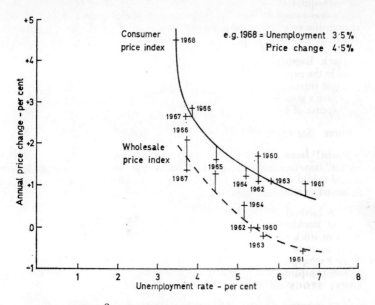

FIGURE 8 PHILLIPS CURVE FOR U.S.A. SOURCE: BLS

Physiocratic School A group of French statesmen and philosophers led by Francois Quesnay (1694–1774) whose thoughts and writings in the 18th century marked the beginning of a science of political economy. The Physiocrats were the first to grasp the conception of a unified science of society. Their studies brought them to believe in a "natural order" based upon property, security and liberty. It was the essence of that natural order that in a free system the particular interest of the individual can never be separated from the common interest of all; therefore restriction is artificial and liberty natural. The Government's duty lay in upholding the rights of private property and individual liberty by removing all artificial barriers and punishing those who threatened the existence of any of these rights. They believed in the concept of free competition, a process resulting in the establishment of the "bon prix", which is the most advantageous price for both parties. From this it followed that both labour and trade must be free. Quesnay argued that "to secure the greatest amount of pleasure with the least possible outlay should be the aim of all economic effort". This is what the natural order aimed at. Alfred Marshall in his *Principles of Economics* (1895) commented that the chief motive of the Physiocrats was not to increase the riches of merchants and fill the exchequers of kings; it was to diminish the suffering and degradation which was caused by extreme poverty—"They thus gave to economics its modern aim of seeking after such knowledge as may help to raise the quality of human life." *See* SINGLE-TAX.

Pick-a-Back Export Scheme A technique, whereby a firm already established in the export field makes its services available without charge to a small firm just entering the market. Thus a small firm obtains the assistance of a large firm's goodwill, experience and "know-how" and is saved the trouble and expense of setting up its own export department.

Piece-Rates *See* TIME-RATES AND PIECE-RATES.

"Pink Form" Issue A compromise between a public issue (q.v.) of shares and a "rights" issue (q.v.) to existing shareholders. Existing shareholders are simply offered special consideration if they apply for new issue shares; special forms are issued to existing shareholders printed, usually, on pink paper.

Placing A method of issuing securities to raise new capital. By this method a firm of stockbrokers, acting on behalf of the company concerned, sells shares or stock to large institutions or other investors. A proportion of the shares must be made available to the public through the medium of the Stock Exchange (q.v.). This method is normally only used in the case of smaller companies. *See* OFFER FOR SALE; PUBLIC ISSUE; RIGHTS ISSUE; STOCK EXCHANGE INTRODUCTION.

Planned Economy An economy in which the problems of production, distribution and growth, are resolved by a central planning authority. *See* LAISSEZ-FAIRE; MIXED ECONOMY.

Planning The plotting of a course of action. Planning may be merely "indicative", involving the collection, processing and distribution of information to others responsible for policy-making and executive action; or it may be "normative", actually involving executive action or enforcement.

Planning Permission A provision of British town and country planning legislation that no development or change in the existing use of land or buildings may be made without the approval or "planning permission" of the appropriate planning authority, e.g. the County Council or the County Borough Council.

Ploughing-Back The re-investment of profits in a company for the purpose of buying new plant or machinery, extending buildings and generally adding to the productive capacity of a company. Often described as " self-financing".

202

Political and Economic Planning (P.E.P.) A research organisation founded in 1931 to study and publish works on economic problems. It has been financed by grants from foundations, contributions from individuals, firms and other bodies.

Political Economy Economic thought regarded as a branch of statecraft. The older, now discarded, name for economics.

Political Science The study of the technique or art of governmental administration.

Pool An association of producers which attempts to control price by the regulation of output, each member firm being allocated a specific output which it may not exceed.

Population, Census of See CENSUS OF POPULATION.

Population, Declining A population diminishing in size. In the case of a country the effect will be to raise the average output per head only if the country was over-populated economically in the first place. Short of mass emigration, a declining population will only occur when the birth-rate falls below the death-rate. An unavoidable effect is the growth in the size of the dependent population consisting mainly of the older-age groups. For the working population, this implies a progressively increasing burden of welfare services. The smaller total market and labour force may mean that the full economies of large-scale production cannot be achieved. Industry would also experience greater difficulty in securing a transfer of labour from declining to expanding industries.

Population, Dependent The whole population of a country minus the working population.

Population, Royal Commission on A Royal Commission set up in 1944 "to examine the facts relating to the present population trends in Great Britain; to investigate the causes of these trends and to consider their probable consequences; to consider what measures, if any, should be taken in the national interest to influence the future trend of population; and to make recommendations." The Commission's Report appeared in 1949 (Cmd 7695). The Commission had "no hesitation in concluding that a replacement size of family is desirable in Great Britain at the present time." They feared the effect of declining numbers among Western peoples on "the prestige and influence of the West" and on the "maintenance and extension of Western values and culture." The Commission recommended an increase in family allowances (q.v.) and income tax reliefs to encourage people to have larger families.

Portfolio The list of securities held by a person or Institution.

Post Office Savings Bank   A savings bank for small savers established under an Act of 1861.   Interest is paid on deposits at a statutory rate of 2½ per cent per annum;   up to £10 can be withdrawn on demand, the withdrawal of larger sums requiring a few days' notice.   Deposits are placed in the hands of the National Debt Commissioners (q.v.) for investment.   Depositors may pay money in, or withdraw money, at any post office in Britain where savings bank business is transacted.   Under the Post Office Savings Bank Act 1966 investment accounts were introduced on which depositors with a minimum balance of £50 in their ordinary accounts can earn a higher rate of interest;   the interest is liable to income tax.   *See* TRUSTEE SAVINGS BANKS.

Post-War Credits   Introduced by the Government in 1941 as an additional method of raising income to finance the War.   Some income tax allowances were reduced and the additional tax credited to the taxpayer for repayment after the War.   About £800 m. were raised in this way.   After the War, it became at once clear that if this huge sum were to be repaid quickly it would merely serve to aggravate the inflationary trends of those years.   Repayments have been gradual;   they may be claimed by a man of 60 or a woman of 55, or by a person suffering hardship or ill-health.   Since 1959, compound interest at 2½ per cent has been payable on outstanding amounts.

Power, Ministry of   Established in 1942 as the Ministry of Fuel and Power, a Ministry made responsible for policy matters affecting the coal, oil, gas, electricity and iron and steel industries, and for the general administration of the statutues relating to those industries.   The Ministry was also responsible under the Nuclear Installations (Licensing and Insurance) Act 1959 for the siting, design, construction, operation and maintenance of nuclear power stations and other nuclear installations in respect of safety.   Commercial nuclear power stations are owned by the Central Electricity Generating Board (q.v.), and experimental reactors by the United Kingdom Atomic Energy Authority.   Absorbed in October, 1969, by the Ministry of Technology.

Predatory Price-Cutting   The selling of a commodity at unreasonably low prices in order to injure or destroy the competition of a competitor.

Preference Share   A share which gives the holder a prior claim over the holders of ordinary shares, both in respect of the payment of dividend and in respect of return of capital if the company goes into liquidation;   preference shares carry a fixed rate of interest (e.g. 5 per cent on the par value of the share).   *See* PARTICIPATING PREFERENCE SHARE.

Preferences, Cardinality and Ordinality of   The cardinal view of utility (q.v.), held by many economists before the 1930s, is that the amount of utility is related to the quantity of commodities already possessed and that changes in utility arising from changes in the quantities possessed can be measured.   During the inter-war years, attention shifted to the ordinal aspect of utility;   the opinion developed that it was unnecessary to assume that utility was measurable and that a more satisfactory theory of consumer behaviour could be constructed simply on the assumption that the utility from different combinations of commodities could be ranked in order of preference by consumers. *See* INDIFFERENCE ANALYSIS; INDIFFERENCE CURVE.

Preferred Ordinary Share A share which carries a right to a fixed dividend, after the payment of dividend to preference shareholders. *See* D E F E R R E D ORDINARY SHARE.

Preferred Stock (U.S.) Shares representing ownership of a business, but the owners of preferred stock have a prior claim on distributed earnings over any claim by common stockholders, and a prior claim on the company's assets if the business is dissolved. Preferred stock has a stated dividend rate; however this dividend must be declared by the company's Board of Directors each time it is due. Dividends are therefore not as certain as in the case of bond interest payments, and a higher rate of return compensates for the higher risk; on the other hand earnings are generally less than for common stock. *See* BOND; CALLABLE PREFERRED STOCK; COMMON STOCK; CONVERTIBLE PREFERRED STOCK; CUMULATIVE PREFERRED STOCK; NON-CUMULATIVE PREFERRED STOCK; PARTICIPATING PREFERRED STOCK; PRIOR PREFERRED STOCK.

Premium The difference between the price at which a security was issued and the price at which it now stands, if the latter is the higher.

Premium Savings Bonds British Government securities issued by the Treasury through the Post Office. No interest is payable to lenders on these bonds, but they are included in a monthly draw for cash prizes. The principal of the Bonds and the prizes allotted are a charge on the Consolidated Fund of the United Kingdom. A weekly £25,000 premium bond prize is given.

Present Worth The capital sum, which, if invested at the time of the commissioning of a plant, would together with the interest earned suffice to pay the annual capital charges on the plant as they occur year by year.

If it is necessary to calculate an average annual cost over the whole life of the plant, the total present worth may be converted to an "equivalent average annual cost" by multiplying by the appropriate annuity rate. Present worth factors and annuity rates may be found from "Inwood's Tables", Archers "Tables of Repayments", etc.

For a 6 per cent interest rate, the present worth factor is given by:

$$\frac{1}{1.06^m}$$

where m = years of life of the plant (assumed for depreciation purposes).
For a 6 per cent interest rate, the percentage annuity rate is given by:

$$\frac{0.06\,(1.06)^n}{(1.06)^n - 1} \times 100$$

where n = term of repayment in years.
The present worth method offers a general and systematic approach to the

problem of allocating a series of irregular costs to the units of a continuous output.

Price The value of a commodity or service in terms of money; an exchange ratio, e.g. three shillings a pound. The term "price" is used in relation to the exchange value of goods and some services; in respect of human services the equivalent terms "wage", "salary", "commission" or "fee" are used. Again the price of borrowing money is called "interest" and the price of hiring land or equipment "rent".

Price Discrimination The charging of different prices to different groups of individuals for the same goods or services. This may occur when there is a geographical separation of markets, the structure of demand in each market being different. It may also occur in respect of railway freight charges. It has also been practised by medical practitioners in communities of wide disparity of wealth. *See* "CHARGING WHAT THE TRAFFIC WILL BEAR".

Price, Equilibrium The price at which the supply of, and demand for, a commodity are equal.

Price Leadership A form of conscious parallelism (q.v.) with regard to prices whereby the price policy of one firm, the price leader, is deliberately followed by others.

Price Level An average of individual prices in any given market.

Price, Long-Run Normal The price of a commodity during the period in which the rate of production is completely adjusted to demand.

Price, Market The price of a commodity during a period in which its supply is fixed.

Price Mechanism System used in a competitive society for the distribution of scarce resources through the agency of price. If too little of commodity A and too much of commodity B is being produced, the demand price for A rises, and that for B falls. The signal is thus given to the productive system to make the necessary adjustments. If competition were perfect these adjustments would continue until marginal cost and price were equal. The prices of all goods and services form an interrelated system; what we are prepared to pay for A depends on the terms which we can obtain for B, C, D, etc. In other words all prices are mutually determined. Price tends to equate the amount sellers are prepared to offer for sale and the amount which buyers wish to buy.

One of Alfred Marshall's greatest contributions to economics was the discovery that pricing problems should be treated primarily from the view point of time. He distinguished three fundamental time periods in pricing:

(1) Market price—the price of a commodity during a period in which its supply is fixed;

(2) Short-run normal price—the price of a commodity during a (longer) period in which the rate of production (per unit of time) is variable but in which there exists a fixed amount of plant.

(3) Long-run normal price—the price of a commodity during the period in which the rate of production is completely variable.

He recognised the roles of supply and demand in the determination of price, but also the long-term influence of costs of production on supply and hence on price.

The price mechanism is defective in that it does not necessarily succeed in regulating supply as required; in that it does not necessarily operate without inflation; and in that it does not automatically adjust social and private marginal net products. In addition, in world commodity markets price has proved a singularly ineffective weapon for achieving reductions in output. Small diminutions in price or demand have produced gluts of astonishing proportions. This has been largely due to the efforts of the small peasant who, faced with a reduction in price, increases his output in order to maintain his income. During the Great Depression, 1929–1935 the world stock of food-stuffs and raw materials increased two- or three-fold while prices declined some 50 per cent or more. Remedies have included proposals for "buffer stocks" (q.v.) and for Government controlled quota arrangements. *See* DEMAND; MARGINAL SOCIAL AND PRIVATE NET PRODUCTS.

Price Ring A loose association of firms for the control of prices by mutual agreement.

Price, Theory of A branch of economics (q.v.) involving studies of the working of the price mechanism (q.v.).

Pricing, Full Cost *See* FULL COST PRICING.

Pricing System *See* PRICE MECHANISM.

Primage Duty A customs duty on imported goods. For example, primage is payable on some imports into Australia charged at 4, 5 and 10 per cent ad valorem according to type and origin.

Primary Employment Employment provided by investment (q.v.) in physical productive assets.

Primary Industry *See* EXTRACTIVE INDUSTRY; SECONDARY INDUSTRY.

Primary Inputs The contributions to production of the three factors of pro-duction—land, labour and capital.

Prime Bill A bill of exchange (q.v.) having an excellent credit risk.

Prime Costs *See* VARIABLE COSTS.

Prime Rate (U.S.) The lowest interest rate payable by borrowers having the highest credit rating (q.v.).

Primogeniture   The principle or rule by which the estate of a father descends unbroken to the eldest son. Inheritance based on this principle works in the direction of a greater concentration of wealth.

Prior Charges   The prior claims of the debenture (q.v.) and the preference share (q.v.) over the ordinary share in respect of capital repayments and interest or dividend distribution.

Prior Preferred Stock (U.S.)   Preferred stock (q.v.) which ranks ahead of any preferred and common stock as to claims on dividends and assets. *See* COMMON STOCK.

Private Costs   Costs necessarily incurred by a firm (q.v.) or individual engaging in the production of goods and services. *See* SOCIAL COSTS.

Private Limited Company   A limited liability (q.v.) business firm with the following characteristics:

    (a) The minimum number of members is two and the maximum fifty (with the exception of persons employed by the company and of former employees);

    (b) It cannot invite the public to subscribe for any shares or debentures;

    (c) It must restrict the right to transfer its shares.

    (d) An annual balance sheet must be submitted to the Registrar of Companies.

There are about 540,000 private limited companies in Britain. *See* COMPANIES ACTS 1948 AND 1967; COMPANY, LEGAL FORMATION OF; PUBLIC LIMITED COMPANY.

Private Placing   The provision of business capital by a finance company, not by way of an ordinary loan but by the purchase of a new issue of debentures or shares.

Private Sector   The "private sector" of the economy is the combination of elements in the economy which are not organs or agencies of central or local government and therefore includes the company sector and the personal sector.

Probability   The degree of certainty of the occurrence of a future event, as given by the equation:

$$\text{Probability} = \frac{\text{Total no. of occurrences of event}}{\text{Total no. of trials}}$$

The answer will lie between 0 (absolute impossibility) and 1 (absolute certainty).

Producer Goods   Goods made for the purpose of producing consumer goods (q.v.) and other capital goods, e.g. machinery of all kinds. Synonymous with "capital goods".

Product Differentiation   Attempts to create differences between products of a similar nature, e.g. breakfast cereals, by introducing distinct brand names, variations in preparation and presentation, and by skilful advertising. The object is to ensure that the product of any one firm is not regarded as a perfect substitute, in the mind of the buyer, for the product of any other firm. If a product establishes itself in the public mind, it may then command a price somewhat higher than another product of similar qualities.

Product, Homogeneous A product of one firm which, in the minds of buyers, is absolutely identical with products of other firms.

Production Activities resulting in a supply of useful goods and services. These activities include mineral extraction, manufacturing, agriculture, transport and communication, wholesale and retail distribution, and the work of civil servants and local government employees.

Production Coefficient The quantity of productive services necessary to produce one unit of a commodity, e.g. if it requires 15 cwts. of coke to produce one ton of pig-iron, then the production coefficient is 3/4. The concept is useful for studying trends.

Production Costs *See* COSTS OF PRODUCTION.

Production Function The relationship between input of production services and output of product, per unit of time. Production functions are descriptive of techniques or systems of organisation of production services. The problem of production consists in selecting the most appropriate production function and then determining the input which will minimise costs.

Production Indifference Curve *See* TRANSFORMATION CURVE.

Production-Mix In a business enterprise, the proportions of different goods produced.

Production Optimum A position in which economic resources are so allocated that the total product could not be increased by any re-allocation of resources and the production of one good cannot be increased without reducing the output of another.

Production Potential Broadly the rate at which the national product of a country can grow given only the physical limitations of manpower, capital and productivity, and assuming that there are no balance of payments difficulties.

Production, Theory of A branch of economics (q.v.) concerned with the study of alternative production methods and the consequences of decisions taken in respect of production methods.

Production, Time Structure of The time interval between a decision to undertake production and the beginning of the outflow of the product; the more capitalistic or "capital intensive" the method of production, the longer will be the time interval. In respect of a power station some 5/6 years may elapse between a decision to build and the initial flow of electricity into the Grid.

Productivity The efficiency with which productive resources, i.e. labour, capital and land, are used; the motive for increasing productivity is to produce more goods at a lower cost per unit of output while maintaining quality. It is not easy to measure changes in productivity, but the relationship of output to man-hours expended is often adopted as a rough guide; this criterion relates to input of labour only, without reference to capital or land, and in certain circumstances may give a misleading picture. The increasing total annual production in Britain has been due partly to an increase in population, but mainly to increasing productivity per man-hour. The rate of improvement in total output and productivity has yet to achieve the targets set by the National Economic Development Council (q.v.) as within Britain's capacity. The main factors contributing to high industrial productivity are:

(a) Adequate buildings, plant and equipment, intensively used and kept up to date by replacement;
(b) Suitably trained labour;
(c) Adequate and steady supplies of raw materials;
(d) Efficient services, e.g. power, transport, etc.;
(e) The best managerial skills and technical know-how applied to the organisation of production and the lowering of costs;
(f) Markets capable of absorbing the whole of the output;
(g) Good employee/employer relationships;
(h) An industrial climate favourable to expansion and confidence in the future;
(i) The abandonment of restrictive practices (q.v.) by both management and men.

The subject of productivity is closely examined in Graham Hutton's book *We too can prosper; the promise of productivity* written at the request of the British Productivity Council (formerly the Anglo-American Council on Productivity—U.K. Section) summing-up the findings of the sixty-six teams who compared American and British industrial efficiency. *See* ANGLO-AMERICAN COUNCIL ON PRODUCTIVITY; BRITISH PRODUCTIVITY COUNCIL; PRODUCTIVITY AGREEMENTS.

Productivity Agreements Agreements between employers and workers aimed at reducing the wasteful use both of capital and of labour; increased rewards to workers are accompanied by new standards of work measurement and new methods of control to ensure that the standards are adhered to. Productivity agreements have proved profitable to both parties, while promoting the interests of the nation. *See* PRODUCTIVITY.

Products, Joint *See* JOINT PRODUCTS.

Profit and Loss Account A summary account incorporating all gains and losses in a business during a given period of trading; the account may thus show a net profit or a net loss. Known in the United States as a "loss and gain account".

Profit Motive In economic analysis, an assumption that in general the financial and investment decisions of private firms are controlled by a desire to increase total long-run profits. Profits permit a return to investors who have risked their capital, provide a source of capital for further expansion, and, in a competitive economy, provide an indication of success.

Profit, Natural Rate of   Term used by the Physiocrats for the necessary rate of profit in industry; now known as "normal profit" (q.v.).   *See* PHYSIOCRATIC SCHOOL.

Profit, Normal   *See* NORMAL PROFIT.

Profit Sharing Schemes   Schemes in which employees share in the profits of the business which employs them.   Usually a proportion of the annual profits is set aside for distribution to employees in the form of a bonus, the bonus itself being proportionate to the individual's wage.   *See* CO-PARTNERSHIP IN INDUSTRY.

Profit-Taking   Sales by "bull" speculators of commodities or shares, following a rise in price, in order to profit.

Profitability of Alternative Projects, Methods of Comparing   *See* COMPARATIVE COST METHOD; DISCOUNTED CASH FLOW METHOD; PAY-BACK METHOD; RETURN ON INVESTMENT METHODS.

Profits   What remains out of business earnings after paying current expenses (costs of production) and providing for the maintenance intact of the money value of the assets of the business.   In the case of an individual employer two further items may be deducted:

(a)   the salary due to the employer himself for his own work, and

(b)   interest on any of his own capital invested in the business.

The remainder may be regarded as "pure profit" which is the reward for taking risks.   Pure profits are more clearly distinguished in the case of "impersonal" enterprises (private and public companies largely) where all salaries due and interest on all capital employed are taken account of fully in the costs of production.

The term "normal profit" appears in economic literature.   This term can be best defined as the least sum which must be paid to the business man (or firm) to induce the investment of capital in any particular process.   Normal profit or expectation is equal to what could be obtained if it was employed in some other way, allowing for different degrees of risk and for any "nonmonetary" advantages or disadvantages.   Economists regard normal profit as a necessary cost of production—a cost necessary to call forth a sufficient supply of that special kind of labour, enterprise.   Profit may include an element of rent or quasi-rent (q.v.).   High profits may be earned in some industries as a consequence of monopoly power, rather than a high degree of uncertainty.   Such profits are not a necessary cost, but an economic rent (q.v.) exacted at the expense of the community.

Profits Tax   A tax imposed from 1937 to 1966 on the profits of trades and businesses carried on in the United Kingdom;   from 1939 to 1946 it was largely replaced by an excess profits tax, only the higher of the two taxes being chargeable.   From 1st April, 1961, the rate was set at 15 per cent.   The Finance

Act, 1965, provided that the profits tax should come to an end on 5th April, 1966; after that date all profits came within the scope of a corporation tax (q.v.).

Program The detailed list of instructions that controls the operation of a computer.

Programme Evaluation and Review Technique (P.E.R.T.) A network analysis (q.v.) technique and a variant of critical path analysis (q.v.). In respect of a project, how long each job or stage is likely to take is given an optimistic and a pessimistic time; statistical methods are used to find the most probable completion time for the project; costs are estimated for each task so that the cost of altering the required completion date may be calculated.

Programmers Persons who prepare a program (q.v.) for a computer.

"Prompt" Cash Payment Cash payment, but one which allows two or three days grace to examine and check the goods and invoices.

Propensities to Consume and Save Concepts developed by John Maynard Keynes (1884–1946) which represent the fractions of the total proceeds or income derived from employment which are, respectively, consumed and invested. The amount which a community spends on consumption depends (a) partly on the amount of its income; (b) partly on the other attendant circumstances; (c) partly on the subjective needs and the psychological propensities and habits of the individuals composing it; and (d) the principles on which the income is divided between them. Keynes defined the principal objective factors which influence the propensity to consume as (a) a change in the wage-unit, i.e. a change in real income; (b) a change in the difference between income and net income; (c) windfall changes in capital values not allowed for in calculating net income; (d) changes in the rate of time-discounting, i.e. in the ratio of exchange between present goods and future goods; (e) changes in fiscal policy, e.g. rate of income tax, tax on "unearned" income, taxes on capital gains, death duties, etc.; (f) changes in the expectation of the relation between the present and future levels of income. Keynes also defined the subjective factors—the motives or objects of subjective character—which lead individuals to refrain from spending out of their incomes. These motives are (a) to build up a reserve against unforeseen contingencies; (b) to provide for future needs—old-age, family education, etc.; (c) to enjoy interest and appreciation, because a larger real consumption at a later date is preferred to a smaller immediate consumption; (d) to enjoy a gradually increasing expenditure; (e) to enjoy a sense of independence and power to do things; (f) to secure a masse de manoeuvre to carry out speculative or business projects; (g) to bequeath a fortune; and (h) to satisfy pure miserliness. Keynes described these eight subjective motives to save as the motives of Precaution, Foresight, Calculation, Improvement, Independence, Enterprise, Pride and Avarice. Apart from the savings of individuals, Keynes also defined the motives for saving by central and local government, by institutions and by business corporations. These are (a) to secure resources to carry out further capital investment; (b) to secure liquid resources to meet emergencies, difficulties and depressions; (c) to secure a gradually increasing income; (d) financial prudence and the anxiety to be "on the right side". *See* MARGINAL PROPENSITIES TO CONSUME AND SAVE, KEYNESIAN REVOLUTION.

Prospectus A document issued by a Company or person wishing to raise capital by public subscription; the minimum contents of a prospectus are defined in the Companies Act 1948. The requirements of the Stock Exchange Council must also be complied with if it is intended to apply to the Council for a quotation (q.v.).

Protection The adoption by the State of special measures to protect an industry from competition. Three types of argument have been used in support of protection:

(a) It may be considered desirable to forgo the economic advantages flowing from the international division of labour for the purpose of making a country self-sufficient in respect of certain commodities, or in respect of all commodities;

(b) It may be thought expedient to impose tarif de combats (q.v.) in order to induce other countries to lower their tariff barriers in respect of one or more commodities. This exception to free trade policy was recognised as permissible by Adam Smith.

(c) It may be thought desirable to give temporary protection to a young and growing industry. This is known as the "infant industry" argument. It is to be found in John Stuart Mill's *Principles of Political Economy*. *See* CLASSICAL SCHOOL; INFANT INDUSTRY; TARIFF (a).

Proxy Variable The taking of unemployment or some other variable as a "proxy" for demand, instead of directly measuring demand forces.

Pty. Abbreviation for "Proprietary" used as part of the names of private limited companies in Australia. *See* LIMITED LIABILITY.

Public Accounts Committee *See* COMMITTEE ON PUBLIC ACCOUNTS.

Public Corporation A corporate body created by public authority, with defined powers and functions, and financially independent. It is administered by a Board. Its capital structure and financial operations are similar to those of a public company, but the stockholders (if any) have no equity interests and no voting rights or power to appoint Board members. The first public corporation to meet this definition was the Central Electricity Board set up in 1926 to promote and control the bulk generation of electricity and to construct and maintain the bulk transmission lines. The British Broadcasting Corporation was established shortly afterwards under a Royal Charter.

Public Finance The provision of money by the community through taxes and rates to be spent by national and local government authorities on projects and schemes of national and local benefit. Public finance has four functions (a) the provision of essential services; (b) the encouragement or control of particular sectors of the economy; (c) the implementation of social policy in respect of social services, and (d) the encouragement of the growth of the economy as a whole.

Public Good A good (q.v.) or service (q.v.) provided for the community by the government or local authority, e.g. education, public health services, libraries, theatres, museums, etc.

Public Issue A method of issuing equities (q.v.) to raise new business funds for capital investment. The company fixes a price for the shares to be issued, and the public are invited through the newspapers to apply for stated amounts of the shares at the specified prices. The company does not sell the shares first to an issuing house, although an issuing house may be retained as adviser. *See* ISSUING HOUSE; PLACING; OFFER FOR SALE; OFFER FOR SALE BY TENDER; RIGHTS ISSUE; STOCK EXCHANGE INTRODUCTION.

Public Limited Company A company which cannot comply with the rules relating to private limited companies (q.v.) and enjoys the following privileges;
  - (a) While it must have a minimum of seven members there is no maximum limit;
  - (b) It can invite the general public to subscribe for its shares and debentures (Stock Exchange permission is required if it is intended to employ Stock Exchange (q.v.) facilities);
  - (c) If the company's shares are quoted on the Stock Exchange their transfer cannot be restricted.

In Britain, there are about 560,000 companies, of which just over 16,000 are public companies. Companies are formed in England, Wales and Scotland in accordance with the Companies Act 1948, and in Northern Ireland under the Companies Act (Northern Ireland) 1932—both Acts are very similar in their provisions. Canadian law takes a similar form. *See* COMPANIES ACTS 1948 AND 1967; COMPANY, LEGAL FORMATION OF; LIMITED LIABILITY.

Public Sector The "public sector" of the economy usually denotes the combination of the central Government, the local authorities and the nationalised industries and other public corporations.

Public Utilities Undertakings which provide essential services to the community, e.g. gas, electricity and water undertakings.

Public Works Roads, bridges, public baths, theatres, multi-storey car parks and other projects undertaking by the government or local authority to provide services for the community.

Public Works Loan Board A Government agency which considers applications for loans by local authorities and certain other bodies. Most of the loans have been made to local authorities for the purposes of implementing capital schemes already sanctioned by Government Departments. The Board is the main source of capital funds for smaller local authorities; larger authorities enjoy larger rate incomes and are more able to raise funds on the open market. The rates of interest charged by the Board are fixed by the Treasury; the rates usually bear a fixed relationship with the Bank Rate and consequently vary with it.

Punter A person who buys and sells quickly, never holding a security for long.

Purchase Tax An ad valorem tax (q.v.) imposed on a wide range of consumer goods in Britain. It was introduced in 1940 to reduce consumption, release resources for war purposes, and provide additional revenue to prosecute the war; today it is essentially a source of revenue while providing another instrument for regulating the economy, either generally or selectively. The tax is generally collected at the wholesale stage in the distribution of goods. *See* REGULATOR; TAXES.

Purchasing Power Parity Theory A theory which asserts that, left to the free play of market forces, the rates of exchange between currencies not linked with gold depend upon the relative purchasing power of the currencies in the countries concerned.

Pure Economics Another name for theoretical economics.

Pure Profit Payment for taking risks. This is a necessary payment to those who invest capital other than in "safe" investments, such as Government stock. *See* NORMAL PROFIT.

Put Options *See* SHARE OPTIONS.

Pyramiding (a) When a tax is imposed at an early stage of production, the effect on the final price when a percentage increase is made at each successive stage of manufacture; (b) the purchasing of the same security on a rising market; (c) the concentration of control over joint-stock companies by a series of controlling interests in holding companies.

Q

Quality Control, Statistical A method of estimating the quality of the whole from the quality of the samples taken from the whole. The method is based upon the laws of chance and has a sound mathematical basis.

Quantity Theory of Money A theory developed by the American economist Irving Fisher (1867–1947), the essentials of which are contained in the equation:

$$MV = PT$$

where M = the amount of money (bank notes, etc. plus bank deposits); V = the velocity of circulation; T = total number of trade transactions; and P = general price level.

From this equation it may be deduced that with V and T constant an increase in M must result in an increase in P. With V and P constant, an increase in M could be offset by an increase in T. With both P and T constant, a decrease in M could be offset by an increase in V. If T is constant, an increase in P may be due to an increase in M or V, or both. The equation is useful in indicating the relationship between the four parameters. *See* CAMBRIDGE THEORY OF MONEY.

"Quarterly Journal of Economics" A journal published by Harvard University.

Quasi-Rent Payment made for a commodity or service for the time being in limited supply. In such circumstances more is paid for a particular commodity or service than would really be necessary to maintain the existing supply. Where quasi-rent exists there is a true surplus, or "economic rent" (q.v.). The quasi-rent may be eliminated either by an increase in supply, if this is practicable, or a fall in demand. The concept of this differential payment or quasi-rent was developed by Marshall.

Queueing, Theory of Theory concerned with the rates at which productive facilities and services should be provided in order to achieve optimum efficiency, i.e. to minimise "queues" or bottlenecks and synchronise better the supply of facilities or services with the demand for them. In management science, queueing theory attempts to describe how customers arrive for a service, how that service meets their requirements in terms of average and variations in service time, how long a customer may have to wait and how long a service unit may be idle. Also known as "waiting line theory".

Quick Assets (U.S.)   Current assets which can be quickly converted into cash.

Quick Assets Ratio (U.S.)   Quick assets (q.v.) divided by current liabilities.

Quotation   (a) An amount stated by a dealer or supplier as the current price of a commodity or stocks; (b) A privilege granted to a Company or Government Department, etc., by the Stock Exchange Council of having the price of a share "quoted" in the Official List of Share Prices.

R

Rack-Rent The highest rent a tenant can be compelled to pay.

Radcliffe Committee A Committee appointed by Treasury Minute dated 3rd May 1957 "to inquire into the working of the monetary and credit system, and to make recommendations". The Committee's Report was presented to Parliament in August, 1959. The committee concluded that the monetary mechanism could not, as operated through changes in the bank rate (q.v.), be relied on to control the economy but should be supplemented by increasing use of physical and other controls, and that there should be more central control over the banking system.

Rally A brisk rise following a decline in the general price level of a security market, or of an individual stock or share.

Rate Deficiency Grant A central government grant to local authorities whose rate-income was below the national average in proportion to their population. A way of giving additional help to poorer authorities. Formerly known as an Exchequer Equalisation Grant, it was incorporated in 1968 in a rate support grant (q.v.).

Rate of Interest The amount of interest due each year in respect of a sum of money borrowed, expressed as a percentage of the total sum borrowed, e.g. 5 per cent per annum (5 pounds per 100 pounds borrowed per annum).

Rate of Return Concept *See* CAPITAL EMPLOYED, RETURN ON.

Rate Support Grant The main channel of Exchequer (q.v.) aid to local authorities, replacing the general grant (q.v.) and the rate-deficiency grant (q.v.).

Rates, Local Local taxes paid to a local authority by the occupiers of property as a contribution towards local services, e.g. education, roads, sewage disposal, health services, libraries, parks, etc. The amount paid by each occupier depends upon his property's rateable value, which is derived from its annual rental value. The rate is expressed as so many shillings and pence in the pound (the "rate poundage") which occupiers have to pay on the rateable value of their property. It is calculated each year by the local authority by dividing the total sum to be raised locally by the estimated yield of a penny rate in the area. *See* DERATING.

Rating A technique often used as a basis for incentive schemes. It involves three related procedures (a) to determine the time required to perform a task; (b) to measure the amount of work in it; and (c) to relate the work value to some scale of cash rewards.

Rationalisation The re-organisation of an industry in order to achieve greater efficiency throughout the whole industry. During the inter-war years, several industries (e.g. shipbuilding and cotton spinning) which had excess capacity through a fall in demand, were re-organised for this purpose, production being concentrated at the most efficient works while the less efficient works were closed down.

Rationing The official control of the right to purchase essential commodities in times of acute scarcity (e.g. wartime), to ensure that everyone shall have a minimum share and yet restrict overall community consumption. It is justified in any circumstances in which rationing by price alone on a free market would have disastrous results for a large section of the community.

Real and Money Terms Real terms take account of the changing value of money, whereas money terms merely reflect such changes. The actual money value of the gross national product over a period of time may increase, but the extent to which this increase is "real" depends upon the change in value of money over the same period. A money value increase may be offset entirely by a fall in the value of money, so that an apparent increase in the money value of the gross national product may be entirely misleading. Real figures are often expressed using a particular year as "the base year", i.e. the year to which the values in other years are related in order to overcome movements in prices.

Rebate A reduction in the price of a commodity, allowed perhaps for prompt payment or the purchase of a large quantity. *See* DEFERRED REBATE.

Receipt Written acknowledgment of the payment of a debt.

Recommended Prices Prices recommended or suggested by manufacturers to retailers, as a guide to retail prices considered appropriate for the goods supplied. *See* RESALE PRICES ACT 1964.

Redeemable Preference Share A share which a company may repay out of its reserve funds. This class of share may be issued by a company only if authorised by its articles of association.

Redemption Date The date on which a loan will be repaid.

Redundancy Unemployment (q.v.) created by the process of change in industry; notably frictional or structural unemployment. *See* REDUNDANCY FUND; UNEMPLOYMENT, TYPES OF.

Redundancy Fund A Fund set up under the Redundancy Payments Act which ensures financial compensation for all workers made redundant following not less than two years' service with an employer. The Fund became operative in

1966; payments are made on a scale based on age and length of service. *See* REDUNDANCY.

Reflation The period of recovery of an economy from a depression, but before a stage of full employment and inflation accompanied by rising prices is reached. *See* INFLATION.

Regional Employment Premium A scheme introduced in September, 1967, to assist manufacturers in development areas (q.v.) providing for a payment to employers in respect of each employee. The objective is to achieve an increase in employment rate (q.v.). It has been estimated that the scheme is worth about £100 million a year to manufacturers in the development areas.

Registered Provident Societies A variety of institutions registered under the Friendly Society Acts, Industrial Assurance Acts, and other Acts. Societies include friendly societies, industrial assurance societies, industrial and provident societies, building societies, trade unions, certified loan societies, railway savings banks, superannuation and other trust funds. These societies are important as media for saving and investment and bestow many timely benefits on their contributors and dependents.

Registrar of Companies *See* COMPANY, LEGAL FORMATION OF.

Regression Analysis A statistical technique used to determine the relationship between a variable x (or variables $x_1 x_2 x_3 \ldots$) and a response y in economic behaviour. If it is reasonable to assume a linear relationship between x and y then the problem is solved by fitting the best straight line to the values of x against y. The best straight line is that which minimises the sum of the squares of the deviations of the observed values from the line; this is called the method of least squares. The process of fitting a curve to a set of observations is called "regression". With only x and y then all that is required is to find the values of a and b in the equation $y = ax + b$ to obtain the best straight line. In practice, there may well be a number of variables all resulting to a greater or lesser extent in a change in the response of y. In this case the problem is to determine the best straight line of the form $y = a_1x_1 + a_2x_2 + a_3x_3 + \ldots a_nx_n + b$. The a's are known as the regression coefficient and b as the residual. A regression of this type is known as a multiple linear regression. If it is not reasonable to assume a linear relationship between the variables and the response, a non-linear function must be fitted. This is a far more difficult process. Although the method of least squares is also used here there are also other techniques, one of the most common being the method of steepest descent. In appropriate cases auto-correlation techniques or spectral analysis may be used. *See* LEAST SQUARES METHOD.

Regulator Measure introduced by Mr. Selwyn Lloyd for producing a quick impact on effective demand for consumers' goods and services, should one be necessary, by raising indirect taxes by anything up to 10 per cent.

Rent (a) A payment made by a person for the use of an asset belonging to someone else; (b) In economic analysis, a surplus accruing to a factor the supply of which is fixed; rent in this sense describes a payment over and above the necessary supply price of a factor of production. Formerly the word was restricted to income received from the ownership of land. *See* ECONOMIC RENT; QUASI-RENT.

Rent Restriction Statutory control of the rents of privately owned dwellings. Legislation controlling rents was introduced into Britain during the First World War; rents were gradually decontrolled between the wars, but full rent control was re-introduced on the outbreak of the Second World War. The Rent Act 1957 allowed the gradual decontrol of rents, but the process was halted by the Labour Government in 1965. The Rent Act 1965 extended rent control to all privately owned rented properties of a rateable value of up to £400 in London and £200 elsewhere, and prevented eviction without a court order from premises of any value. In disputes between landlords and tenants, a local rent officer attempts to negotiate a "fair" rent; if either party refuses to accept his decision the case may then be referred to a Rent Assessment Committee whose verdict is binding.

Rent, Ricardo's Theory of A proposition that the rent of a piece of land is the excess of the yield of that piece of land over that of the worst land in cultivation. Ricardo considered that land at the margin of cultivation yielded no rent; indeed if rent was charged the land would not be cultivated. Farmers would have to pay more for the use of more fertile land, and the excess yield over that of "no-rent" land would be its rent. Thus, the net return to farmers on a unit of land of any given fertility would tend to be the same. Ricardo regarded the rent of land as a surplus, or economic rent (q.v.). The ready conclusion that may be drawn from this theory is that as the world's population increases so landlords will receive every-growing sums of unearned economic rent. This may be ultimately true, and is true in certain areas. But only a fraction of the land of the world suitable for agriculture and building has yet been brought into use. Ricardo's theory arose out of the condition of his time in which land was demanded mainly for corn; he did not foresee the growing demand for land for alternative uses such as building which would introduce another element into agricultural rents—a payment to keep land out of an alternative use.

Rentier A person whose income is "unearned", i.e. derived from the ownership of capital by way of interest, rents or dividend, rather than "earned" in the form of a salary, commission, fee or wage.

Representative Firm A concept sometimes used in economics, a representative firm may be described as a firm that has had a fairly long life and fair success, which is managed with normal ability, and which has normal access to both the external and internal economies available to producers of the class of goods involved. As with the concept of the "average man", the possibility of locating the representative firm in any given situation is fraught with difficulties. The concept was first developed by Alfred Marshall (1842–1924).

Reproductive Debt That part of the National Debt (q.v.) covered by real assets, in contrast to Deadweight Debt (q.v.).

Resale Price Maintenance A trade practice binding shopkeepers and dealers to sell goods at prices laid down by the manufacturer or other supplier. The principal effect of resale price maintenance is that it eliminates price competition between distributors of price-maintained goods. Formerly, in Britain, a manufacturer could refuse to supply a trader who failed to comply with his prescribed prices. In addition, the collective enforcement of resale prices by trade associations (q.v.) was widespread; if a trader reduced the price of one line of one manufacturer, his name might be placed on a "stop list" and as a consequence he might be unable to obtain supplies of a wide range of goods made by other manufacturers.

In 1947, the Lloyd Jacob Committee reviewed the question of resale price maintenance. It was recommended that no action be taken which would deprive an individual producer of the power to prescribe and enforce resale prices for goods bearing his brand, but that collective sanctions should be made illegal. In 1956, the Restrictive Trade Practices Act prohibited the collective enforcement of resale price maintenance. At the same time the Act strengthened the power of the individual manufacturer to enforce resale prices set by him.

In 1964 the practice of resale price maintenance was again reviewed by Parliament and on this occasion it was decided to abolish all resale price maintenance save in those instances where a manufacturer could demonstrate that its retention for his goods was in the public interest. The result was the Resale Prices Act 1964 (q.v.).

Resale Prices Act 1964 Described as "an Act to restrict the maintenance by contractual and other means of minimum resale prices in respect of goods supplied for resale in the United Kingdom." The Act states that "any term or condition of a contract for the sale of goods by a supplier to a dealer, or of any arrangement between a supplier and a dealer relating to such a sale, shall be void in so far as it purports to establish or provide for the establishment of minimum prices to be charged on the resale of goods in the United Kingdom". The Act does not preclude a supplier from publishing recommended prices (q.v.) for his goods, but it is unlawful for dealers to withhold supplies from a dealer because he has sold such goods below the recommended price. It is however legal for a supplier to withhold goods which have been sold as "loss leaders" (*See* LOSS LEADER). The Restrictive Practices Court may rule that any good or class of good is exempted for the purposes of the Act, but in every case it must be established that the resulting detriment to the public as consumers or users of the goods in question arising from the Act would outweigh any detriment to them resulting from the maintenance of minimum resale prices of goods. *See* RESALE PRICE MAINTENANCE.

Research-Intensive Description of industries in which there is a high ratio of expenditure on research in relation to the value of net output, e.g. the aircraft and electronics industries. *See* CAPITAL-INTENSIVE; LABOUR-INTENSIVE.

Reserve Bank of Australia The central bank of Australia, formerly known as the Commonwealth Bank of Australia.

Reserve Bank of New Zealand The central bank of New Zealand.

Reserve Currency A currency commanding general acceptability held by individual countries to meet their financial commitments. Normally, reserves consist of gold and certain key reserve currencies, mainly the U.S. dollar and the British pound.

Reserve Price A minimum price at or below which a seller will withdraw an article from sale.

Reserves Money held back by a company and not distributed in dividends for the purpose of strengthening the financial position of the company, providing for future developments and against unknown contingencies. A useful distinction may be made between revenue reserves, representing amounts withheld from profits but which could be made available for distribution as dividends at the discretion of the directors, and capital reserves which are not available for distribution as dividends for legal reasons. The Companies Acts specify some items as capital reserves, and the memorandum and articles of a company may specify that certain profits shall be capital reserves.

Resident Sterling Sterling currency held by residents of Sterling Area (q.v.) countries.

Restricted-Hours Tariff Tariffs offering low rates for supplies of electricity which are restricted automatically by time switches to certain off-peak hours of the day. *See* TARIFF (b).

Restrictive Practice (a) Any inefficient working method or system which is difficult to alter, due either to opposition from the management, the workers, or both. The practice may be perhaps unnecessary overtime working, for which the management is primarily responsible; or it may be a set of traditional working practices for which the unions are primarily responsible.

(b) A practice in restraint of trade or production. Among firms such practices as common prices, collusive tendering, allotment of sales or output quotas, division of markets, exclusive dealing and loyalty rebates to customers may be employed.

Restrictive Practices Court A Court set up in 1956 by the Restrictive Trade Practices Act of that year. This Act requires the registration of a wide range of restrictive agreements among producers and traders, and established the principle that price fixing and other restrictive arrangements are contrary to the public interest, unless the contrary is proved. Thus producers and traders wishing to operate such restrictions have to show that what is proposed is *positively* in the public interest. The Court examines and passes judgment on cases brought before it by the Registrar of Restrictive Practices. The Restrictive Trade Practices Act of 1956 was also important for prohibiting the collective enforcement of resale price maintenance (q.v.).

Between 1956 and 1965, the Restrictive Practices Court passed judgment on 138 agreements. Among those it found contrary to the public interest were schemes operated by the Associated Transformer Manufacturers, the Linoleum Manufacturers and the British Bottle Association. In a price-fixing case heard before the Court eight galvanised tank manufacturers were fined a total of £102,000.

Retail Prices, Index of *See* INDEX OF RETAIL PRICES.

Retailer A dealer (q.v.) selling goods in relatively small quantities to private consumers. The Census of Distribution and Other Services (q.v.) in 1961 revealed that Britain had about half a million retail establishments, or about one for every 100 inhabitants. *See* WHOLESALER.

Return on Investment Methods Methods of comparing the profitability of alternative projects. Among the formulae used are:

$$\frac{\text{Total gross Income before Depreciation}}{\text{Number of years of life} \times \text{Initial outlay}} = \begin{array}{l}\text{Average gross annual in-}\\ \text{come for n years per } \pounds\end{array}$$

$$\frac{\text{Total Net Income}}{\text{Number of years life} \times \text{Half Initial Outlay}} = \begin{array}{l}\text{Average net annual income}\\ \text{for n years per } \pounds \text{ of average}\\ \text{Investment over n years}\end{array}$$

The most serious defect of these methods is that they fail to take account of the incidence of income. Clearly the earlier the proceeds are received the more quickly they may be utilised for further investment.

Revenue Reserves *See* RESERVES.

"Review of Economic Studies" The Journal of the Anglo-American Economic Study Society, published three times a year.

Ricardo's Theory of Rent *See* RENT, RICARDO'S THEORY OF.

Rights Issue The offer of new shares by a company to existing shareholders. Each shareholder has the right to subscribe to the new shares up to a given proportion of the shares he already holds, on the basis of, say, 1 for 1, 3 for 5, etc. The shareholder may either accept the offer himself, or may assign part or all of his "rights" to someone else by means of a "letter of renunciation" (q.v.). Such "rights" are valuable as the new shares are offered to shareholders at a price below the current market price. The making of a "rights" issue by a company is a cheap and convenient way of raising additional capital (q.v.), particularly if the amount required is moderate in relation to the amount already issued. *See* OFFER FOR SALE; PLACING; PUBLIC ISSUE.

Ring Trading Auction sales in which traders form a ring around a caller.

Risk Chance of injury or loss. There are two types of risk:
    (a) insurable risk, e.g. fire, burglary, etc.;

(b) non-insurable risk or uncertainty, e.g. the risk of loss through changes in the future demand for goods. This type of risk or uncertainty may be reduced by, inter alia, hedging (q.v.). *See* UNCERTAINTY.

Risk Capital   Capital subject to considerable risk. Also called "venture capital". *See* SECURITY CAPITAL.

"Roundabout" Methods of Production   Description of capitalistic methods of production in which products pass through many stages before completion.

Round-Lot   Usually one hundred shares, being the normal unit of trading on the stock exchange (q.v.). *See* ODD-LOT.

Royal Economic Society   A Society which has for its object the general advancement of economic knowledge. It was founded, under the name of the British Economic Association, at a meeting held at University College, London, on November 29th, 1890. Its formation was the outcome of a circular, prepared by the Cambridge economist Alfred Marshall in consultation with others, entitled *Proposal to form an English Economic Association*. The Society became incorporated by Royal Charter in 1902. The Royal Economic Society's official publication, the *Economic Journal*, published quarterly, is intended to reflect the various shades of economic opinion, and to be the organ, not of one school of economists, but of all. The Journal numbers among its contributors leading economists of all countries.

Royal Mint, The   A government department responsible for the provision of coins for circulation in Britain. Since the middle of the 16th century all coins in Britain have been struck at the London Mint. The Mint currently operates under the Coinage Act of 1870. Its main functions are:
(a) the coinage and issue of token silver and bronze pieces on account of the Government;
(b) minting of coinages required by British Colonies and Dependencies; and
(c) the manufacture of naval, military and other medals.

Royalty   Compensation for the use of a patent, copyright, or other property, often calculated as a percentage of the sales value of the article or service.

Rubber Exchange   A London market in rubber housed in the London Commodity Exchange. Trading is all by private treaty and consists largely of "futures".

Running Costs   Operating costs, which include the cost of raw materials and power, labour and supervision. It excludes capital charges and other overheads. *See* CAPITAL CHARGES; FIXED COSTS; OVERHEADS; VARIABLE COSTS.

S

Safeguarding of Industries Acts 1921-26 Acts introducing import tariffs to protect and encourage home industries which, while unimportant in themselves, might be regarded as providing key products essential in more important manufacturing activities in Britain.

Sales Forecasting The estimating of sales, in value or physical units, for a specified future period. *See* FORECASTING; MARKET RESEARCH.

Sales Tax A tax imposed at a uniform rate on all goods at the point of retail sale, other than exempt goods. In Australia, in which an ad valorem sales tax is generally levied, exempt goods include basic foodstuffs, clothing, building materials, educational books and other essential goods. In Canada a sales tax is imposed on goods manufactured or produced in Canada and on the "duty-paid" value of goods imported into Canada. However most foodstuffs, raw materials and implements used in the primary industries are among those articles exempted from sales tax. *See* AD VALOREM TAX; PURCHASE TAX; TAXES; TURNOVER TAX; VALUE-ADDED TAX.

Sales Turnover The words "turnover" and "sales" are really synonymous. The term turnover is a literal expression deriving from the "turnover" of stocks.

If a company begins its trading year with stocks valued at £100,000 and ends it having sold finished products to the value of £1 m. then it has "turned over" (i.e. bought, converted and sold) its initial stock ten times; its turnover is £1 m.

"Save As You Earn" A contractual savings scheme operated by the Department for National Savings. Individuals may save up to £10 per month, through deductions from pay, or by standing orders on banks and the Giro (q.v.), or in cash over Post Office counters. After five years savings attract a tax-free bonus, or a larger bonus if left in for a further two years.

Saving The withholding of money from expenditure on goods and services. The amount saved out of any given income depends upon the Propensities to Consume and Save (q.v.), and out of any addition to income on the Marginal Propensities to Consume and Save (q.v.). In discussing the national economy, however, economists frequently use the term "saving" for expenditure of a special kind—the employment of income in the creation of new capital. Thus saving is identified with investment in real assets, and not with the "hoarding" (q.v.) of money which is simply the non-expenditure of money held. Adopting this definition the savings and investment of a community can never diverge.

Savings Equal Investment A maxim of Lord Keynes (1884–1946) who defined savings and expenditure on capital goods or investment (q.v.) as being of necessity equal to one another. The logic of his argument was as follows:

Income = Expenditure on consumption goods and savings.

Output = Output of consumption goods and investment.

Since Total Income = Value of Total Output; and

Expenditure on consumption goods = Output of consumption goods.

Savings = Investment.

Savings, Point of Zero A level of disposable income at which it is all consumed. Above this point, out of each additional unit of income a varying percentage will be devoted to consumption and the remainder saved; below that point dissaving will occur, i.e. past savings will be used up and debts incurred.

Say's Law of Markets A law formulated by the French economist J. B. Say stating that every increase in the supply of goods is a corresponding increase in the demand for goods so long as producers have directed their production in accordance with each other's wants. Hence, it was argued, a general over-production of goods cannot occur. For a barter economy, this is a truism. Under modern conditions, however, the exchange of products takes place in two stages—first of all the exchange of a producer's product for money, and, subsequently, the exchanging of money for another producer's product. The second part of this operation may be postponed. If a sufficient number of buying decisions are postponed, the demand for goods may become temporarily restricted without necessarily curtailing the volume of production. In the long run, a reduction in the velocity of circulation of money would have a serious effect on demand, prices and production. Say formulated his law of the market in 1803. His view was generally accepted by the Classical School (q.v.) and it was not seriously questioned until the Great Depression, 1929–35 (q.v.) when John Maynard Keynes (1886–1946) effectively challenged its validity under modern conditions. *See* KEYNESIAN REVOLUTION.

Scale of Preferences The quantitative expression of a consumer's tastes.

Scarcity A relative term, indicating shortage in relation to demand. It is only because of scarcity that price exists.

Scheduled Territories Another name for the Sterling Area (q.v.).

Scottish Agricultural Securities Corporation A financial institution which makes loans to farmers for periods of up to sixty years at fixed rates of interest. *See* FINANCE CORPORATIONS.

Scottish Banks The Scottish banks comprise the Bank of Scotland, British Linen Bank, Clydesdale Bank Ltd. and The Royal Bank of Scotland. They transact virtually all the commercial banking business in Scotland, where they maintain a clearing system.

Scrip Abbreviation for the word "subscription". *See* SCRIP CERTIFICATE; SCRIP DIVIDEND.

Scrip Certificate A provisional certificate for shares or debentures in a company, or for Government bonds. The scrip certificate is issued when the allotment money is paid; in due course it is exchanged for the share certificate (q.v.) or bond when all the instalments have been paid. *See* SCRIP; SCRIP DIVIDEND.

Scrip Dividend The distribution by way of dividend of shares or debentures. The power to issue "scrip dividends" must be contained in the articles of association (q.v.) of the company concerned.

Scrip or Bonus Issue of Shares The issue of additional shares free of charge to shareholders in proportion to the shares they already hold. This may be done when a company increases its capital by using some of its profits for this purpose and feels that the previously issued share capital does not give a true picture of the amount of capital actually employed by the firm. Indeed the gap between the nominal and market value of its shares may have become misleadingly large, with dividends expressed as a high percentage of nominal capital.

If a company makes a scrip or bonus issue to shareholders of one new £1 share for every £1 they hold and at the same time announces that there will be no change in the amount available for dividend payments, all that happens is that a shareholder who previously held one £1 share worth, say, £3.50 on the market now holds two £1 shares worth £1.75 each. The dividend, expressed as a percentage of nominal capital, would be halved in these circumstances. Thus a scrip or bonus issue does not add to the capital available to the business concerned and may be regarded as a book-keeping transaction.

Seasonal Tariff A tariff for the supply of electricity in which a higher price per unit of electricity applies during the winter months than during the summer months. *See* TARIFF (b).

Secondary Industry Or manufacturing industry, the processing of raw materials into finished products. *See* EXTRACTIVE INDUSTRY.

Secular Stagnation A low level of economic activity over a considerable period of time.

Secular Trend Any general tendency of values in a time series to increase or decrease over a period of years. Various methods of estimating a secular trend are available; the method of least squares may be used. *See* LEAST SQUARES METHOD.

Securities Stocks, shares or bonds. They are in two main forms:
   (a) Bonds; fully-paid stock, shares, stock units; and unnumbered shares; and
   (b) Partly-paid stock or shares.
   See CUMULATIVE PREFERENCE SHARE; DEBENTURE; DEFERRED FOUNDERS' OR MANAGEMENT SHARES; DEFERRED ORDINARY SHARE; NON-VOTING SHARE; ORDINARY SHARE; PREFERENCE SHARE; PREFERRED ORDINARY SHARE; REDEEMABLE PREFERENCE SHARE; SHARE; STOCKS AND SHARES.

Securities and Exchange Commission (U.S.) The supervisory body of the New York Stock Exchange.

Securities Management Trust An agency set up by the Bank of England and the commercial banks, during the Great Depression 1929–35 (q.v.), for the purpose of assisting industry. *See* FINANCE CORPORATIONS.

Security Capital Capital subject to a minimum amount of risk, as opposed to risk or venture capital. *See* RISK CAPITAL.

Select Committee on the Nationalised Industries A House of Commons Committee set up in 1956 and comprising members drawn from all political parties to conduct enquiries and report from time to time to Parliament on the nationalised industries. The object is to provide Members of Parliament with information complementary to that published in the industries' Annual Reports and Accounts. The Committee provides the nationalised industries themselves with the opportunity to explain to Parliament what their problems are, how they are tackling them, and the ways in which they might be helped in carrying out their functions. The Committee has reported on the North of Scotland Hydro-electric Board, the National Coal Board, the Air Corporations, British Railways, and the gas and electricity supply industries.

Selective Credit Controls An instrument of monetary policy to limit or encourage the use of credit in specified types of activity. For example, the Government, through the Bank of England, may request the commercial banks to give priority when making advances to firms in the export trade or firms wishing to invest in new capital equipment. Another example is the regulation by the Board of Trade of the terms on which hire-purchase transactions may be carried out, particularly in respect of the proportion of the purchase price which must be put down by buyers as a deposit and the length of time over which hire-purchase instalments may be spread. Another selective control technique, now abandoned, was the control exercised by the Treasury through the Capital Issues Committee (q.v.) over the raising of new capital.

Selective Employment Tax A payroll tax (q.v.) introduced into Britain in 1966, designed to encourage the release of labour from services thus making more labour available for the expansion of manufacturing industry. All employers in the public and private sectors pay a levy on each worker on their payrolls, but some qualify for refunds and others for a refund plus a premium. Thus employers may be placed in three categories:

(a) Employers who pay the tax without refund, e.g. those in the construction industry and services generally.

(b) Employers who have the tax refunded or counterbalanced, e.g. those in transport, agriculture, extractive industries, and in the public services including nationalised industries.

(c) Employers who receive a premium (refund of tax plus an additional amount) being those engaged in manufacturing industry.

The collection of contributions from employers began on 5th September, 1966; the payment of refunds and premiums began the following February, 1967. Initially the tax was at a rate of 25 shillings a week for men, with reduced rates for women, boys and girls; premiums amounted to 32 shillings and sixpence a week for men with reduced rates for women, boys and girls. From 1st April, 1968, the payment of premiums was restricted to manufacturers in the development areas (q.v.) and subsequently abolished. *See* REGIONAL EMPLOYMENT PREMIUM.

Self-Financing Ratio The amount of capital required for new investment by an organisation obtained from its own earnings (i.e. from depreciation funds, profits and surpluses) expressed as a percentage of total capital requirements. The electricity supply industry provides about half of its capital needs from internal resources; the balance required comes from external borrowings by the Electricity Council (q.v.).

Self-Liquidating Advances Bank advances to customers which are for the purpose of tiding over a temporary shortage of funds only, e.g. when the farmer is faced with a heavy outlay of wages during the "seed-time to harvest" period, the loan being repaid when the crop is sold.

Selling Agency, Common An agency serving a group of otherwise independent firms, the purpose of which is to avoid undercutting of prices.

Selling Costs Costs incurred in creating, retaining or expanding a market for a product. These costs include the cost of advertising; earnings and expenses of commercial travellers; costs of market research; and the various inducements by way of stamps, give-aways and specially reduced prices offered by firms to attract customers.

Diminishing returns are a feature of selling costs, mainly because the best potential markets are exploited first and subsequent marginal sales involve the sacrifice by purchasers of increasingly important alternative wants.

Sensitive Market A market in which market prices fluctuate widely in response to good and bad news.

Serfdom A system of employment in which men worked partly for themselves and partly for a lord, tilling a part of the lord's fields, paying him out of the produce raised, and being under an obligation to serve as soldiers when required under the lord's command.

Service In economic science, a useful function fulfilled by a person, or organisation, and for the benefits of which consumers are prepared to pay a price. Payment, like service itself, may be direct or indirect. *See* GOOD.

Service Industry Industry (q.v.) producing or supplying a service (q.v.) as distinct from a good (q.v.), e.g. the catering industry.

Settlement Day *See* ACCOUNT DAY.

Share The individual portion of a company's capital owned by a shareholder. Shares are divided into different classes according to their terms of issue. *See* COMMON STOCK (U.S. AND CAN.); CUMULATIVE PREFERENCE SHARE; DEFERRED, FOUNDERS' OR MANAGEMENT SHARES; DEFERRED ORDINARY SHARES; NON-VOTING SHARES; ORDINARY SHARE; PARTICIPATING PREFERENCE SHARE; PREFERENCE SHARE; PREFERRED ORDINARY SHARE; PREFERRED STOCK (U.S.); REDEEMABLE PREFERENCE SHARE.

Share Certificate A certificate which is evidence of a person's ownership of shares. As soon as it is issued the seller's certificate is cancelled by the company concerned. Should the seller have disposed of only a part of his holding he receives a new certificate for the balance.

Share Indices, The Times Share indices designed to provide a yard-stick for the performance of an average portfolio of shares held by an average investor and invested in an average selection of shares. They also show what happens to some of the major elements of a general portfolio, e.g. those shares of companies making capital goods or consumer goods.

Each index number is a weighted arithmetic average of the prices of all the stocks and shares included in that index. Each index is weighted according to the market capitalisation of the companies included in it. Each stock or share is allowed an importance proportionate to the market value of the total issue of that stock or share. *The Times* Industrial Share Index covers the prices of 150 ordinary shares (50 shares from large companies and 100 from smaller companies). The prices used for computation of the indices are taken from the list of Stock Exchange Closing Prices recorded in *The Times* each day.

Full details of the composition and compilation of the index numbers are given in the booklet *Share Indices: The History, Methods of Calculation and First Revision of* The Times *Stock Exchange Indices* (1964) obtainable from *The Times* Publishing Company Ltd.

Share Options Options which confer the right to buy or sell a block of stock at a predetermined price within a given period. Option dealings on the London Stock Exchange were suspended indefinitely in 1939, and they were not resumed until October, 1958.

"Call" options give the right to buy shares at a future time. "Put" options confer the right to sell shares at a future time.

Shares, Method of Issuing *See* OFFER FOR SALE; OFFER FOR SALE BY TENDER; PLACING; PUBLIC ISSUE; RIGHTS ISSUE.

Shift   The normal period of attendance at a mine or factory by one wage-earner in one day.

Ship Mortgage Finance Company Ltd.   A company formed in 1951 to assist in financing shipbuilding in Britain. Under the management of the Industrial and Commercial Finance Corporation Ltd. (q.v.) it makes loans to British and foreign shipowners to assist in the construction of ships in British shipyards. It may also subscribe share capital in shipping companies and will arrange ship leasing transactions. In 1963, it was appointed agent for the Government's Shipbuilding Credit Scheme. *See* FINANCE CORPORATIONS.

Shipping Conference   An association of ship-owners the purpose of which is to fix rates to be charged.

Short   A description of a buyer or holder of securities (q.v.) who has contracted to deliver at some future time more of a particular stock than he holds; the "shorts" are usually those who have sold in anticipation of a drop in prices, hoping to be able to buy at a lower price in time for delivery. *See* LONG.

Simultaneous Maximum Demand   The maximum demand of two or more consumers for a service, e.g. supply of electricity, taken together at the same time.

Single Tax   A proposed tax on that part of land values known as the "unearned increment" (q.v.), the view being taken that land is the only equitable field for taxation. The Physiocrats favoured a single tax—an "impôt unique" —on land, arguing that the cultivation of land was the only work really productive of wealth, since the assistance of nature caused it to yield a surplus. This surplus, the excess of the value of the produce over its cost, was called the "produit net". The bulk of this "produit net" was given to landlords as rent; hence the case for a single tax falling on this surplus. *See* PHYSIOCRATIC SCHOOL.

The great American exponent of a single tax on land was Henry George (1839–1897), a writer, economist and philosopher. His book *Progress and Poverty: an Inquiry into the Cause of Industrial Depressions and of Increase of Want with Increase of Wealth* appeared in 1880. George rejected Malthusian theory—that population tends to increase faster than the means of subsistence— conventionally offered as an explanation as to why, despite the increase of productive power, wages tended to the minimum of a bare living. Land being held as private property would produce in a stationary population all the effects attributed by Malthusian doctrine to a growing population. George submitted that it was the advance of rents that explained why wages did not advance. Further, that the continuous advance in land values was responsible for periodic industrial depressions. He claimed that his investigations showed that nothing short of making land common property could permanently relieve poverty and check the tendency of wages to the starvation point. Private property in land, instead of being necessary to its improvement and use, stood in the way of improvement and use and entailed an enormous waste of productive forces. The recognition of the common right to land would, however, involve no shock or dispossession, but be reached by the simple and easy method of abolishing all taxation save that upon land values. George held that the change proposed would enormously increase production; secure justice in distribution; benefit all classes; and make possible an advance to a higher and nobler civilisation. *See* MALTHUSIAN THEORY OF POPULATION.

Single-Use Goods Goods used up in a single process of consumption or production.

Sinking Fund A fund built up by equal periodic instalments in order to accumulate a certain sum by a given date for some specific purpose, e.g. the replacement of a physical asset. The interest arising out of the sinking fund investment is itself periodically re-invested and allowed to accumulate with the periodic contribution of principal. The sinking fund instalment, consisting of an annual payment, is equal to the original capital cost of the asset multiplied by a sinking fund factor equal to:

$$\frac{i}{(1 + i)^n - 1}$$

where i is the rate of interest, and n the plant life expressed in years. *See* DEPRECIATION; DEPRECIATION FUND METHOD.

Site Value Rating The levying of local rates on owners of land rather than occupiers. It is claimed that site value rating would encourage owners to make their land available for development, that it might often prove unprofitable for landowners to hold on to land for speculative reasons, and that it might tend to retard the rise in land values. It is argued, however, that if the principle was introduced in Britain considerable difficulties of valuation would arise because of the complicated system of land tenures, the artificial restrictions imposed by contract or by statute, the imprecise nature of development plans and the lack of reliable evidence upon which valuations can be based. The principle is, however, applied in other countries.

Slavery A system in which men, who have no civil rights, work for and are kept by their masters and owners, either badly or well, receiving no wages.

Sliding Scales A system of wage payments in which the wages paid are linked with the price of the finished product or to the index of retail prices (q.v.). The object is to protect the worker against the erosion of the real value of his wages through inflationary price increases.

Social Account An organised arrangement of all transactions, actual or imputed, in an economic system.

Social Accounting The compilation of accounts for particular groups within the nation—the sectors of the economy. The organisation of statistics into a set of social accounts has become normal practice and is the framework on which is built the presentation of the statistics for the United Kingdom in the annual Blue Book "National Income and Expenditure" published by the

Central Statistical Office. The principal advantage of such a framework, it is claimed, is that it displays the mutual relations between the different parts of the economy, and the different forms of economic activity, in a way the statistics of aggregate national income and expenditure alone cannot do. The essential sectors into which the economy is divided are:

(a) a "personal" or household sector, displaying the transactions of members of the community in their capacity as final consumers;

(b) a "productive enterprises" sector, recording the transactions of industrial and commercial undertakings whether publicly or privately owned;

(c) a sector for recording the transactions of the organs of government, both central and local, with the rest of the economy; and

(d) a "rest of the world" sector, recording international transactions.

Further information on this topic is given in *National Accounts Statistics: Sources and Methods* (1968) issued by the Central Statistical Office.

Social Benefits The value of gains accruing to the community as a consequence of the establishment of an industry, factory or facility, although the new development may not have taken place with that aim or purpose. Benefits may include increased opportunities for employment, steadier employment, improved roads, improved shops and amenities, elimination of a swamp or removal of unsightly existing premises.

Social Capital Assets belonging to the community as a whole, rather than to private persons or industries, e.g. schools, hospitals, roads, etc.

Social Class A group of persons conscious of certain common traits and of certain common ways of behaviour which distinguish them from members of other social classes with other traits and other ways of behaviour. Thus English society may be viewed as consisting of numerous classes—farmers, teachers, artists, civil servants, skilled artisans, labourers, and so on. But all these are the sub-strata of the classes into which society has been traditionally divided. In Britain four classes are usually distinguished; a so-called "upper-class" consisting largely of the old landed aristocracy, still highly regarded but not quite as rich and powerful as in days gone by; an "upper middle class" consisting of the most prosperous and influential sections of the community and from which most members of the British Government are drawn; a "lower middle class", much more numerous than either of the above, consisting of many highly intelligent and educated people but dependent largely upon earned income to sustain their standard of life; finally the "working class", numerically larger than the three previous classes together, consisting largely of skilled and unskilled manual workers depending upon wages for their standard of living. The "upper class" and the "upper middle class" own and control a considerable portion of the nation's capital. It is this fact, rather than intelligence, education or culture, which tends to perpetuate the "two nations"; the extremes of wealth and poverty are by no means as sharp as they were, but they are still considerable.

Social Costs Costs which do not appear in the accounts of a company, e.g. the costs to the public caused by air pollution, water pollution, noise and congestion, or the provision and maintenance of roads by the public for private distribution purposes. If a company is required by legislation to prevent or minimise its contribution to, say, air pollution then the cost of doing this will appear in the accounts of the company. In this instance a general and difficult to measure social cost will have been converted into a specific and accurately measured private cost. *See* PRIVATE COSTS.

Social Credit A theory developed by Major C. H. Douglas, a Canadian engineer, in the 1930s with the purpose of achieving permanent prosperity through a reform of the monetary system. He attributed the causes of social and economic evils to an insufficient supply of money. His remedies were to increase the purchasing power of consumers by reducing prices, subsidies being paid to retailers; or to increase purchasing power by means of a variable "national dividend", paid to everyone. The Social Credit Movement, which Douglas founded, only sought to help capitalism to work, not to replace it.

Social Economics A branch of applied economics which deals with problems of social importance such as wages and the standard of life; housing and sanitation; provision for children, the sick and the aged; unemployment; state regulation of industrial conditions; welfare institutions and social insurance.

Social Engineering The introduction of social and economic changes in a community through centrally co-ordinated planning.

Social Insurance The collective insurance of members of a community through the State for a variety of social benefits in times of illness, old-age and unemployment. The development of social insurance in Britain dates from the National Insurance Act, 1911, which provided insurance against sickness and disablement on a compulsory and contributory basis for most lower paid workers, and introduced a limited scheme of unemployment insurance which was subsequently widened. In 1925 the Widows', Orphans' and Old Age Contributory Pensions Act provided the first national scheme of contributory pensions. Following the Second World War, a more comprehensive scheme of social insurance was introduced which embraced the whole population. The scheme was based on a plan prepared by Sir William (later Lord)Beveridge which appeared in his famous Report on Social Insurance. The scheme embodied in the National Insurance Act 1946 was compulsory and contributed to by employees, employers and the State; the "self-employed" also became compulsory contributors. Benefits are payable in respect of sickness, unemployment, widowhood and old-age; retirement pensions are payable to men at 65 and women at 60 years of age; maternity grants and funeral grants are also payable. *See* BEVERIDGE PLAN; FAMILY ALLOWANCES.

Social Philosophy A branch of philosophy concerned with the validity of social ideals.

Social Psychology The study of individuals in their interactions with one another, and the study of group behaviour.

Social Sciences   Sciences concerned with all phases of human activity, e.g. economics, social institutions, law and justice, criminology, penology, anthropology, etc.

Social Service   A service, subsidy or payment rendered by, or on behalf of, the community, to an individual or to a family for his or its exclusive use. A social service contains an element of redistribution of income and resources. Social services in Britain include the following: (a) education; (b) insurance; (c) housing, subsidising and provision of; (d) health (hospital, medical, dental services, etc.); (e) national assistance; (f) old people's services; (g) children's services; (h) family allowances (although these are subject to income tax); (i) food subsidies; (j) rent restriction; and (k) legal-aid and advice.

Social Survey   A first-hand investigation and analysis of the economic, sociological and other related aspects of a selected community or group. A survey may have as its object: (a) the provision of material scientifically gathered from which social theorists may draw conclusions, and/or (b) the formulation of a programme of amelioration of the conditions of life and work of a particular group or community. Well-known reports include those of: (a) Le Play, who in the 19th century studied European working men's family budgets; (b) Charles Booth and associates who undertook in 1886 studies reported in "Life and Labour of the People in London"; (c) the Kellogg Survey in the United States in 1909; (d) the Rowntree surveys of the City of York in 1900, 1936 and 1950; (e) the 1934 London School of Economics "New Survey of London Life and Labour"; (f) the Rowntree and Lavers survey of "English Life and Leisure" published in 1951. Many social surveys conducted today are confined to the investigation of a particular phase of community life, such as crime and delinquency, housing, health, education or recreation.

Socialism   A social system in which the means of production, distribution and exchange are wholly or substantially owned by the State. *See* CAPITALISM; MARXIST SOCIALISM.

Socialist Economics   As defined by G. D. H. Cole, a form of practical economics concerned not merely with attempts to describe and analyse what happens under certain underlying conditions but also with the discovery of what ought to happen in the interests of the general well-being of society and of its members. For Socialists, he argued, the traditional distinctions between "pure" and "applied" economics, and between economics proper and welfare economics, simply do not exist.

Sociology   The science of society which, according to the English sociologist Ginsberg, comprises:

  (a) the study of the various forms, institutions, and growth of social groups;
  (b) the discovery of interrelations between these phenomena;
  (c) the formulation of empirical generalisations or laws of social growth;

(d) the interpretation of these laws in terms of their eventual connection with ethical theory.

Economics is a branch of Sociology.

Soft Currency A currency with a relatively unstable or declining value in international exchange. For many years following the Second World War, sterling and most European currencies were "soft", while the United States dollar was recognised as "hard". *See* HARD CURRENCY.

Sole Proprietor, The The commonest type of business unit in which a single person is responsible for raising the capital, organising and managing the business, and undertaking the risk. A very high proportion of the 700,000 shops and service establishments in Britain are in the hands of sole proprietors. A similar position exists in the United States and Canada. The main advantages of this type of business unit are (a) the self-interest of the owner can be a great driving force making for efficiency, (b) changes can be introduced without the need to consult anyone else and (c) the proprietor knows both his staff and customers personally. Sole proprietorship has been described as an opportunity "to work as hard as you like, for as long as you like, for as little as you like". Many small firms have very short lives—the main cause of failure is insufficient capital.

South Sea Bubble A popular name for a series of wild financial projects originating with the incorporation of the South Sea Company in 1711. The Company had grandiose schemes for developing South American and Pacific trade and for taking over the national debt (q.v.); its shares rose to ten times their nominal value and then suddenly collapsed.

Special Areas Areas of mass unemployment which the Special Areas Act 1934 sought to assist. One of the results of this Act was the introduction of Government financed trading estates in four areas—the North East, West Cumberland, Scotland and South Wales.

Special Buyer The representative of a firm of discount brokers which conducts open market operations (q.v.) in Treasury Bills on behalf of the Bank of England (q.v.). The Bank does not itself deal directly with the market.

Special Deposits A monetary control device first used in the summer of 1960 as a counter measure against inflationary pressure. The London Clearing and Scottish banks were required to make "special deposits" with the Bank of England amounting to 1 per cent (½ per cent for the Scottish banks) of their total deposits; these "special deposits" were not classified as "liquid assets" and the capacity of the banks to extend credit to customers was reduced. Special deposits were required between June, 1960, and December, 1962; they were again required in May, 1965, and July, 1966. Deposit requirements have risen as high as 3 per cent of total deposits. Such deposits are not at free disposal of the banks lodging them, and can only be withdrawn with Bank of England permission. The measure was introduced as a means of making traditional weapons more effective by preventing the commercial banks from defeating open-market operations (q.v.) by selling their holdings of Treasury Bills (q.v.).

Special Drawing Rights (S.D.Rs.)   An international reserve currency system created by the International Monetary Fund (q.v.) in October, 1969. It provides for a new type of money (known as "paper gold") to serve by agreement of the free world nations as the first international legal tender. S.D.Rs. are used along with gold and dollars as monetary reserves; they are not held by individuals or private businesses but used in transactions between governments and central banks.

Specialisation   A leading characteristic of all communities, specialisation is a feature of increasing complexity in modern industrial communities. Land is devoted to its most suitable role. Some areas are more suitable for certain types of farming than others; some areas are not suitable for farming at all. Throughout the world areas tend to specialise in the production of such commodities as cotton, tobacco, sugar, rubber, tea, cocoa, citrus fruits, etc. The location of the mining industries is determined by mineral resources. The location of manufacturing industry is influenced by a variety of considerations. (*See* LOCATION OF INDUSTRY, FACTORS INFLUENCING). Labour specialises by entering an enormous variety of occupations (*See* DIVISION OF LABOUR). Capital takes a variety of specialised fixed forms (dams, oil refineries, coal mines, blast furnaces, shoe factories, etc.). The effect on production, productivity and unit costs of all this specialisation is profound.

Specialists (U.S.)   Name for Wall Street stockjobbers.

Specie Points or Gold Points   The extreme points of variation in a rate of exchange under the gold standard (q.v.).

Specified Currency   Currencies approved under the Exchange Control Regulations for the purpose of paying for exports from Britain by countries outside the Sterling Area (q.v.).
   Non-specified currencies are also acceptable provided they are freely convertible into sterling (e.g. Spanish pesetas). Sterling from an external account is also an approved method of payment.

Speculation   The buying of something cheap at one time for the purpose of selling the same thing dearer at another time. Speculation may be described as "arbitrage through time"; instead of buying in one place and selling in another, commodities are bought at one time and sold at another. The difference between arbitrage through space and arbitrage through time is that in the former the prices in the various markets are known, while in the latter prices at future dates can only be estimated. Whilst in a sense all deals are speculations the term is generally limited to circumstances where profit is made because the same thing has different prices at different times. John Maynard Keynes in his *General Theory* commented, "Speculators may do no harm as bubbles on a steady stream of enterprise. But the position is serious when enterprise becomes the bubble on a whirlpool of speculation."

Split Pricing The practice of selling a product uniform in quality and other characteristics at different prices, because it is branded or packed differently, or distributed through different channels, or both.

Spot Market A market in which goods are sold for immediate delivery.

Spot Payment Payment in cash by way of an immediate settlement.

Spot Price The price of a commodity for immediate delivery, as distinct from its "forward" price for delivery at some future date.

Spot Purchase The purchase of commodities or currency immediately available, as distinct from forward or future transactions.

Squeeze Stock exchange term to describe a situation in which "bears" (q.v.) are forced into losses. *See* CREDIT SQUEEZE.

Stag A person who applies for a number of shares (q.v.) in a new issue, with the intention of selling quickly to make a profit.

Stagnation Thesis An argument developed in the 1930s that in a rich country continuing to increase in wealth (through accumulation of capital and technical improvements) opportunities for further and further profitable capital development will tend to decline, while the propensity to save will be at least maintained, and that this combination of circumstances is likely to produce a chronic tendency to under-employment of the country's resources.

Stale Cheque Cheque (q.v.) which is six months old, or older.

Standard and Poor's Indices (U.S.) United States Index numbers of the prices of stock exchange securities.

Standard International Trade Classification (S.I.T.C.) A classification of industrial activities for statistical purposes, useful in promoting uniformity and comparability in official estimates.

Standard of Living The degree of material well-being of a community, or of different classes or groups within a community. *See* NATIONAL INCOME.

Standing Orders Orders given to a Bank by a customer instructing the Bank to make payments for such regular items as insurance premiums, subscriptions, periodical instalments, etc.

State Bank (U.S.) A banking institution carrying on business under the laws of one of the States of the United States of America; it may be a commercial, private or savings bank. *See* NATIONAL BANK.

Static Theory *See* EQUILIBRIUM THEORY.

Statistical Methods Defined by Professor A. L. Bowley as "devices for abbreviating and classifying numerical statements of facts in any department of inquiry and making clear the relations". *See* ECONOMIC STATISTICS.

"Statistical News" A quarterly publication of the Central Statistical Office, providing a comprehensive account of current developments in British official statistics.

Statistician A person versed in, or engaged in collecting and tabulating, statistics.

Statistics As a singular noun, the term "statistics" indicates the study that has for its object the collection and arrangement of numerical facts or data, whether relating to human affairs or to natural phenomena. As a plural noun, it refers to facts which can be put into a numerical form, e.g. unemployment statistics. *See* ECONOMIC STATISTICS; STATISTICAL METHODS.

Statistics of Trade Act 1947 An Act providing for the annual holding of a census of production (q.v.), and for the carrying out of a census of distribution (q.v.) in any year decided upon by the Board of Trade.

Statist Index, The An index covering the price movements of forty-five commodities, e.g. food and raw materials.

Sterling Area A group of countries which tie their currencies to sterling rather than to gold, and keep most of their exchange reserves in the form of balances with the Bank of England. The group was originally formed in 1931, when the United Kingdom went off the gold standard (q.v.), and consisted mainly of Commonwealth countries. With the necessity for exchange control during and after the Second World War, the area became more clearly defined. The Exchange Control Act 1947 gave the sterling area official recognition, being described as the "scheduled territories". At the end of 1968, the scheduled territories comprised the United Kingdom and its colonies; all Commonwealth countries, excluding Canada; the Irish Republic; Iceland; Jordan, Libya; Kuwait; South Africa and South West Africa; and Western Samoa.

The main attributes of the sterling area are:

(a) Payments in sterling between members are generally free from control;
(b) Members hold sterling balances in London;
(c) The gold and dollar reserves of the whole area are held, on behalf of the area, by the United Kingdom;
(d) Members tend to follow the same policy in relation to the dollar area (q.v.) and other hard currency areas.

Sterling Balances Liquid sterling funds held in London, in bank accounts or short-term investments, by overseas traders, investors, central banks and other official bodies. Some are held by private individuals and companies; most are held by international organisations, governments and central banks abroad. Total sterling liabilities to countries and international organisations now exceed £5,000 m.

Stock Dividend (U.S.) A scrip or bonus issue (q.v.).

Stock Exchange An auction market for the purchase and sale of securities such as stocks, bonds and shares. It thus provides a convenient arrangement for persons to invest money in large business enterprises and to liquefy their investments at any time by selling their securities. In the United States there are three national stock exchanges accounting for some 90 per cent of the total trading on exchanges throughout the nation. These are: (a) the New York Stock Exchange, the principal security market in the United States, whose beginnings may be traced back to 1792; (b) the American Stock Exchange, formerly known as the Curb Exchange as its early trading was conducted for many years in the open street; and (c) the National Stock Exchange, opened in 1962. All three exchanges are located in New York City. The principal exchange in the United Kingdom is the London Stock Exchange.

The London Stock Exchange is part of the financial machine that is called "The City"—The City of London—perhaps the greatest monetary centre in the world. Besides the London Stock Exchange, there are other Exchanges in many cities and provincial towns. They are all simply markets for the stocks and shares of companies and of the Government. At the beginning of 1963, the total market value of the stocks and shares quoted on the London Stock Exchange alone amounted to over £55,000 m., including £18,000 m. British Government Stock.

Like so many of the most famous British Institutions, the Stock Exchange developed slowly, in response to the needs of the changing business world. In the 17th century, the Government and many trading enterprises, being unable to raise sufficient money from their own sources, invited the public to put up the money they needed. The Government, and the companies which were formed, issued stocks and shares which were bought and sold. Those who held Government Stocks received each year a fixed rate of interest. Those with shares in a Company received a share in the annual profits (if any). People began to make a living by bringing together buyers and sellers of stocks and shares, and thus a market—a Stock Exchange—was formed. In the latter half of the 17th century, the stockbrokers found a meeting-place in the Royal Exchange. Later they moved and carried on their business in the coffee houses around Change Alley. In 1773 a meeting of stockbrokers decided to take over a building at the corner of Threadneedle Street and Sweeting Alley and over its door inscribed the title "The Stock Exchange". There are now about 3,500 members of the Stock Exchange, representing over 400 separate firms.

The Stock Exchange is governed by a Council of 36 Members, a third of whom are elected every year from among the Members, by ballot. The Council regulates the procedures of the Stock Exchange and secures the maximum protection of Members and public alike. For example, before the shares of any enterprise can be dealt in on the Stock Exchange, permission must be obtained from the Council. The motto of the Stock Exchange is "Dictum Meum Pactum"——"My word is my bond". *See* BOURSE; COMMISSION BROKER; ODD-LOT DEALER; SPECIALISTS; STOCK BROKER; STOCKJOBBER; TWO-DOLLAR BROKER.

Stock Exchange Introduction The introduction of one or more classes of the securities of a company on to the London Stock Exchange. A company seeking this privilege must instruct its broker to submit an application, setting out the particulars of the securities for which a quotation is sought. Such an application must ultimately have the approval of the Stock Exchange Committee on Quotations. The Stock Exchange regulations relating to the advertisement of an introduction, arranging for supplying jobbers with shares to make a free market, etc. must be carefully complied with.

Stock Purchase Warrant A certificate giving the holder the right to purchase a specified number of stocks or shares at some future time at a fixed price.

Stock Turn The average rate at which stock is turned over in a year, calculated by dividing sales by stock or selling price. *See* TURNOVER.

Stockbroker An agent buying or selling securities on behalf of his clients. He also gives advice to his clients on request and attends to the transfer of the legal title to securities. When negotiating a transaction on the Stock Exchange, a broker does not disclose whether he has buying or selling instructions. The broker makes enquiries regarding the price of a security with stockjobbers (q.v.) dealing in that particular stock. Two prices are quoted by a stockjobber, the lower being the price at which he is prepared to buy from the broker and the higher being the price at which he is prepared to sell. The stockbroker charges a commission on the shares which he sells and buys for his clients.

Stockholders' Equity (U.S.) The total equity (q.v.) interest that stockholders have in a corporation (q.v.).

Stockist A dealer (q.v.) who has been granted special buying terms by a manufacturer of goods in return for undertaking to hold specified stocks of these goods.

Stockjobber Member of the London Stock Exchange who buys and sells stocks and shares. Stockjobbers are essentially "wholesalers" and have no direct dealings with the public, as distinct from stockbrokers (q.v.) who buy and sell on behalf of members of the public. Out of some 3,500 members of the London Stock Exchange, there are about 700 jobbers divided among 80 firms.

Most jobbers specialise in one of the main groups of the 9,000 or so different securities (q.v.) quoted on the floor of the Exchange. Some deal in the "gilt-edged" market, others in the "Kaffir" market, or in steel, bank, shipping, oil, property and brewery shares.

The spread between the buying and selling price which a jobber quotes is known as the "jobber's turn"—but profit is not automatic and the market highly competitive.

Stockpiling The purchase and accumulation of strategic raw materials.

Stocks Materials and fuel, work in progress and finished goods on hand for sale held by trading enterprises for business purposes. Over a period of years, the level of stocks in the economy tends to rise as national output rises; in the short-term, stock levels may fluctuate very considerably. The book value of stocks changes in two ways, through: (a) stock appreciation and depreciation arising from changes in the prices at which stocks are valued; and (b) physical increases or decreases in stocks. In Britain, the book value of stocks is equal to about one-third of annual national output.

Stocks and Shares Terms which tend to be used interchangeably, the distinction becoming blurred. Stocks, however, denote money lent to a government, local council, or company and involving a fixed rate of interest; shares denote part-ownership of a company's capital, issued on a variety of terms, and yielding variable returns. The main groups of stocks and shares are: (a) gilt-edged, i.e. government issues and a number of securities grouped with them ; (b) foreign government bonds; (c) American and Canadian shares; (d) banking, insurance and shipping; (e) breweries; (f) commercial and industrial; (g) iron, coal and steel; (h) financial, land and property; (i) investment trusts; (j) rubber and tea plantations; (k) oil; (l) mining—South African, Rhodesian, Canadian, Australian, West African and others; (m) cables and transport.

Stocks and Shares Prefixed or Affixed "A", "B", etc. Stocks or shares which carry special rights, or a special limitation of rights, such as being "non-voting". *See* NON-VOTING SHARES.

Stop-Go A characteristic of British economic policy since the Second World War which has led to perpetual oscillation between periods of expanding aggregate demand to reduce unemployment and boost production, and periods of contracting demand and rising unemployment to eliminate balance-of-payments deficits.

Stop List A list of "offenders" against the resale price rules of trade associations; the persons on the list are unable to obtain supplies of the goods involved. *See* RESALE PRICES ACT 1964.

Stop-Loss Order An order to a stockbroker (q.v.) to sell securities when a stipulated price has been reached on a falling market. By using "stops", holders of securities limit their losses in a declining market.

Stream Days In respect of plant, time efficiency (q.v.) expressed as operating days per year.

Strike The voluntary and collective withdrawal of labour from a place of employment. Opposite of lock-out (q.v.).

Striking Price The predetermined price at which shares can be dealt in during the life of an option (q.v.).

Subscribed Demand Tariff A tariff for the supply of electricity consisting of a unit charge and a charge related to the demand the consumer wishes to subscribe for. *See* TARIFF (b).

Subsidiary Company A firm under the control of another firm through stock ownership.

Subsidies Grants of money to particular industries or groups of individuals by the State.

The purpose of such payments may be to promote exports of a particular commodity—export subsidies; to assist local authorities to provide homes below their economic cost—housing subsidies; to keep the price of food-stuffs below market price—food subsidies.

Subsistence Theory *See* WAGES, THEORIES OF.

Substitution The replacement of a commodity or service by another commodity or service.

Supplementary Costs *See* FIXED COSTS.

Supply   The amount of a commodity or service which will be offered for sale at a given price per unit of time. *See* DEMAND; ELASTICITY OF SUPPLY.

Supply and Demand Curves   A graphical presentation of supply and demand functions, showing on the one hand how much of a commodity will be supplied per unit of time at any given price, and on the other how much of a commodity will be bought per unit of time at any given price; the equilibrium price is the price at which there will be just sufficient demand to take the whole of the supply off the market. If conditions change, and more will be offered for sale at any given price than before ("an increase in supply"), the equilibrium price will be lower than before. Conversely, if less is offered at any given price ("a decrease in supply"), the equilibrium price will be higher than before. Corresponding changes in the equilibrium price will take place if there is an increase or decrease in demand. Figure 9 shows a combination of two normal supply and demand curves, with the equilibrium price shown at Q. *See* SUPPLY CURVE; DEMAND CURVE.

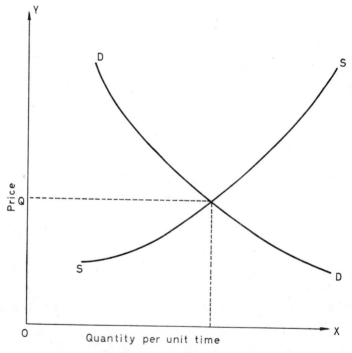

FIGURE 9   SUPPLY AND DEMAND CURVES

Supply and Demand, Laws of   In respect of goods and services:
  (a) If, at the price ruling, demand exceeds supply, the price tends to rise; conversely, when supply exceeds demand the price tends to fall.
  (b) A rise in price tends to contract demand and expand supply; conversely, a fall in price tends to expand demand and to contract supply.

(c) Price tends to a level at which the demand is equal to the supply, i.e. to an "equilibrium price".

The term demand refers to "effective demand". These laws or tendencies are a fair description of what happens in most situations; but there are exceptions, at least in the short term. In a period of growing shortages (due to famine or national emergencies) a rise in price of a certain commodity might be accompanied by an increase in demand, if it is feared that the price will rise higher still for a long period. A fall in share prices may not be accompanied by an immediate increase in demand if potential buyers are confident that prices will fall lower still; conversely a rise in share prices might not stimulate an increase in the quantity for sale, if potential sellers have grounds for believing that prices will rise higher still. *See* PRICE MECHANISM.

Supply Curve A graphical presentation of a supply function, $x = \phi(p)$, showing how much of a commodity will be supplied per unit of time at any given

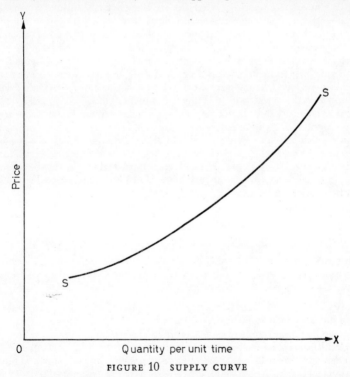

FIGURE 10 SUPPLY CURVE

price, providing that the other influences governing supply remain unchanged. The supply curve is referred to axes OY and OX along which prices and supplies are respectively measured. It is an economic convention that supply curves are referred to a vertical price axis. In normal supply curves x increases as p increases, i.e. the supply function, $x = \phi(p)$, is monotonic increasing.

245

The shape is generally concave to the origin, but the precise form depends on the commodity and the elasticity of supply. Generally supply expands with an increase in price, although a trend cannot continue, of course, if production is unable to keep pace with demand or there is no more of a commodity available. In exceptional circumstances supply curves may be regressive, less being offered at a higher price. This could happen if supplies were withheld because of an expectation that prices will rise even higher. This condition would only hold, however, for a relatively short period. Figure 10 shows a normal supply curve under conditions of perfect competition (q.v.). The terms "expansion" and "contraction" of supply are reserved for changes in supply attributable to changes in the price of the commodity only; the amount supplied at any given price remaining constant. The terms "increase" or "decrease" in supply are reserved for changes in supply attributable to changes in the state of supply; more or fewer goods being supplied at any given price than formerly.

Supply Curves, Regressive, Negative or Backward Sloping A graphical presentation of an abnormal market situation in which the fall in the price of a good or service leads to an increase in the supply of that good or service, or conversely an increase in price leads to a fall in supply, at least in the short term. For example, it has been observed that a fall in the price of an agricultural product has resulted in increased production. The explanation may be that if prices are low a farmer may work with greater energy to produce a large crop with the object of maintaining his standard of living. Conversely, when prices are likely to be high he may plan a smaller output. In the longer term, poor prices will tend to reduce the number of farmers in business, while high prices will have the reverse effect. To take another example, an increase in wages in a particular occupation may result in a reduction in the number of hours worked (by way of reduced overtime) and total output may be reduced, at least until such time as the total labour force has been increased as a result of the more attractive wages. *See* Figure 11.

Supply Expenditure Expenditure provided for in the British Government's Civil and Defence Estimates; this represents only a part, though a large part, of total public expenditure.

Supply Schedule A table giving the supply (q.v.) of a commodity or service at various prices, while all other factors determining supply remain unchanged. *See* DEMAND SCHEDULE.

Supply Services An item in the Budget comprising the ordinary expenditure of the British Government Departments. It includes all defence expenditure, grants by the Government in support of local authority revenues, the National Health Service, agricultural subsidies and most of the aid programme. From 1966–67 it also included the Selective Employment Tax premiums and refund payments. Estimates of all this expenditure have to be submitted to and voted by Parliament annually.

Surcharge *See* IMPORT SURCHARGE.

Surplus In the nationalised industries, another term for "profit". *See* BALANCE OF REVENUE; ECONOMIC RENT; RENT (b).

Surplus Value A description accorded by Karl Marx to that portion of the value of the results of human labour which accrue to people other than the workers or producers in the form of profits, dividends, rent, etc. All value, argued Marx, is the result of human labour, and the worker should enjoy the full fruits of his endeavours.

Surtax An additional income tax imposed on British residents at a progressively increasing rate according to the size of their personal incomes above a specified level; the broad effect of allowable deductions for tax purposes is that surtax does not become payable on earned income until the latter reaches about £5,000 per annum, depending on the personal allowances due. *See* INCOME TAX, PROGRESSIVE.

Swaps A City expression, meaning the exchange of sums of money of the same currency but on different terms—for example, selling francs for delivery now while simultaneously buying them back for delivery in three months' time. *See* CURRENCY SWAPS.

Sweating System The exploitation of labour by means of low wages, excessive work stints, and poor working conditions.

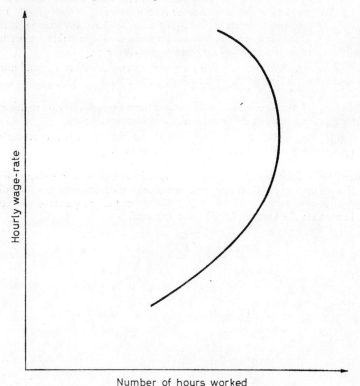

FIGURE 11   BACKWARD SLOPING SUPPLY CURVE

G.D.E.T. — 9

Switch Dealer A dealer (q.v.) who disposes to others goods that one trading party does not wish to receive from another trading party under, say, a bilateral trade agreement. The activities of these dealers injects some flexibility into bilateral trade agreements which oblige trading partners to keep their trade with each other in approximate balance. *See* BILATERAL TRADE.

Switch Selling Advertising one model and trying to sell a more expensive one. The offer or advertisement of a "cheap" commodity is used to arouse consumer interest; persuasive salesmen then concentrate on selling dearer models to customers who have shown interest.

Switching The transfer of investment between different classes of securities. Switches are of three fairly distinct kinds:

(a) Policy switching—made to take advantage of future possibilities in relation to an investor's requirements. It may involve the redistribution of a portfolio;

(b) Coupon switching—made to take advantage of immediate possibilities of profit;

(c) Anomaly switching—switching between securities of comparable maturity to profit from some fleeting anomaly in their prices. The purpose is always a profit on trading without any change in the broad pattern of an investor's portfolio. Large stakes are needed to show a profit on the fine margins available.

Generally, switching helps to even out prices and makes a contribution to the smooth functioning of the gilt-edged market.

Syndicate (a) An association between two or more firms to carry on together a joint activity without the formation of a separate legal entity.

(b) A ring formed by London discount houses for the purpose of tendering for agreed quotas of Treasury bills at uniform rates.

Systematic Soldiering Conscious restriction of output by a working group. A term used by F. W. Taylor, a pioneer of scientific management, to describe control over output by a working group, when the group's standards were lower than management hoped for or expected.

T

Take-Over Bid An offer addressed to the shareholders of a Company by an individual or Company, to buy their shares at a named price with a view to securing control of the Company.

Talon A slip attached to dividend and interest coupons (q.v.) for the purpose of applying for further coupons when necessary.

Tap Issue The issue of bills and securities by the Treasury direct to Government Departments and other buyers at a special price, without going through the market. *See* TREASURY BILLS.

Tap Stocks Securities (q.v.) which are always available; the term is applied also to government securities which are sold by the government departments holding them when they reach a certain market price. Tap stocks may be short- or long-dated. Exchequer $6\frac{1}{4}\%$ 1972 is an example of a "short tap"; Treasury $6\frac{3}{4}\%$ 1995/98 is an example of a "long tap".

Tare The weight of the packing or container of an article. This must be deducted from the gross weight to find the actual or net weight of the article.

Tarif de Combat A tariff used as a bargaining counter in attempting to secure trade advantages.

Tariff (a) A duty or tax charged by a country on its imports from other countries; a customs duty (q.v.). The duty may be imposed on an "ad valorem" basis, as a percentage of the value of the goods, or by way of a specific amount per unit of weight or volume. The tariff may be used to protect home industries from the competition of foreign producers, or it may be adopted to reduce the total imports bill a country has to pay. (b) method of charging for services, e.g. supplies of gas or electricity. *See* BLOCK TARIFF; BULK SUPPLY TARIFF; FLAT-RATE TARIFF; INSTALLED LOAD TARIFF; LOAD/RATE TARIFF; MAXIMUM DEMAND TARIFF; RESTRICTED HOUR TARIFF; SEASONAL TARIFF; SUBSCRIBED DEMAND TARIFF; TIME OF DAY TARIFF; TWO-PART TARIFF.

Tax, Average Rate of The rate of tax paid by the individual computed as follows:

$$\frac{\text{Total income tax}}{\text{Total income}}$$

Tax Avoidance Term used to describe not only illegal evasion of tax obligations but also the entirely legal ways by which a person may so arrange his affairs as to minimise, or even eliminate, tax liability on his property and income.

Tax, Marginal Rate of The amount of tax a person pays on the last unit or increment of income received.

Tax, Progressive *See* INCOME TAX, PROGRESSIVE.

Tax, Proportional *See* INCOME TAX, PROPORTIONAL.

Tax, Regressive A tax which takes a larger percentage of income from people the smaller their income.

Tax Reserve Certificates Non-negotiable securities in which corporations and persons can invest any funds set aside for payment of tax until the date when tax is due to be paid (when they can surrender the certificates to the revenue authorities in payment of the tax) and earn interest in the meantime.

Tax, Selective Employment *See* SELECTIVE EMPLOYMENT TAX.

Taxable Income That part of income liable to tax. It is arrived at by deducting from assessable income (gross income) all allowable deductions.

Taxation, Adam Smith's Canons of Smith's canons of taxation were as follows:
- (a) the amounts people paid in taxes should be equal, i.e. proportional to their incomes;
- (b) there should be certainty with regard to the amount to be paid;
- (c) there should be convenience of payment and collection;
- (d) economy should be observed so that taxes should not be imposed of a kind where the cost of collection was excessive.

Taxation, Purposes of The purposes of direct and indirect taxation are broadly:
- (a) to provide the public authorities with the revenue required for meeting the cost of defence, social services, interest payments on the national debt (q.v.), municipal services etc.;
- (b) to give effect to economic policy, the objects of which may include:
  - (i) increasing the economic welfare of the community as a whole by reducing the inequality of incomes;
  - (ii) reducing or increasing purchasing power through increasing or reducing purchase taxes (q.v.);
  - (iii) checking the imports of a commodity from abroad in order to help to correct an adverse balance of payments (*See* IMPORT SURCHARGE);
  - (iv) influencing the rate of economic growth of the nation.

Taxes A compulsory financial contribution by a person or body of persons towards the expenditure of a public authority. Taxes on income (i.e. on wages, salaries, profits, dividends, rent and interest) and on capital are known as "direct" taxes. Taxes on commodities or services are known as "indirect" taxes. In Britain, the indirect taxes on tobacco, oil and alcoholic drinks account for over 70 per cent of the revenue from this source. Other indirect taxes include purchase taxes, entertainment taxes and import duties. Purchase taxes are ad valorem (q.v.) taxes and were first introduced into Britain during the Second World War. Rates are a local indirect tax on property. *See* CAPITAL GAINS TAX; COMPANY TAXATION; CUSTOMS DUTY; EXCISE DUTY; PURCHASE TAX; RATES, LOCAL; SELECTIVE EMPLOYMENT TAX.

Technical Development Capital Ltd. (T.D.C.) A company formed in 1962 to provide finance for the commercial exploitation of technical developments and innovations. Its formation was among the recommendations of the Radcliffe Committee (q.v.). The company's shareholders comprise over forty leading insurance companies, investment trusts and merchant banks. The primary objective is to help medium-sized and small businesses to accelerate the commercial exploitation of technical innovations rather than to finance research or development. The company is therefore prepared to support at an early stage projects having attendant high risks. Usually most of the finance required is made available on secured loan terms, repayable over a reasonable period. While a share in the equity of any project is expected, majority control is seldom sought. *See* FINANCE CORPORATIONS; INNOVATION.

Technical Efficiency The combination of the best and most modern production techniques, efficient management and a highly skilled work-force. *See* ECONOMIC EFFICIENCY.

Tender Offer in writing to execute work or supply goods at fixed prices. *See* QUOTATION.

Tenor The period of time stated on a bill of exchange (q.v.) before payment is due.

"Term" Loans Fixed loans for a definite term of years.

Terminable Association An association of producers, each producer retaining the right to terminate its membership.

Terminal Markets In London, markets in which trading is confined to "futures", i.e. the making of contracts for the delivery of commodities at some specified future date.

Terms of Trade The relationship between the prices of exports and imports. It may be expressed as an Index:

$$\text{Index of Terms of Trade} = \frac{\text{Price Index of Exports}}{\text{Price Index of Imports}}$$

251

The price index of exports measures the change in the aggregate value of a representative selection of exports as compared with the corresponding value in a base year; similarly the price index of imports measures the change in the aggregate value of a representative selection of imports as compared with the corresponding value for the same base year. If the prices of imports rise in relation to the prices of exports, then the terms of trade have moved against the exporter.

Test Discount Rate One of the essential elements of the discounted cash flow method (q.v.) of investment appraisal. The British Government has asked the nationalised industries to use a common test discount rate of 8 per cent for all new investment (q.v.), i.e. new investment projects will need to show either that receipts will be greater than costs, discounting future returns at 8 per cent per annum, or that there is some special social or wider economic justification for the investment.

Theoretical Economics A branch of economics (q.v.) concerned with the development of economic laws and hypotheses, based upon the analysis of economic activity. *See* APPLIED ECONOMICS; ECONOMIC LAW.

Theory of Variations *See* EQUILIBRIUM THEORY.

Thermal Efficiency The total calorific content of the useful heat or energy produced by a plant, expressed as a percentage of the calorific content of the total fuel consumed.

The Three "C's" Character, capacity and capital. Three important factors in evaluating the soundness of an individual or a business firm as a credit risk. *See* CREDIT.

The Three "L's" Luxury, leisure and longevity. Three problems presented to society as the long-term result of economic growth.

The Three "S's" Simplification, standardisation, and specialisation. Three important factors in achieving high productivity.

"The Times" Share Indices *See* SHARE INDICES, "THE TIMES".

Ticket or Name Day Day prior to settlement or account day (q.v.) on the Stock Exchange (q.v.) when stockbrokers make out tickets bearing the names of their clients and details of shares bought during the previous account period (q.v.). These tickets are passed on to the stockjobbers from whom the shares were obtained. The stockjobbers pass on the tickets which finally reach the stockbrokers who first sold the shares. Arrangements are then made for payment for the shares and their legal transfer. The following day, accounts are settled.

Tied Shop   A shop of which the proprietor is financed by a company on condition that he supplies only the products of that company. In the brewery trade, a "free house" is one in which the proprietor is not so tied.

Tight Times   Times prescribed by management for the completion of certain tasks, which are barely adequate.

Time and Motion Study   An analysis of the methods, materials, tools and equipments used, or to be used, in the performance of a piece of work with the purpose of (a) finding the most economical way of doing the work; (b) standardising the methods, materials, tools and equipment; and (c) accurately determining the time required by a qualified and properly trained person working at a normal pace to complete the task.

Time Deposit (U.S.)   A bank deposit withdrawable only after giving specified notice; not unlike a British deposit account (q.v.). *See* DEMAND DEPOSIT.

Time Efficiency   The fraction of the total time available during which a plant is in productive operation. *See* CAPACITY; LOAD FACTOR; STREAM DAYS.

Time Limit   In respect of transactions of stocks and shares, a limit imposed by a customer in respect of the time in which a broker may carry out an order. Thus an order may stipulate:

G.T.W.	Good this week
G.T.M.	Good this month
G.T.C.	Good 'til cancelled

If an order is endorsed "buy or cancel" it means that if the order is not completed within the same day as given, the order is automatically cancelled.

Time-of-Day Tariff   A tariff for the supply of electricity which, in its simplest form, has a high rate in the day-time and a low rate at night. *See* TARIFF (b).

Time Rates and Piece Rates   Common bases of wages payments. Under time rates a worker receives a fixed sum per hour; under piece rates he obtains a fixed sum for a given output. It is claimed that time-rates encourage careful work and individual attention, while piece-rates favour high-speed production of a repetitive nature.

Times Covered   *See* DIVIDEND COVER.

Tithes   Originally the tenth part of the produce of the soil paid to the clergy. The Tithes Commutation Act 1836 commuted tithes into money rent. In 1936 tithe rent charges were extinguished and sixty-year redemption annuities substituted.

Token Coins Coins of which the legal value is higher than that of the metal contained in them.

Town and Country Planning Community planning of developments in town and country with the aim of achieving a socially desirable balance between the many competing uses to which land may be put, and to ensure that public and private development is carried out with the least possible harm to amenities. Planning activities in Britain have included: (a) the provision of urban amenities in the countryside for the agricultural population; (b) the preservation of historical monuments and the creation of national parks; (c) schemes for the redistribution of industry and the building of new towns (q.v.); (d) the creation of green belts (q.v.) to restrain the outside spread of towns and cities; (e) slum clearance and development schemes; (f) the provision of sports facilities, airfields and highways.

Trade Association A body of persons formed for the purpose of furthering the trade interests of its members.

Trade Bill A commercial bill used in transactions actually involving goods. *See* FINANCE BILL.

Trade Boards *See* MINIMUM WAGE LEGISLATION.

Trade Cycle Alternating periods of trade boom and depression, especially characteristic of 19th century business activity in Britain when cycles of this nature occurred at fairly regular intervals. Lord Beveridge in his "Full Employment in a Free Society" (1944) examined the cycles of business activity from 1792 to 1913 revealing intervals of from five to eleven years between one boom and the next, with an average of eight years. During boom periods employment, wages, prices, profits and production rise together, only to decline during the ensuing slump. While all, or nearly all, industries are simultaneously prosperous or depressed, fluctuations occur most sharply in the production of capital goods. The long drawn out depression from 1920–1939, between the two World Wars, differed in character from previous periods. A short period of boom after the First World War was followed by acute depression. Unemployment in the years 1920–1928 averaged one and a half million. Superimposed on this came the Great Depression of 1929–35 in which unemployment rose to the unprecedented heights of almost three million, declining only slowly. By 1939 unemployment had decreased to about one and a quarter million. The Great Depression was more severe and more world wide than any other. All capitalist countries were affected. In very marked contrast, the period following the Second World War has been one of boom; unemployment in Britain has rarely exceeded 500,000 or 2 per cent of the working population. Some areas have suffered a higher percentage of unemployment than this, such as Scotland, North and North-West England, South Wales and Northern Ireland where special problems exist and special measures have been introduced. In large parts of England, notably the South-East, the unemployment percentage has been little above one per cent. *See* ACCELERATOR; DEVELOPMENT AREAS; DISTRIBUTION OF INDUSTRY ACT 1945; GREAT DEPRESSION (1929-35); GROWTH AREAS; LOCAL EMPLOMENT ACTS 1960 TO 1966; MULTIPLIER; SPECIAL AREAS.

Trade Cycle, Theories of the   Theories adduced by economists to explain fluctuations in trade have included:

(a) *"Real Causes" Theories* (i) Attempts to explain the trade cycle in terms of harvest fluctuations attributable to the weather. One of the most famous of these theories was the "sunspot" theory of William Stanley Jevons (1835-1882). Jevons traced cyclical trade fluctuations to cycles in harvest yields; in turn he correlated the harvest fluctuations with the appearance of spots on the face of the sun, it being argued that sunspots influence the weather and hence harvest yields. This and other climatic theories are no longer accepted as primary explanations of trade movements; (ii) Theories that fluctuations in capital-producing industries are due to the fact that the demand for their products is a derived demand (q.v.). *See* ACCELERATOR, THE.

(b) *Psychological Theories*   Theories that business men are influenced alternately by waves of optimism and pessimism. When trade is good people are optimistic, buying more while prices rise and production is stimulated. When trade is poor pessimism prevails buying is reduced, prices fall and production is depressed. The importance of these theories lies in the light they throw on the forces which tend to accentuate fluctuations, even if they do not themselves produce them. John Maynard Keynes (1883-1946) attached great importance to the psychological influences affecting the propensities to consume and save (q.v.).

(c) *Monetary Theories*   Theories that stress the role of the quantity of money and credit, and the rate of interest, in influencing business activity. The view that the trade cycle (q.v.) is a purely monetary phenomenon has been held by Ralph G. Hawtrey (1879-) who regards the Bank Rate (q.v.) as the mainspring of cyclical change. A reduction in Bank Rate and other short-term interest rates encourages merchants to carry larger stocks of goods and stimulates trade generally; an increase in interest rates has the reverse effect. Hawtrey argues that by raising the Bank Rate a stop can be put to any boom, and by reducing the Bank Rate we can end nearly all depressions. The first proposition finds agreement in the Government White Paper on Employment Policy of 1944, although the Paper expresses doubt that changes in the rate of interest at the bottom of a depression will have any decisive effect on the course of trade.

(d) *Over-Production and Under-Consumption Theories*   Numerous and diverse theories but all may be described as theories of the deficiency of effective demand. John A. Hobson (1858-1940) argued that in good times profits increase without a corresponding increase in the wages level and the purchasing power in the hands of the general public. Surplus profits are invested and productive capacity is greatly enlarged; but there is no market to carry off the increased supply of consumers' goods and a crisis persists until the surplus of stocks is worked off.

(e) *Saving-Investment Theory* A theory that consumption depends on the level of income, and that this in turn depends on real investment. Now saving, i.e. the abstention from the purchase of consumers' goods, is a pre-requisite for investment. Thus saving, consumption and investment depend on one another, together determining the level of total income. For full employment of resources to be maintained it is essential that the effective demand for goods and services should be sufficient to absorb all the output of the economic system. When saving is not translated into investment, the demand for goods is insufficient to cover all that is being produced; output falls and unemployment results. Between the two World Wars savings tended to exceed investment with adverse effects on employment. In these circumstances, incomes tend to fall until saving is once more brought into equality with investment. This may be at a level which is socially unacceptable. The solution lies in stimulating investment and hence incomes and effective demand.

Trade Gap, Crude Defined as imports c.i.f. (q.v.) minus exports and re-exports f.o.b. (q.v.).

Trade Mark The use of a brand name or other device to relate a commodity to the firm owning, producing or distributing it. *See* PRODUCT DIFFERENTIATION.

Trade-Off (U.S.) Or balance of advantages and disadvantages, e.g. between inflation and unemployment. Hence "trade-off ratio", e.g. the ratio at which the benefit from a given increase in employment more than cancels the harm from a given amount of inflation. *See* PHILLIPS CURVE.

Traders (U.S.) A small class of members of the New York Stock Exchange, they buy and sell stock on their own account with the hope of making speculative profits.

Trades Union Congress A body representing most British trade unions (q.v.); its objects are to further the interests of its members and improve the economic and social conditions of workers. Founded in 1868 it is an important channel of communication and consultation between the Government and unions.

Trade Unions Combinations of workers formed for the purpose of taking collective, as distinct from individual, action against their employers for the improvement of pay and other working conditions. Most unions also develop "friendly society" activities offering their members additional insurance against sickness and accident. There are two types of union; (a) craft unions, members of which are all engaged in the same—or one or two closely associated—occupations; (b) industrial unions, members of which come from branches of a particular industry.

Trading Account A business account the purpose of which is to indicate gross profit on trading alone, without taking into account the overhead expenses.

Trading Banks (Aust.) Name for the Australian commercial banks.

Trading Certificate A certificate issued by the Board of Trade without which a public limited company cannot commence business.

Tradition The sum of all the ideas, habits and customs that belong to a people and are transmitted from generation to generation—the social "heritage".

Transfer Cost What must be offered to attract a supply of a factor of production away from alternative avenues of employment. This sum of money is the necessary supply price of that factor in its new employment.

Transfer Deed A legal document by which ownership of stocks or shares is transferred from a holder to a purchaser. *See* TRANSFER FORM.

Transfer Earnings The amount that any factor of production (q.v.) could earn in the best paid alternative use.

Transfer Form A document used in a new system for transferring the ownership of stocks and shares which came into effect in Britain on 26th October, 1963. Under this system, a buyer of shares does not normally have to sign a form of transfer. The broker acting for the buyer simply completes a transfer form and sends it with the seller's share certificate to the registration office of the company. On the other hand, a seller of shares will need to sign a transfer form authorising the company to remove his name from its records so that the buyer can in turn be registered.

Transfer Payments Payments made by public authorities which are not made in consideration of goods and services currently produced, e.g. national assistance payments, unemployment benefit, grants to students, family allowances, interest paid on the national debt.

Transformation Curve A graphical presentation showing the alternative productive possibilities of a given supply of factors of production (q.v.). A transformation curve is a "maximal" concept plotting all those combinations of goods which can be produced if all resources are fully employed; any point within the curve corresponds to possible combinations of products using resources at less than full employment. Figure 12 shows the relative quantities of consumer goods (q.v.) and capital goods (q.v.) which may be produced from given amounts of labour and materials.

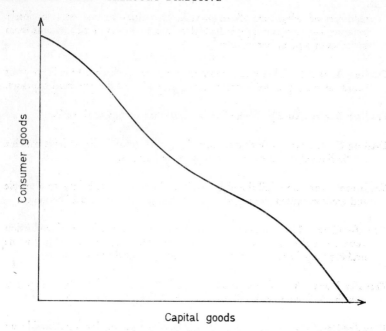

FIGURE 12 TRANSFORMATION CURVE

Treasury Bills Short-term bearer securities, with a maturity usually of 91 days, issued by the Treasury (q.v.). Tenders are invited every Friday for the Bills to be issued in the following week. The effective yield is the discount at which they are sold, that is to say the difference between the price at which they are sold and their redemption value. These are known as "market" Treasury Bills. They must be distinguished from "tap" Treasury Bills which are those Bills issued directly, not through the tender, to Government departments, including the Issue Department of the Bank of England (q.v.), the National Debt Commissioners (q.v.) and the Exchange Equalisation Account (q.v.). The raising of money by the Treasury through the issue of Treasury Bills enables the British Government to meet its weekly commitments which are ultimately paid for by taxation. The taxes do not come in at an even rate, however, a large part coming in at the end of the financial year; hence the need for short-term borrowing.

Treasury Deposit Receipt Largely replaced the Treasury Bill (q.v.) in Britain during the Second World War. Each week the Banks were advised as to the amount of Treasury Deposit Receipts they were to take up. The system declined in post-war years. By the beginning of 1952, the Treasury Deposit Receipt had disappeared.

Treasury Directive Instruction or request by the Treasury (q.v.) to the banks in respect of the volume of bank advances. It has become an important additional instrument of monetary policy.

258

Treasury, The The central department in the British Civil Service, functioning as the technical controller of the public purse. The treasury is divided into three sections—supply, establishment and finance—corresponding to its three functions of supervising the activities of other spending departments, supervising the appointment and pay of civil servants and preparing details of financial policy. In October, 1969, the department acquired responsibility for medium and long term economic assessments.

Treaty of Rome 1957 The governing instrument of the Common Market, officially titled the "Treaty Establishing the European Economic Community" signed at Rome on March 25, 1957, by France, Germany, Italy, the Netherlands, Belgium and Luxemburg. The negotiation of it began in Brussels in June, 1956. The Treaty, which with its protocols runs to 378 pages in the standard English text, has six parts:

Part I, Principles, which states and elaborates the overriding aim of promoting a "harmonious development" by "establishing a Common Market and progressively approximating the economic policies of member States."

Part II, Basis of the Community, which defines the Common Market in four sections by providing for (1) a Customs Union and the abolition of internal tariffs and quotas; (2) a common agricultural policy; (3) free movement of persons, services and capital; (4) a harmonised transport system.

Part III, Policy of the Community, which in four sections provides for (1) common rules of competition and laws affecting it; (2) co-ordination of economic policies; (3) harmonised features of social policy; (4) a European Investment Bank.

Part IV, The Association of Overseas Countries and Territories, which associates former and present colonial territories of the Six with the Community.

Part V, Institutions of the Community, which governs the Council, Commission, Assembly, etc. and voting.

Part VI, General and Final Provisions, which gives the Community "legal personality" and regulates establishment of the Institutions and the entry into force of the Treaty.

There are also protocols covering certain special interests of individual member States and certain individual products requiring special treatment.

The Treaty lays down the length and stages of the "transitional period", during which the aims of the Community will be gradually attained. *See* EUROPEAN ECONOMIC COMMUNITY.

Triffin Plan Named after Professor R. Triffin of Yale University, a proposal to convert the International Monetary Fund (q.v.) into a world central bank. Features of the proposal are: (a) The reserves of each member country would include deposits at the International Monetary Fund in terms of a new unit of account; (b) each country would hold 20 per cent of its official reserves in this form; (c) payment between members would normally be made in terms of these new deposits; and (d) while these deposits would be increased to meet the growing demands of world trade, the size of the annual increase in deposits would require the prior agreement of the member countries.

Truck System The practice of paying workmen by means of orders on certain shops, or in kind, instead of with money.
This has been forbidden by the Truck Acts of 1831, 1887 and 1896.

Trust A combination or amalgamation of large firms exercising monopoly control over the commodity produced. Government legislation may be introduced to protect consumers, e.g. the anti-Trust legislation in the U.S.A. The Sherman Anti-Trust Act 1890, dissolved the great oil and tobacco trusts, although both were later reconstituted. *See* VOTING TRUST.

Trustee Savings Banks Local savings banks for small savers, managed by boards of honorary trustees and managers. Two departments are maintained for (a) ordinary, and (b) special investment; the deposits in the special investment department receive a higher rate of interest. The Trustee Savings Bank Act, 1964, enables the banks to operate a current account service by means of which depositors can issue cheques on non-interest bearing accounts. *See* POST OFFICE SAVINGS BANK.

Tucker Committee A Committee on the Taxation of Trading Profits which presented its Report (Cmd. 8189) in April, 1951.

Turn A Jobber's "turn" is the difference between his buying and his selling price. He may make a profit or loss.

Turnover The total receipts for goods sold by a trader during a given period.

Turnover Ratio In a business, the ratio of the value of annual sales to the value of fixed investments.

Turnover Tax A tax imposed on the sale of a commodity every time it changes hands. *See* AD VALOREM TAX; SALES TAX; TAXES; VALUE-ADDED TAX.

Two-Dollar Broker (U.S.) A broker who makes a livelihood by executing orders for commission brokers during busy periods. The broker charges commission for his services, which at one time was $2 for every 100 shares or stocks bought or sold.

Two-Part Tariff A composite charge for gas or electricity comprising a fixed charge per accounting period and a charge per therm or unit of gas or electricity consumed. The underlying principle is that the fixed minimum charge should cover roughly the fixed costs (q.v.) of production and distribution, and the charge varying with consumption should cover the variable costs (q.v.) of production.

U

Uncalled Capital Authorised capital remaining uncalled on shares issued to the public. The uncalled capital may be regarded as reserve capital. *See* CAPITAL—AUTHORISED, NOMINAL OR REGISTERED.

Uncertainty In economics, non-insurable business risk; the unpredictability of the outcome of much of business activity. The risks of theft, fire and flood to a large number of businesses can be calculated and insurance offered against them. In this way this class of risk can be converted through insurance into a known cost to the firm. Other business risks cannot be so provided against, e.g. the unforeseeable effect of political decisions on the markets for certain goods. These risks or uncertainties must be borne by the entrepreneur (q.v.). In private competitive enterprise profit is regarded as the reward for bearing uncertainties. *See* EXPORT CREDITS GUARANTEE DEPARTMENT.

Under-Population A condition when the marginal product of labour is greater than the existing average output per head for the country as a whole. Thus, if the population were slightly increased, the average output per head would be raised. *See* OPTIMUM POPULATION; OVER-POPULATION.

Underwriting The act of insuring or guaranteeing. In the new issues market, underwriters guarantee, for a commission, that the money required will be forthcoming; if the public does not subscribe fully to the new issue the underwriters take up the remaining shares or stock. *See* INSURANCE.

Unearned Income Income from capital investments, ownership of land and savings. It includes interest and dividends, rent and income derived from deposits in the Post Office, Trustee and other savings banks, National Savings Certificates and bank deposits. Such income is taxed at a higher rate than "earned" income in the United Kingdom.

Unearned Increment A phrase used by John Stuart Mill (1806–1873) to describe the increase in the value of a piece of land which is not due to any expenditure on improvements by the owner, but due to other factors.

"Uneasy Triangle", The A reference to the three-cornered incompatibility between a stable price level, full employment and free collective bargaining. It has been argued that theoretically Britain can have any two of these desirable things, but that neither theoretically nor in practice is it possible to have all three simultaneously. Full employment means high bargaining power for workers and competition between employers to obtain and retain suitable amounts and qualities of labour. High earnings not linked with individual productivity raise costs and swell demand, and under the influence of "push and pull", prices rise. Prices have outstripped the increase in national productivity since the Second World War, to the detriment of those living on fixed, or relatively fixed, incomes and to the constant hazard of Britain's export drive. Fortunately, other countries to whom we export have suffered inflation too. Of course, reasonable stability of the value of money while retaining free collective bargaining by trade unions could be obtained, but only at a level of unemployment unacceptable in post-war society. Another much more acceptable alternative is that restraint should be exercised in demands for higher wages, provided that not only wages are held in check but also all other incomes and prices, in an effort to dampen inflationary trends; but even if nationally negotiated wage-rates are linked with national productivity there remains the eroding influence of "wage drift" (q.v.) as a result of which actual earnings run well-ahead of national rates. It is likely therefore that an inflationary trend cannot be stopped, but at least some contribution can be made to slowing it down. *See* INFLATION; NATIONAL INCOMES POLICY.

Unemployment A condition of involuntary idleness.

Unemployment Benefit Financial assistance to those genuinely seeking work, but unable to find suitable employment.

Unemployment Rate The number of persons capable of working and willing to work but unable to find suitable employment, expressed as a percentage of the total number of persons available for employment at any time.

Unemployment, Types of Economists distinguish the following types of unemployment:

(a) *Disguised Unemployment* A slackening of total effective demand may not be fully reflected in the increase of persons registered as unemployed for two reasons: (i) workers may be put on "short-time", thus reducing the number of hours worked per person and avoiding redundancy, and (ii) employers may retain a greater number of men than they require during what is believed to be a temporary recession in order to keep teams together and to have sufficient labour available when demand revives. *See* ACTIVITY RATE; PAYROLL TAX.

(b) *Unemployables* Individuals who, suffering from a mental, temperamental or physical disability, are unable to find or follow any normal employment. The number of such individuals is relatively small. They are no longer included in the published figures for unemployment.

(c) *Frictional Unemployment* This type of unemployment consists of individuals who are temporarily unemployed, although there may be an overall unsatisfied demand for labour in the country, because they are not offering the right skills at the right time in the right place to meet that demand. Mobility or re-training may provide a solution. A more stubborn problem exists if the person displaced by the introduction of a labour-saving device such as a computer, is too old to find another place, and perhaps another kind of work, in industry.

(d) *Seasonal Unemployment* Unemployment which arises in particular trades and industries through seasonal variations in activity. For example, bad weather often causes a temporary suspension of work in the building industry; seaside resorts offer little employment during the winter season; agriculture provides seasonal employment at times of harvesting, potato-lifting and fruit gathering.

(e) *Structural Unemployment* Unemployment which arises in particular industries through a major and more or less permanent fall in demand for the products of those industries. Between the two World Wars, this type of unemployment was prevalent in three declining industries—coal-mining, ship-building and cotton.

(f) *Mass Unemployment* Unemployment affecting many trades and industries arising from a fall in the total volume of effective demand for goods and services of all kinds. It is associated with the trade cycle (q.v.) and is sometimes called "cyclical unemployment". The Great Depression, 1929–35 (q.v.), and indeed the whole period between the two World Wars, provided an unprecedented example of this type of unemployment. The problem was not confined to Britain, affecting all industrial countries. *See* FULL EMPLOYMENT.

Unfair Competition Competition which appears to violate the standards of fairness or honesty generally held by a community. Some of these standards may be embodied in legislation, e.g. safety regulations, food and drugs regulations, etc. Conduct sometimes described as "unfair competition" is not necessarily unlawful conduct; a plea often advanced is that certain imports from countries enjoying a lower standard of living constitute "unfair competition" because "cheap labour" is used in their production, placing manufacturers in the importing country at a disadvantage.

Unissued Capital Authorised capital which has not been issued. *See* CAPITAL —AUTHORISED, NOMINAL OR REGISTERED.

"Unit of Account" of Common Market Under the Common Market rules a "unit of account" is equivalent to an American dollar and represents that value in gold.

Unit of Currency The standard monetary unit in use in a country. Some examples are given in Table 4.

Unit Trust A method of investment by which money subscribed by many people is invested on their behalf by a management company; the investment and management is subject to the strict legal provisions of a trust deed. The investments acquired are held by a trustee which may be a bank or an insurance company. The management company and the trustee are parties to the trust deed which defines their respective responsibilities and contains the rules for the operation of the trust. Unit trusts are subject to the Prevention of Fraud (Investments) Act 1958. Net income is paid to all investors in the trust in proportion to the size of their holdings. *See* INVESTMENT TRUST.

United Nations Children's Fund (U.N.I.C.E.F.) United Nations organisations set up to help countries meet the urgent needs of their children through well conceived long-term programmes. Aid is given only at the request of the government concerned. The main fields of U.N.I.C.E.F. aid are (1) health services; (2) family and child welfare; (3) disease control, and (4) nutrition.

TABLE 4

EXAMPLES OF UNITS OF CURRENCY

COUNTRY	Unit of Currency	COUNTRY	Unit of Currency
AUSTRALIA	Dollar (100 cents)	MOROCCO	Dirham (100 Francs)
AUSTRIA	Schilling (100 Groschen)	NEW ZEALAND	Dollar (100 cents)
BELGIUM	Franc (100 Centimes)	NORWAY	Krone (100 Öre)
CANADA	Dollar (100 Cents)	PORTUGAL	Escudo (100 Centavos)
DENMARK	Krone (100 Öre)	SPAIN	Peseta (100 Centimos)
FRANCE	Franc (100 Centimes)	SWEDEN	Krona (100 Öre)
(WEST) GERMANY	Deutsche Mark (100 Pfennig)	SWITZER- LAND	Franc (100 Centimes)
GREECE	Drachma (100 Lepta)	U.K.	Pound (100 pennies)
HOLLAND	Florin/Guilder (100 Cents)	U.S.A.	Dollar (100 Cents)
ITALY	Lira (100 Centesimi)	YUGO- SLAVIA	Dinar (100 Paras)

In addition the Fund helps countries survey the needs of their children, establish priorities and plan programmes, and provides emergency aid for children suffering from catastrophes, such as earthquakes, floods and droughts.

United Nations Conference on Trade and Development (U.N.C.T.A.D.) An organisation set up by the United Nations to assist the less developed nations, defined as those countries with a gross national product per head of less than $600 a year. It seeks to accelerate the growth rate of the less developed countries to not less than 5 per cent per annum. The Conference endeavours to do this by arranging aid and finance, and by promoting trade. In respect of finance special drawing rights have been made available at the International Monetary Fund (q.v.) to assist the less developed countries when faced with an unexpected slump in their export receipts. The first U.N.C.T.A.D. meeting was held in Geneva in 1964.

United Nations Educational, Scientific and Cultural Organisation (U.N.E.S.C.O.) A United Nations organisation which came into being in 1946 whose aim is the expansion of education as a tool for progress in the world's developing countries.

Unrequited Exports Exports which are not exchanged for current imports, but the value of which pays interest on loans raised abroad, or profits on investment made in the home country by foreigners.

Usance A time fixed by custom for the payment of a bill of exchange (q.v.).

User Cost A term introduced by Lord Keynes to describe the reduction in the value of capital equipment due to its being used as compared with its not being used.

Usury The charging of an exhorbitant rate of interest on a loan. Until 1854, the Usury Laws prohibited a higher rate of interest than 5 per cent per annum.

Utility The capacity of a good or service to satisfy a human want. Utility cannot be measured in any definite quantitative form; it is sufficient to be able to say, however, that the utility of commodity A > B > C, and so on. *See* UTILITY, TOTAL.

"Utility" Goods Goods produced cheaply for the home market in a limited range of patterns or designs during the Second World War and the years immediately following.

Utility Optimum A position in which the satisfaction of a community cannot be increased, and the satisfaction of one member of the community cannot be increased without reducing the satisfaction of another.

Utility, Total The total satisfaction derived by a person from the consumption of a commodity or a service. There is no way in which to measure total utility.

V

Valorisation Schemes Schemes to safeguard the interests of producers by keeping up or maintaining selling prices, e.g. the inter-war Brazilian coffee valorisation scheme under which supplies of coffee were deliberately destroyed.

Value To an economist, the "exchange value" or price of a commodity or service, i.e. the power it possesses of acquiring other goods or services by means of exchange. However treasured a thing may be to an individual, if that thing cannot be exchanged then as far as the economist is concerned it has no value. Value depends in the first instance on demand in relation to supply. Alfred Marshall (1842–1924) likened value to the keystone of an arch, balanced in equilibrium between the contending pressures of its two opposing sides, the forces of demand on the one side and those of supply on the other. He visualised the amounts and prices of the several agencies of production as mutually determining one another—"when several balls are lying in a bowl, they mutually determine one another's position".

Value-Added Tax A tax levied on net business turnover. It differs from a turnover tax in eliminating from the taxable "base" the cost of inputs such as material and labour. It is a tax on the "value added" to a group of inputs by the operations of the firm. This "value added" is the difference between the untaxed selling price of an article or service and the unit cost of production.

Value Analysis *See* VALUE ENGINEERING.

Value Engineering The application of the technique of value analysis, the object of which is to obtain the same performance out of a product at a lower cost by achieving economies in the cycle of product design and manufacture. Economies are sought by questioning the usefulness of every part and operation in the manufacture of the product, and its costs in proportion to usefulness.

Value Judgment A decision involving basic issues of fairness, justice or morality. An economist is no more fitted to make such judgments than anyone else; he is concerned solely with the relationship between means and ends, whatever the nature of those ends might be.

Value of Service Principle A basis for charging for services which may be adopted by a monopolist who enjoys the power to discriminate between markets. A monopolist adopting this principle will divide the total market served by him into a number of minor markets, exacting the maximum gain from each market. In respect of railway rates, this principle has led to elaborate schemes of classification, both for passenger and for goods traffic. *See* COST OF SERVICE PRINCIPLE.

Value, Theories of Theories devised to explain the exchange value or price of commodities and services. These have included:

(a) *Labour Theory of Value* A theory that commodities are sold in ratios determined by the amount of labour expended on producing them. This was a fair observation for freely reproducible goods in a labour-intensive economy, but confused cause and effect. This theory was expounded by Adam Smith (1723–1790), David Ricardo (1772–1823), Karl Marx (1818–1883) and others.

(b) *Cost of Production Theory of Value* A theory which states that the value of a commodity is governed by the cost of the various factors employed in its production. This theory is simply a restatement of the labour theory of value expressed in monetary terms. Again the argument is from the side of supply, i.e. that cost determines price. The plausibility of this theory arises from the fact that under free competition between freely reproducible goods, a high rate of profit on any class of commodity will attract new producers into the field. The addition to the supply will tend to reduce the price until it is equal to the cost of production, including normal profit (q.v.). Conversely, low profits or a loss will drive producers out of the market, and once again price will tend to equal the cost of production, including normal profit. The theory does not account, however, for the value of goods which are not freely reproducible, or for the depressed value of goods due to a change in taste or fashion, or for the price of goods supplied under monopolistic conditions.

(c) *Marginal Theory of Value* A theory expounded by William Stanley Jevons (1835–1882), Léon Walras (1834–1910) and Carl Menger (1840–1921) which states that the value of any commodity or service is determined by its marginal utility for any particular purpose. Thus value depends on relative scarcity, or on demand in relation to supply. This theory satisfactorily explains the value of all goods whether freely reproducible or not, and whether the goods are supplied in highly competitive conditions or not; yet it does not preclude the view that in the case of freely reproducible goods, produced in competitive conditions, their values in the long-run are derived from the values of the factors of production which enter into their manufacture. Thus, although costs do not determine values or prices directly, they have an indirect influence through their effect on the supply curve (q.v.).

Variable Any quantity which varies.

Variable Costs Costs which vary directly with variations in the volume of output. The major variable costs involved are those of labour and material. Also known as "prime costs". *See* FIXED COSTS.

Variable Proportions, Law of If the quantity of one productive service is increased by equal increments, from zero, the quantities of the other essential productive services remaining fixed, the resulting increments of product will increase for a period, then become constant, and then decrease. Thus increasing, constant and diminishing returns may be regarded as an aspect of the law of variable proportions—as a movement towards or away from the optimum. The law relates to quantities per unit of time and is essentially technological. It is applicable, of course, to those cases in which the proportions of productive services are variable. *See* Figure 13; (a) in the 1st stage, from the origin out to the point at which the average product curve reaches a maximum, the marginal product reaches a maximum and then decreases; (b) in the 2nd stage, the curve of the marginal product reaches zero, this being the point at which the total product reaches a maximum; (c) in the 3rd stage, the marginal product is negative, and the total product curve eventually reaches zero. Also known as the Law of Diminishing Returns.

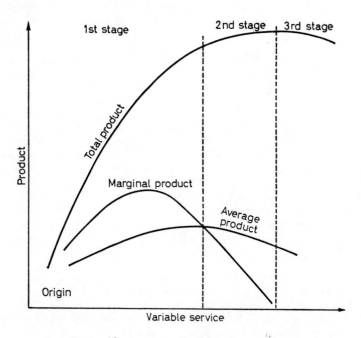

FIGURE 13   LAW OF VARIABLE PROPORTIONS

Variables, Endogenous and Exogenous   An endogenous variable is a variable explained within a theory; thus the price of oranges is an endogenous variable being determined within the framework of the theory of price. An exogenous variable is one that impinges on a theory from the outside; thus the state of the weather is an exogenous variable which will influence the price of oranges. Exogenous variables are sometimes referred to as autonomous variables.

Velocity of Circulation The average number of times that each unit of money (whether in the form of coins, notes or bank deposits) changes hands in the course of a year. In other words:

$$\text{Average velocity of circulation} = \frac{\text{Volume of spending per year}}{\text{Total volume of money}}$$

The velocity of circulation is taken into account in the Quantity Theory of Money (q.v.). In the "equation of exchange" $MV = PT$, where M is the quantity of money, V the velocity of circulation, P the price level, and T the total volume of transactions. With T constant, an increase in the quantity of money will not raise the price level proportionately if V falls. The velocity of circulation is not constant, changing in boom and depression. A feature of the Great Depression, 1929–35 (q.v.), was a reduced velocity of circulation. Those who thought recovery could be stimulated by increasing the quantity of money were disappointed by the unexpected decline in the velocity of circulation of the new money. Money became less active. The velocity of circulation is influenced by such fundamental factors as savings and investment, the total quantity of money and the amount of new money, the movement of interest rates and security prices, and many other factors.

The income velocity of money differs from the transactions velocity above as it excludes both financial transactions and a considerable volume of intermediate transactions. It takes account only of payments to dealers for goods and services. Income velocity measures the number of times per year that a unit of currency completes the circuit from income to purchase of goods and services and back to income again. Sometimes called circuit velocity.

Venture Capital *See* RISK CAPITAL.

Vernon Report (Aust.) The Report of a Committee set up in 1962 by the Australian Government, under the chairmanship of Sir James Vernon, on the state and prospects of the Australian economy. The Report, published in 1965, covered subjects as diverse as taxation, tariffs, foreign investments, economic planning, wage fixing and migration. The main theme was that Australia had a growth potential of 5 per cent per annum over the decade 1965-75, without excessive balance of payments problems or foreign domination, providing the Report's recommendations were implemented. These were: (a) the Government should set up an advisory committee on economic growth; (b) the Government should evolve policies directed at long-term rates of growth for the economy as a whole, and these should be made public; (c) the annual rate of new foreign investment should not exceed $A300 million a year, to prevent overseas control of Australian companies accelerating to unhealthy limits; (d) a strengthening of the position of the Reserve Bank; (e) the conducting of a full-scale inquiry into monetary policy along the lines of the Radcliffe report in the United Kingdom; (f) a target for net immigration of 100,000 persons per annum; (g) to maintain past rates of improvement in productivity, investment as a proportion of gross national product would have to increase by 2 per cent to 26 per cent; (g) manufacturers needed to export more if this sector was to increase its contribution to productivity growth; (h) more married women should be encouraged to enter the work force; (i) a wages policy should be introduced; (j) saving would need to be higher in order to boost investment and some of this extra saving would have to be generated through higher taxes. The immediate reaction of the Federal Government was unfavourable.

Vertical Disintegration An opposing trend to vertical integration, being a situation in which an isolated process has an optimum scale of operation much greater than that required by the other processes of manufacture and, therefore, tends to be undertaken by a specialist firm which supplies a number of firms in the main industry. *See* HORIZONTAL INTEGRATION; VERTICAL INTEGRATION.

Vertical Integration The amalgamation of firms engaged in the different stages of production of the same commodity to achieve greater economic strength and profitability. Although the units may be far apart, geographically, both the sources of raw materials and the outlets for the products are assured. The American Steel Trust consists of firms engaged in transport, coal and iron-mining, steel production and rolling. A high degree of vertical integration may occur within the same establishment. An integrated iron-and-steel works provides a leading example of integration in so far that coke-ovens, blast furnaces, steel-making furnaces and rolling equipment are all in close proximity to each other. A considerable saving in fuel is effected by passing metal from one stage to another while it is still hot. In addition, gases produced in blast furnaces and coke ovens can be used to provide heat and power for other parts of the plant. Metal scrap can be readily returned to the steel-making processes. Transport savings are also considerable. Also known as "vertical combination". *See* HORIZONTAL INTEGRATION; VERTICAL DISINTEGRATION.

Viability The ability to meet financial obligations. It is used in relation to the balance of payments (q.v.) to signify the ability of a country to meet the payments due to other countries in respect of the import of goods and services without the assistance of special loans. A country is "viable" if it is able to pay its way unaided.

Virement The power to transfer items from one account to another. The re-allocation of public expenditure by Government Departments requires specific Treasury (q.v.) sanction.

Visible Trade *See* BALANCE OF PAYMENTS.

Voluntary Unemployment A description given by Keynes to unemployment directly due to the "withdrawal of their labour by a body of workers because they do not choose to work for less than a certain real reward".

Vote on Account A statement of expenditure proposals which the British Government presents to Parliament in mid-February each year; it provides the first official indication of the shape of Central Government spending in the coming financial year. The purpose of the Vote on Account is to provide the Government with authority for expenditure in the new financial year until the passing of the Appropriation Bill. The statement covers only the Civil Estimates and the Defence (Central) Estimate; it does not cover expenditure which is authorised under permanent legislation, principally Consolidated Fund services, including interest on the National Debt and Consolidated Fund loans, nor the main Defence Estimates.

Voting Trust A permanent form of trust (q.v.) in which a number of competing companies agree to assign the whole of their stock to a group of trustees, receiving in exchange trust certificates representing the valuation of their properties. The trustees are thus able to exercise complete control over all the companies. This form of organisation was prevalent at one period in the United States until held to be illegal by the Courts. Perhaps the most familiar example was that of the Standard Oil Company which adopted this form of control during the years 1879–92. Following a decision of the Supreme Court in 1892 the organisation was reconstructed to take the form of a holding company (q.v.).

W

Wage Drift The gap between nationally-negotiated wage-rates and actual earnings which tend to be much higher; this difference is due to overtime payments, bonuses and other incentives. In view of the significance of the trends in wage-rates and actual earnings in the national economy, variations are often expressed in percentage form. This is calculated:

$$\left(\frac{E}{M} - 1\right)100$$

where E = ratio of average earnings at end of period to those at the beginning; and M = corresponding ratio in respect of wage-rates.

Wage-Fund Theory *See* WAGES, THEORIES OF.

Wage Payments and Incentives *See* CO-PARTNERSHIP IN INDUSTRY; MINIMUM WAGE LEGISLATION; PROFIT SHARING SCHEMES; SLIDING SCALES; TIME RATES AND PIECE RATES; WAGE-RATE; WAGE-RATE, STANDARD; WAGES, THEORIES OF.

Wage-Rate The basic minimum rate of payment for a certain occupation, generally expressed as the rate per hour.

Wage-Rate, Standard Uniform wage-rates agreed between employers and trade unions through the process of collective bargaining (q.v.).

Wages A comprehensive term covering all the different forms of earnings of labour.

Wages Councils *See* MINIMUM WAGE LEGISLATION.

Wages, Theories of Theories seeking to account for the level of wages in a community. The main theories which have been advanced are as follows:
(1) *Subsistence theory.* Of French origin, this "iron law" of wages asserted that if wages rose above subsistence level an increase in population would inevitably follow, thus forcing wages down again to subsistence level. In many parts of the world, in which the standard of living is very low, this problem persists; nevertheless, the advanced industrial countries have demonstrated that this "law" is not inevitable and that rising wages can be associated with a falling birth rate.

(2) *Wage-Fund Theory.* A theory advanced in the early 19th century that the amount available for wages is limited by the amount of capital; thus there is a definite "fund" from which wages are paid, and if some get more, others get less. Wages depend, therefore, upon the proportion that the working population bears to capital. The idea of a fixed wages fund is a fallacy, but the proportion between labour and capital does influence directly the productivity of labour, and ultimately the level of real wages.

(3) *Marginal Productivity Theory.* A current theory that wages tend to be equal to the value of the marginal product of labour. The marginal product is the additional income that would accrue to an organisation from the employment of one extra man (or alternatively the decline in total income from the dismissal of one man). It is profitable to continue to employ additional men until the value of the marginal product is equal in value to the wage. If wages are increased, men will tend to be dismissed until the value of the higher marginal product is equal to the higher wage, other things remaining the same.

Waiter Uniformed attendants stationed about the Stock Exchange, or "House". A derivation from the old coffee house days.

Waiting Line Theory *See* QUEUEING, THEORY OF.

Walks Cheques payable at the London Offices or branches of banks which are not members of the Clearing House, e.g. Overseas and Foreign Banks and Merchant Banking Houses.

Wall Street Or simply "the Street", a reference to the New York financial community concentrated in the Wall Street area of Manhattan, New York City. *See* WALL STREET CRASH (1929).

Wall Street Crash (1929) The collapse of prices on the New York Stock Exchange in 1929 which precipitated the Great Depression, 1929–1935 (q.v.), in the United States and throughout the capitalist world. Excessive speculation in stocks and shares had raised prices to abnormal heights.

Wants A craving or desire for mental and physical pleasures and satisfactions.

Warranted Growth Rate The rate of economic growth at which planned investment is equal to planned saving; a requirement for stable growth.

Washington Agreement An Agreement made on 6th December, 1945, under which the United States loaned to Britain the sum of $3,750 m. This sum was to be repaid over 50 years, beginning in 1951, at 2 per cent per annum. Under the Agreement, British debt from the First World War was to be cancelled and the Lend-Lease account considered settled. Two other clauses under the Agreement forbade Britain to impose quantitative restrictions on American imports which were not also imposed on imports from other sources, and required Britain to make sterling freely convertible at an early date. *See* CONVERTIBILITY OF STERLING.

Watering Stock The issue of securities to an extent un-warranted by the assets of a company.

Ways and Means Advances Short-term loans made by the Bank of England (q.v.) to the British Government. These loans form part of the Government's short-term or "floating debt" (q.v.).

Wealth Goods and other assets in existence at any time which command a market value (i.e. price) if offered for sale; this implies that such assets have utility and scarcity value, and that it is possible to transfer their ownership from one person or body to another. Economic science is concerned with the production and distribution of wealth defined in this way, and not with assets which have value in the mind of the owner only. Wealth is a fund of goods which can be consumed; it represents stored up facilities for the satisfaction of future wants.

Welfare Economics A branch of economics (q.v.) concerned with studying the extent to which economic activity maximises human welfare, and the evaluation of public policies relating to the economy designed to achieve that end. A term first associated with the work of the British economist, A. C. Pigou. *See* ECONOMIC WELFARE; MARGINAL SOCIAL AND PRIVATE NET PRODUCTS; SOCIAL ECONOMICS.

Welfare State A nation that provides minimum standards in respect of education, health, housing, pensions and other social benefits, etc. when the individual means of certain sections of the population may be inadequate to provide these standards. The development of welfare in Britain had its origins in the 19th century with early factory legislation.

Whitley Councils *See* JOINT INDUSTRIAL COUNCILS.

Wholesale Markets Chiefly markets for foodstuffs and raw materials.

Wholesaler A dealer (q.v.) who buys and stocks goods for re-sale to others; an intermediary between manufacturer or supplier and retailer (q.v.). *See* BREAKING BULK.

Widening Investment *See* INVESTMENT, WIDENING.

Wieser's Law of Costs A law formulated by Friedrich von Wieser (1851–1926), an Austrian economist, that the cost of a commodity is the alternative foregone in producing it. *See* OPPORTUNITY COST.

Window Dressing A practice once engaged in by most banks, the effect of which was to show in their monthly statements a higher cash ratio than they normally maintained. This was achieved by calling in some of their loans to the money market for the purpose of showing a greater amount of cash in the statement. This practice came to an end in 1946 on the recommendation of the Bank of England (q.v.).

274

"With Particular Average"   A type of marine insurance policy which covers partial loss through marine risks and other risks such as theft and pilferage. *See* "FREE OF PARTICULAR AVERAGE".

Work Study   A generic term for those techniques, particularly method study and work measurement, which are used in the examination of human work in all its contexts, and which lead systematically to the investigation of all the factors which affect the efficiency and economy of the situation being reviewed in order to effect improvement.

Working Capital   The net liquid resources of a business, i.e. the current assets minus the current liabilities.

Working Classes   An antiquated term used to describe those who work for weekly wages and are in the lower income groups.

Working Control   Theoretically the ownership of 51 per cent of a company's voting shares and stocks, giving effective control over the company's affairs; in practice effective control may sometimes be exerted through ownership of much less than 50 per cent of the stocks and shares, depending on the character and distribution of the other shareholdings.

Works Councils   Joint councils consisting of management and employees formed for the purpose of discussing matters of mutual concern not covered by specific trade union agreements.

World Bank   *See* INTERNATIONAL BANK FOR RECONSTRUCTION AND DEVELOPMENT.

World Health Organisation   A United Nations organisation formally established in 1948 which has as its basic objective—"the attainment by all peoples of the highest possible levels of health". Its work is guided by the World Health Assembly composed of representatives of all member states.

X Y Z

Yield The percentage return on capital. The gross flat yield on a security is the annual amount receivable in interest expressed as a percentage of the purchase price; the net flat yield is the gross flat yield less income tax at the standard rate.

If, as is nearly always the case, the market price of a share differs from the nominal value, the yield is calculated according to the following formula:

$$\frac{\text{Nominal Value} \times \text{Dividend}}{\text{Market price}} = \text{yield per cent}$$

For example: "A" Co. £1 shares, market price £3.75, dividend 15 per cent:—

$$\frac{1.00 \times 15}{3.75} = 4 \text{ per cent yield.}$$

If securities are redeemed at a known date, the gross redemption yield comprises the gross flat yield together with an annual apportionment of the calculated capital gain or loss; the net redemption yield is similar to the gross redemption yield except that income tax at the standard rate is deducted from dividends, and any capital gains tax (q.v.) from the capital appreciation. *See* DIVIDEND.

York-Antwerp Rules International rules which provide uniformity in the administration of marine insurance.

Zollverein A German word meaning "a customs union". It was applied to the customs union of German states established in 1833 under the leadership of Prussia. The "zollverein" had two distinct features: (a) the abolition of all duties between the different States which joined it, and (b) the formulation of a common policy towards other countries. It was an act of economic union which preceded political union.